VICKI GOTSIS (

Dance In The Fire of Life!

Women who walk through the fire of life leave sparks
of light wherever they go, illuminating the path for the
future generation of women to come.

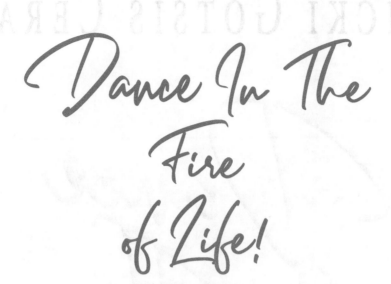

Dance In The Fire of Life!

Copyright © 2019 Vicki Gotsis Ceraso

ISBN: 9781090264268
Imprint: Independently published

ICK *Publishing*   **VGC Publishing**
VickiGotsisCeraso

Published By ICK com. llc Publishing House©
Edited By ICK Publishing & Vicki Gotsis Ceraso
Cover Design and Book Design By ICK Publishing©

Dance In The Fire of Life!

This is a work of nonfiction. No names have been changed, no characters invented, no events fabricated.

Women who walk through the fire of life leave sparks of light wherever they go, illuminating the path for the future generation of women to come.

Dedications

I dedicate this book to my family.

To my loving Husband and my fellow life adventurer,
Bruno Ceraso for his unconditional love and devotion to me
and to our family and for his unwavering belief and
encouragement which has allowed me to spread my wings,
follow my path and shine my light.

To my THREE HEARTS; my awe-inspiring sons, Joseph,
Rick and Paul for their constant expression of love,
their pride in me and my work and for being
my greatest source of inspiration.

~ Vicki Gotsis Ceraso

What people are saying...

Re-Ignite The Embers Of Your Life

Vicki's story was heartfelt and relatable. I was totally immersed and blessed to be given such an enlightening gift...So well written and powerful. I would absolutely read it over and over again as it continues to give further hidden gems of wisdom and inspiration.

The introduction entices you gently to continue reading. I loved the closing poem. It touched my soul and inspired me to continue to feed my unique light...My personal message from Vicki's story was the courage to believe in myself and that I 'have the power' to begin to use and trust my unique tools.

Nancy Perri, Australia

Vicki reaches into the depths of you and ignites a truth of what life, this precious animation skilfully shows you how the "Call" to be the Truth of you is the greatest journey a
person can take... You can feel Vicki's passion as you read her story.

Vicki's style is passionate, insightful and commanding of Truth. You feel her desire for your triumph as her words leap off the page and into your heart. There is so much gold in this story that to read it once would be an injustice to yourself.

It is still rare to hear people openly talk about Being instead of directing you into doing. What Vicki is doing is she is calling for fellow travellers to just emit their own Light and soon that Light will join with others as a beacon of Hope.

The demographics of the reader is not limited to just women, this is a story that is reaching out to souls, not gender. Vicki's own heartfelt quest is a catalyst to others igniting their own flame.

The introduction immediately sang to my soul immersing me into the wisdom that was unfolding through Vicki's story. There were times when you could almost imagine that Vicki's narrative was a wise mother whispering into the heart of her child all the secrets that could be found within the soul for that child to live a meaningful life.
The poem at the end repeats this wisdom and reinforcing that it is not what life does to you that determines the truth of you it is the truth of you that creates the meaning of your life.

Thank you, Vicki, for being a Lighthouse that provides a safe passage for all those who read this story and desire something greater than the sum of their present beliefs about themselves.

Dr Rosemary McCallum, Australia

Totally inspiring from start to finish, want more of it now Vicki's chapter was very easy to read and easily relatable. I feel it could've gone on for further chapters and chapters as I was totally immersed, need the book!

As I read this book my mind wondered to whom I would introduce it to. I feel there are many people who are yet to experiencing empowerment and self-love and really have no way of identifying how they can go about it.

Dolly Yanevski, Australia

I experienced a true relationship with the author. The authors' purpose, challenged and pivotal moments prompted me to think of my own journey...both the Introduction and the closing were very impactful...The purpose of Vicki's chapter was to highlight to us to be the "light". That shook me a little because it reminds me of why I do what I do. If not the US then who right? The author is saying we collectively have a responsibility yet the author does not shy away from hers. Its almost as if she is saying let's do this together.

Myrtha Dubois, USA

Vicki's powerful chapter gave me an experience of pure soul-felt inspiration of being understood in my darkest hours, reminding me I am never alone; I am overflowing with power to triumph over tragedy if I only allow myself to experience that high level of hope and love: and I am worthy of all life has to offer. Her chapter left my heart singing and soaring!

Vicki's chapter is beautifully crafted, richly written and easy to understand. I especially adore her passion that jumps off each page and her gorgeous poetry that every woman needs to have on a card, tucked into her purse /wallet. Her authentic voice is thought-provoking and wonderfully relatable.

I would recommend Vicki's chapter to all women because of the valuable pearls of wisdom and empowering feminine perspective she so beautifully captures. Too many women doubt their dreams, natural gifts, talents, their ability to thrive beyond current challenges, their capability to financially prosper. Vicki's chapter addresses all of that, helping the reader to believe and succeed!

I loved how Vicki set up her chapter with such thoughtful, purposeful care so that the reader can fully receive the incredible value she shared in the life lessons she's learned.

The greatest impact for me was the need to recognize the power we have to overcome the greatest challenges and achieve our deepest potential. What spoke deeply to me is Vicki's utmost confidence that we are here on purpose, for a purpose! And that our experiences -positive and painful- help us to discover what that is!

Her truth truly touched me, especially her devotion and love for her son despite all the doubts within her and around her. I also especially LOVE Vicki's message about trusting our own internal guidance system that all of us have, and all the powerful tools we have at our fingertips to overcome and thrive!

Marlene Elizabeth, USA

Vicki writes in an incredibly articulate way. Her ideas and thoughts were clear and easy to understand. I was presented with a variety of concepts that encompass Soul Searching, Life Lessons, Unique Individuality, Love, Connectivity and Awareness of who we are as human beings, and the impact we can have, not only to the people around us but to the world as a whole.

It engages your mind in a way that gives you the confidence and belief that you have the ability to make people feel better and leaving an everlasting impression by simply being in their presence. The reader is encouraged to have a positive outlook towards every single situation in your journey through life. To really and truly RISE UP and make that change.

Realising that your INNER LIGHT is the beautiful soul that lives within you. That is the light, that can and will leave a shining memory on those that you encounter.
After reading this chapter, it will leave you with new-found confidence, so powerful, that it will lead you into greatness!

This is an incredible read.... it is motivating, inspiring and empowering. It is a chapter that should

What people are saying...

be read by everyone. Whether it is to find your voice, to discover what you stand for, to unleash your superpower or just to make that positive difference in the world you live in.... it is one that you should grab with both hands and read!!

"I am ready to go out there and elevate myself to be that person that people will never forget how I made them feel"

Shimon Bohbout, Australia/Singapore

At The End of Nature's Illuminated Path

This chapter is filled with such beautiful words and imagery. It was captivating. "An inspiring story"

Tarra Bulum, Australia

"Poetically, captivating imagery that takes you on a journey where you feel the intense connection between Mother Nature and life itself."

Anna Nanos, Australia

"I was moved by this inspirational story, it is a raw and genuine reflection of a life lived ....The story speaks to women who second guess their choices in life, and that their hopes and dreams are worth striving for no matter what!"

Noula Fillis, Australia

Marica is an exceptional writer. Her style resembles the flow of a beautiful poem, full of imagery and heart. Such a moving account of one woman's journey back to her true self. I just wanted this chapter to keep going on and on.

Despina Yarros, Australia

The Real Heroine Epidemic

The story kept me engaged and emotionally invested the entire time ...The author's call for women to speak up and realise their own worth ... resonated with me, as well as the struggles the author described in feeling as though women must constantly apologise for simply taking up space in the world... It was a perfect balance between powerful and emotional, with a small touch of humour...

Sarah Yarak, Australia

This story touched my heart in a profound way...an impactful statement about wanting women to feel inspired and have the courage to live their lives as freely and fearlessly as they can.

Debbie Chandler, UK

Laurie's unique take on 'recognition, understanding, and acceptance of the expanded role as a still-relevant woman' and not allowing herself to be defined by the normal, expected female roles was so inspirational!

Samantha Ryan-Smith, Australia

My big take away from Laurie's chapter was that women should make their own contributions in the world and should not allow anyone else to take this away from them.

Julie Stevens, USA

Don't Wait For 'Something'

Reading Jenny's story gave me insight into how hard growing up in an ethnic household with this very special gift was for her. Her story touched my heart…..Her persistence and determination gave her the strength to continue and follow her spiritual path and what makes her so special.

France Deville, Australia

Jenny's chapter was well written and showed powerful expression...I felt I was with her along her journey...loved it Jenny, well done! Can't wait to read it again!

Francesca Thorne, Australia

...took me on a journey of re-living what my own childhood was like...it was emotional and beautiful,….. with bursts of humour mixed in. It felt the connection of such emotion married with humour, brilliant! Down to earth real raw, honest and funny…. Opened my heart and changed my perspectives…..felt layers of the uncertainty of who I am, stripped off.'

Sara Merckel, Australia

Dodging The Fire Balls Of Domestic Violence

It serves as a stark reminder that we can never fully comprehend the experiences of one's life and how it has affected them or others. Through story and understanding we can unite to create healing.

Dale Gray

No longer can men hide behind outdated and obsolete cultural or religious doctrine that leads to physical, emotional or spiritual abuse of women.

Danielle Aitken

She allowed the story to open up with the feeling of 'hope' around a new life with her husband then packed a punch just like that first hit to the side of her head.

Natalie Drenovac

The chapter shows only 3 moments in time. The magnitude of what she's survived hits even harder when considering this was her life for 8 years.

Kylie Dayman

Dare to Believe

" Danielle has the ability to take you on a journey of potential and discovery through her words'"
"The main message is one of human potential…..the things discussed in this chapter are designed to inspire people to believe in themselves and create their own changes"

Phillip Aitken

"We can change direction in our lives at any time, and many times"

Tara Bulum

"The most important message is that we are all in charge of our destiny" "We all have the power to change our lives for health and wellness and most importantly peacefulness..."
I would recommend it to …."young or old, male or female. Anyone who has suffered loss or hopelessness looking to improve their own spiritual well being."

Michelle Bennett

What people are saying...

"Very insightful, written from a very knowledgeable position ""I think the main message was hope, and the belief that with the right help we can achieve almost anything"

Jean Pemberton

"Your determination without hesitation, fearless and firmly grounded, belief in your purpose gives me the courage to stand behind my words with fearless conviction" "Thank you for sharing Danielle, you've got me reaching for the sky""

Marcia Grahovac

My Journey to Self-Identity

"Even if you feel there is a lot of work to do and it will be hard, there is always hope."

Nancy Becher, USA

"It is a love story with all the complexities, complications and beauty while emphasizing the dichotomy of a twin while seeking individuality."

Linda Curtis, UK

"How she overcame the struggle of self-identity, rose above and began helping others with her coaching."

Kelly Doiron, Canada

"It is not easy but it is important to gain greater clarity and insights so you can discover the real you."

Lisa Anna Palmer, Canada

"It's important for each person to have a strong sense of their own identity to succeed and be happy."

Cheryl Strickland, Canada

Fear Crippled Me...

I am impressed by the strength she has found to turn her life around.

Denise Plant, Spain

Beautifully written ... makes the reader sometimes feel almost like they are standing next to Linda... After reading this I can sum up in one word how I am feeling- inspired.

Jade, Ibiza

Very well written ... like the intricate detail, Linda has gone into... I think every reader will take something away ... to enrich their lives ... to conquer their fears....The closing paragraph is particularly moving where she describes the passing of her beloved partner ... Linda is determined to use her grief to propel her forward and seize every amazing opportunity.

Claire Bailie, England

I would recommend this story to others, especially those with anxiety, eating disorders or other related issues...The chapter was entirely inspirational.

Jane Hodgetts, UK

I was cheering when by 51 she was able to break through her limiting fears and start to enjoy life, it is never too late to change your life...I would recommend this story to those suffering in silence with feelings of low self-worth, fear to do new things, and wanting to feel free.

Carol Davies, Canada

I would recommend this ..easy read story .. to people who are having struggles because it is an inspiring and motivating reminder that things can and do change...didn't know the struggles she had been through … I am amazed at her transformation … having been so fearful in the past...you can't assume anything about somebody's life … we can make massive strides in a short space of time.

Lucy Davies, UK

Dancing with the Devil

The story was very easy to read and grabs you from the very beginning….it made me want to know more about her life and exactly how she managed to become the woman she is now after going through such a traumatic experience.

Daniela, Petrevski, Australia

This chapter is an incredible eye-opener.

Natalie, Australia

This chapter was so well written I envisioned her every movement.

Maria Iliadis, Australia

I was hooked from the first few lines. Easy but sad to read. Emotional. Couldn't stop reading it.

Marica Borg, Australia

Intro made me feel like I was right there watching but not able to help her.
It was engaging from first intro.

Debbie Potaka, Western Australia

Very deep... showed determination and courage and how at the lowest point in her life she came through to be the woman she is today.

Nancy Seldon, Australia

I found this story inspiring, a story of triumph or adversity, the awakening of a women's spirit.
We have the power to make changes take back our broken lives and move forward.

Ester D'Elesio, Australia

I wanted to read more about the experiences and delve deeper into the authors' trauma.

Josie Kirby, Australia

This depicts a woman that was so emotionally and physically tormented by an abusive predator.

Stacey Vlahos

What people are saying...

The Blood Moon

Such a beautiful teaching, the metaphors used in this piece to bridge Mother Nature and the cycles we each undergo bought much clarity and ease of understanding. I loved the way Prasanna, shared the earth's path first and then ties it into her own experience...creating a depth of sharing... Highly enjoyable and valuable.

Amalia, USA

It touches me when I yet again realise that nature is showing us exactly how we should live our lives! I truly enjoyed this story by Prasanna as the wise goddess she is... Prasanna's writing captured my attention from get go and I would certainly read more from her. I feel really comforted by the way she writes... What she is writing about is a missing piece of our female lives today... Prasanna's writing is so comforting. She gives a cuddle and says everything will be alright in her text. She holds you in a motherly way so you feel encourage to follow your own inner wisdom through her stories.

Gigi Lindros, Australia

Dancing in the Fire with the Goddess

It is a beautiful story of her life journey to discover herself and her experiences can definitely help others to move through their challenges and obstacles in life to heal oneself and empower oneself to walk on this path of truth to discover who we are... The story is well written that you see yourself reliving the author experience as your own... Definitely recommended to anyone who is awaken and ready to walk on this spiritual path to discover oneself and live the truth of who they are here for.

Sophia Ly Phi, USA

I love reading about how she learned through her life, step by step. So surprised that a "girl" of 16 could follow her intuition and led where she needs to be. Surprised by the affirmation that one can be led to divorce for one's higher good and everything work out... Anyone who is on the spiritual path, or even considering it would enjoy this story for the inspiration and the gems of knowing spread throughout the story.

CG, USA

Inner Pearl Diving.

Extremely enjoyable and thought-provoking...I want to read it again and again. I recommend this to many people who feel they are stuck in a rut ...Sue shows you that there is always an answer ... Absolutely, totally inspirational.

Caroline Beasley, Derby. UK

She conveyed a lovely message that was clear... For people who are struggling or in need of inspiration, I would recommend it... I found the body of the text more enthralling.

Phillip Aitken, Australia.

I was impressed with her positive take on life, in the belief that if life gives you lemons, you make lemonade... I would read it again and I would recommend this chapter to those who are stuck or struggling with life.

Jean Pemberton, Victoria, Australia

I feel that Sue's story is one that a lot of people could engage with in their daily lives...I would definitely recommend this story to others especially someone who is struggling with either health issues or life's challenges as it would give them strength to read how someone else has turned their life around.

Wendy Keegan, England

Sue gave us some very insightful reasons why a woman who looks talented, smart and having great success, can still carry all the wounds of a negative childhood and not believe in herself... There was a compelling introduction, personal anecdotes illustrated the author's message very well, and the conclusion gave us definite solutions to follow... Sue gives us a message of hope that we can change our lives by believing in ourselves, making self-care and self-love a priority and being grateful for all we have in life.

Carol Davies, Canada

We Never Walk Alone

I would recommend this story to others, it demonstrates that even in the darkest of moments of depression there is hope...Childhood sexual abuse and being raised with domestic violence are terribly traumatising events which can leave life long consequences...What is uplifting is that Jo was able to crawl her way out of a dark place and find the light she has been searching for.

Debbie Clarke, Australia

I felt the introduction was very impactful without being "graphically unacceptable" and the ending very graceful and soft...I found the story very easy to read and follow. The flow of it was excellent. Jo has shown the raw emotions she experienced to portray to the reader who may have experienced the same or going through it...all the emotions that Jo has written about will be a great help to others out there who are going through the same.

Michele Cali, Australia

I liked very much the honesty about the story and the courage that Jo is telling the deepest part of her life story... we are not victims... we can take our lives into our own hands and trust our intuition. I love the title "you Never walk alone ". The closing paragraph gives a lot of hope and a feeling of hope which really touches me.

Petra Brumann, Germany

The Wondrous Magic Of Life

I found the introduction and closing paragraphs were both impactful and encouraged me to re-think the way in which I view life and challenges I face......be open to giving and receiving....I do not need to change myself to fit into the "norm"....I can make changes at anytime....I am in control and make the decisions in which I direct my life.

This was an inspirational and enlightening chapter Kathie has written. I really enjoyed reading the personal insights about accepting help from others, keeping a positive mindset and being at one with your mind and body.

Benjamin Carter

What people are saying...

...Very engaging.....advice and guidance provided were based on authors personal observations and feelings...the author explained the strategies that worked for her in her life.

It entices you to keep reading to learn more about the authors life lessons.....can apply the techniques in my life. I think....it would help some people open their eyes to their true abilities and gifts.

Comparing lifes to 'magic' is a very uplifting statement and leaves the reader in a very positive mood.

Penelope Pavlou

I felt it was written from the heart, inspiring and optimistic. It spoke directly to the reader making it personal and impactful. Kathie shares her story in a touching way, empowering others to find their strength.... it was candid and sincere.

Main messages..........mindfulness, power of the mind, positivity, respect, and Love, for oneself....do not let fear restrict your life and that no matter where your life takes you, that's exactly where the universe wants you to be in order to learn your lessons. I would recommend this to anyone searching for answers.

Terri Tonkin

The writer felt honest and her style of writing was engaging. It was clear the author shared an honest account of her experience with chronic fatigue. I myself have experienced similar symptoms and I respect Kathie's method in taking control of her life, mind and body. The 7 step ritual ....is clear and can be followed by anyone who reads and chooses to take part.

I would recommend the story to ....sufferers of chronic fatigue, mental health, anxiety and depression. I feel as though this would be the best audience considering its overall positive messaging and guide for support.

Lasting impression.....Believe in yourself, you have the answers within you, be open to receiving, you have strengths to be shared.

Christina Psevdos

Your Time as a Caterpillar has Expired

I would hope that people read Angie's story and realise that they can get up again and survive.

Karen Frohloff, Australia

By the end I felt that there was hope and that change was to be embraced.

Gerard J Browne, Australia

It has a strong message of believing in yourself, overcoming obstacles ...

Raewyn Wise, New Zealand

Well written story that touches upon a lot of everyday life journeys

David Grahame, Australia

I was struck by the courage and resourcefulness

Scotty Brimstone, Australia

I liked that it gave an exercise that was very practical. Thought provoking and appealed to my emotional connection.

Mark Thompson, New Zealand

Some points really pulled at my heart strings. Stories such as Angie's really open one's eyes and give encouragement.

Doug Spencer, Australia

Pippies On The Beach

I was fully engaged, wanting to know the outcome and how she got through that period of her life. I was involved emotionally, felt sad at times, worried and joy at her survival and positive impact… It's a positive story for a person thriving despite hardship… It would be a good story for emerging adult females to know what life can be like and that they can make it. She is a positive role model.

Andrea McMahon, Australia

It brings to my mind that life is hard, that there are people out there that are not invested in your growth and that you cannot allow it to stunt your growth… It was a lovely story.

Julie Ramchander, Australia

I saw a woman who believed in herself despite the challenges and refuses to be beaten by anything. I saw wisdom, truth, and determination to be the women she wants to be. A powerful message about forgiveness and it is never a bad time… The words were everyday words and that made the narrative very readable.

Jhaiya Naikkar, Australia

Phoenix Rising

The text is like a gift… inspires you to keep moving forward despite challenges. Very easy to read, touches of humor in amongst some very personal stories. Have read it a few times – always powerful…. not the usual self-help book. It is raw, honest and a treasure to read. Engaging from beginning to end. Leaves you … inspired to move and pass on the baton that this author has given the reader through the story.

Teresa Defazio

"I enjoyed reading the short stories immensely, they struck a nerve in me and woke me up from my current apparent depression which is something so foreign to me."

Jade Wilson

I couldn't stop crying but felt impelled to keep reading through the chapter. … touched me to the core and I also felt 'lighter' after reading it. … the introduction you're at my heart strings and as I read through the story it made me realise that we ALL can conquer things in life with a positive mindset.

Suzie Scaffidi

Stepping Out From Behind The Shadows

This story lets people know we are all different and we can all overcome hiding in the shadows and stepping out into the light if we want to and are prepared to do what it takes.

Eleni Szemeti, Australia

I read her chapter three times and each time I felt emotional…this is a story of coming to terms with one's self-belief and confidence.

Christine Williams, Australia

What a privilege to be able to see the unfolding of a real hero. The challenges of early life can scar us forever and Pina so beautifully took me on a journey that made me hold my breath at the enormity of her pain and fear.

Rosemary McCallum, Australia

What people are saying...

The story was easy to read...I could not put it down....I would read it again...If this story could be shared with year 7 - year 9 school girls, it would be amazing!

Sarah Susac, Australia

Engaging and beautifully expressed...totally relatable.

Tara Bulum, Australia

Pina's message is 'be fearless in believing in you...in eliminating insecurities...anything is possible when you believe in yourself.

Lorene Roberts, Australia

I felt her pain and her courage inspired me...I loved it.

Loretta Drago, Australia

Everything Happens to Reveal Our Purpose

It's expressed in a loving and nurturing way. I could feel each revelation and unfold beautifully... Reminded me to look at things with and from a different perspective...

SRWolf, Australia

I would recommend this story to women who question their lives as being a mistake or to women who blame their childhood backgrounds, to those who have felt neglected emotionally by their upbringing.

Marica Grahovac, Croatia

I was touched and saddened by the raw honesty of this piece... written as a reflective narrative which really expressed the thoughts, fears, and experiences of a young girl at various ages... Tara had not only survived but was able to take the valuable lessons from the journey.

Danielle Aitken, Australia

It was engaging and beautifully expressed... highlights important lessons and wisdom that are valuable for all of us...

Pina Cerminara, Australia

Tara's story brings to light what is happening right now in so many households... Tara made me feel like I was reading her own very personal diary... Her writing style is warm and simple, there is no pretentiousness – you can almost imagine a child of various ages reading from that diary... We all need this story because we have all had our authentic self in one form or another violated when the parts of us that were not acceptable to others – were cast into the shadows of our psyche.

Dr. Rosemary McCallum

I experienced so many emotions reading this chapter... so compelling...I was so full of admiration for a woman who has literally been through hell and has emerged as a strong, amazing woman...Tara's story shows us that no matter how terrible our circumstances are, we can rise above and beyond them if we have total faith and commitment in ourselves.

Samantha Langridge, Australia

Don't Be Afraid To Dance Alone.

I was amazed and connected with her chapter. I felt connected to her words and experiences. Being single over forty and desiring to be married has been a challenge especially when everyone around you is getting engaged... Truly an inspirational chapter... Loved how transparent the author was about loneliness and depression. My god, I can relate to every word.

Tosha Barnes, USA

I was engaged. It kept my attention. I wanted to know what was coming next, and how she felt in the situation she described… I enjoyed learning more about the author… She expressed real feelings about difficult situations and how she has grown from them. Someone in a difficult place would find comfort, I believe, in the author's perspective.

Angela, USA

You Were Born To Shine

Very relatable, raw & emotional. An inspirational story….I recommend it to teenagers and young adults to show them that you don't have to stay in the status quo, do what makes you happy and that there are pivotal moments in life.

Jo Firman

Julie's story triggered many pivotal moments in my life & standouts of me giving up my significance.

Janene Babauskis

Primary emotion was empathy, I am that woman too, maybe not quite as far along the road of self-acceptance but definitely a fellow traveller

Jane Zeeher

The story was beautifully written, authentic, humble & powerful. We would all benefit from reading it.

Nanette Abbott

Written in a way that two close friends would pour their hearts out to each other with no judgement.

Toula Bradshaw

I would recommend it to anyone. We have all been told who we are, who we should be and how to act in life. This is a lesson in breaking free, of being led and what is 'expected'.

Brenton Opperman

Dance of a Warrior

"It inspired me, allowing me to look back on my life and things I still try to hide from to be strong for others at the risk of my own health."

Karen Thomas, USA

"I literally cried, got angry, screamed from getting the news, and celebrated when Holly became defiant... This story is not merely about Crohn's, death, or being sick. It's about our fight, our attitude, being able to find our reason, and our voice for living despite everyone against our success. It's about positioning to win no matter what!"

Martha Dubois, USA

"I really had no idea about the mental and spiritual journey while going through a chronic sickness. I love how she kept choosing to proactively love herself on her journey despite not seeing the direct results of it until the end."

D.W, USA

What people are saying...

The Naked Hustle

I experienced goosebumps, recognised some things and was almost in tears. All our dreams can come true if we have the courage to pursue them.

Nanette, Netherlands

It was captivating and enjoyable... a person driven to succeed.

Brenton Marriott, Adelaide Australia

This is a powerful and moving reminder that nothing is permanent and that we all have the power within to find the life we deserve. I was touched and motivated to incorporate new outlooks into my own life.

Michelle Bush, USA

The opening chapter made you want to read more. It can be read by everyone. Unfortunately, abuse is common and this would help them better to understand what their friends are going through.

Leeanne Braund, Australia

A wonderful inspiring read for anyone who feels they have no hope or no option for a break-free life.

Monika Edmonds, Australia

It was enjoyable as it is a real-life experience someone had the courage and openness to share with others.

Mark Carn, Australia

Domestic Violence comes in all forms - as the author stated, she didn't have any black eyes, however, it was still abuse, just in a different form.

Helen Hall, Australia

From Darkness Into Light

The story tells me of a resilient child that carried into her adulthood. When I read the story of her illness as a 12-year-old, I experienced her pain, anguish and determination to overcome what life had gifted her at this time. I say gifted, as because of this illness and near-death experience Adrienne was able to grow, learn about herself and later on teach others.

The story shows us the great strength and fortitude from a young girl. I related to the story and understood the battles she would have to continually overcome to move forward. As I have nursed this type of patient and a husband had head injuries.

Margie O'Kane, Australia

Inspiration, hope. Delight...deepens my understanding of the level of determination she has drawn on, the process that has been operating within her...Eminently readable, full of hope, of ideas. I will read it again. I would recommend it to people who experience early life health challenges, have had a stroke, or are experiencing despair... In the hope that people struggling might find a sense that things can go well even in overwhelming circumstances.

My take away message: Hope. Possibility. Dig deep & find the mettle you may not know is there. Adrienne recognised the qualities in herself that helped her respond so effectively.

Bev Henwood, Australia

Become The Diva You Were Born To Be

I found it very easy to read and full of truth and great advice. It kept me engaged right to the end. I couldn't put it down. I could so relate to so much of what you shared and I know that many women will too. This is an inspiring story that empowers women to find their truth and show up.

Pina Cerminara

Kristina has an enormous capacity and energy which she uses to connect with people of all walks of life. She has a wonderful love of people and life which is infectious and gives us all hope through drive and tenacity we can achieve our goals.

Jennifer McNamara

Kris has a lot of great strengths including confidence, great communication skills and loves to connect with people. Her past hasn't defined her. It has made her the strong woman she is today.

Kylie Farrugia

Explore Your Life – Renew Your Power

'Louise's share is amazing...she truly understands the meaning of giving of yourself and inspiring others she comes into contact with to be the best they can be….easy to understand and read...I think mature aged would appreciate Louise's story from all over the world as we all experienced many of the things Louise rights about.'

Karen Miward, Australia

'This touched my inner being and reinforced that we are all connected and through this story, it inspires me to go out and do more and be more… I see Louise as an incredible role model to all, young and old and one who will continue on as life's journey with enthusiasm, love, compassion and gratitude…'

Jenny Lovett, Australia

'The chapter was well written, easy to understand, engaging, funny at times and therefore very enjoyable. The combination of ideas and personal examples i s very powerful. I would read it again.'

John Sautelle, Australia

Flag & Barrel

Eloquently written and a heartstring puller….it highlights that whatever your past and present may be, you can always have a future...a great guideline for anyone who is not experiencing the best of times.

Jenny Baini, Australia

Her lesson to us is that everything happens for a reason, learn from your experiences and move on...if you change your perspective on life, you can learn from difficult times...my big take away was that asking for help is not a sign of weakness, instead, it is a sign for help.

Margie O'Kane, Australia

Love that Francesca is so passionate about 'family' and keeping the family stories alive regardless of whether they are happy or challenging. They have taken place and therefore they are important. This is what legacy is all about.

Becky Stimopoulou, USA

CONTENTS

CONTENTS

Acknowledgements

To my parents Ekaterini (Kathy)and Photios Gotsis (Fred) for filling my mind and soul with the belief that I can do anything I put my mind to and for instilling the qualities of courage and tenacity into my being. (Dad, I wish you were here to witness the unfolding of what I have created upon the foundations of your belief in me).

To my beautiful sister, Anna Nanos for always being a loving support for me and for my family and for instilling me with the peace of mind that I can rely on her for anything I need.

To my dear friends, Linda D'Abate and Nancy Perri whose unwavering love, support, friendship and belief in me has propelled me forward and ensured I strive higher with every goal.

I would also like to mention Irene Pro from ICK Publishing who has gone over and above in ensuring the integrity and the sincerity of this beautiful book is kept in its original form and for her personal love and friendship that has blossomed with every call.

I would be amiss to not mention my soul sister, Laurie Roberts Vallas who through her love and genuine friendship has been by my side throughout this entire project and has recognised our friendship as an invaluable treasure that is steeped in mutual love and respect.

I would like to also dedicate this book to the younger girls and women in my life in the genuine hope that this book and my work will inspire them to reach for their goals and to follow their own unique light.

They are:
Sarah Ceraso, Katie Ceraso, Alesia Kapoulitsas, Celine D'Abate, Zoe Chryssikos and Isabel Bartolucci

To all my clients, I thank you for trusting me and allowing me to grow and learn from your vulnerable shares.

To my Dance In The Fire Of Life Co-Authors, I have such deep love and gratitude to each and every one of you for hearing my heartfelt call and for resonating with my vision for this book and for women globally. Due to our shared journey throughout Dance In The Fire Of Life, we will be forever joined by the invisible thread of deep sharing, understanding, love and sisterhood.

My final dedication goes to THE woman who has a call in her heart to DO more, to EXPERIENCE more and to BE more. I invite her to see every pivotal moment in her unique life as a Pearl of Divine Wisdom waiting to adorn her with its brilliant glow.

~ *Vicki Gotsis Ceraso*

Foreword

by Dr Rosemary McCallum

Life is full of delicious twists and turns if you can just put down your "shoulds" and "have tos" long enough and observe the clues that draw to you like minded people. People who leave an impression on you and are on the same passionate path to be a difference maker within the world. A person who has a burn deep within their being to become a catalyst to lift others up so that the world may see their Light.

Such a woman crossed my path late last year as we shared a phone conversation in which she revealed her passion and her vision for creating a space where women could rise into their own magnificence. As we spoke, I recognized that familiar burn that accompanies a difference maker. There is a subtle urgency in their essence. A drive that is irrefutably present in their energy as they speak their passion and describe their visions.

There is also that underlying frustration as those with such sight find that sometimes the people, they are sharing with find it hard to step out of their orchestrated life and leap for the stars. Sadly, all too often, those trapped in the conformity of certainty can seek to stifle the creative passion of those of us who have an insatiable yearning to wander paths untrodden. But for those who know their heart, those fearful voices fall on deaf ears. The phone call left me inspired and elated to know that here was another woman whose vision was raising her higher than the naysayers. This passionate woman with a burning cause was Vicki Gotsis Ceraso.

At the time I knew nothing about Vicki's history, or her accomplishments nor would that have made an impression on me as I am only ever listening to the heart of those I share with. The rhetoric of their accomplishment means nothing if I can't hear that passion for being a difference maker. The call ended with an arrangement to catch up in the new year.

Now one must laugh at how the Universe powerfully orchestrates the next chapter in one's life. At the beginning of this year two women whom I admire deeply asked me if I could review their writings for a book that they were contributing to. Knowing the hearts of these two magnificent women, I was honoured to be asked. It then became apparent that they were two of the 27 amazing women who were contributing to Vicki's powerful book *"Dance in the Fire of Life"*

So, who am I to review these powerful writings and recommend you read these stories? What gives me the credibility to encourage you to allow the gold of the messages within this book to seep into your soul and awaken the possibilities of the truth of you?

My name is Rosemary McCallum and for over 30 years I have been passionate about activating the exceptional in people. I came to this path all those years ago, a broken, self-mutilating manic depressant who contemplated suicide on a daily basis. Like Alice, I fell into a hole so deep that there was no way out. I tried and fell, and I tried and fell as inside a voice cried out hysterically "Can you hear me screaming?"

Life led me to study behavioural therapy, mainly because I wanted to understand why I was the way I was. It left me intellectually informed but emotionally empty. There just had to be more to the mystery of this thing called "life". I wandered endlessly in the desert of "what is my purpose?" I clung onto something! I didn't know what the something was at the time, but whatever it was it kept beckoning me forward out of the dark. I was hanging on for dear life as I tried to climb a mountain of shale that kept shifting under my feet. I sought everything outside of myself for the answer but in my busyness, I was deaf to the small voice that beckoned me inwards. Until one fateful day, I decided enough was enough and I gave up. I gave up seeking answers from others, gave up trying and just surrendered to the force that faithfully would not let go of this emotionally drowning person I had become.

This part of me that was so much stronger than my hapless mind finally led me to the door of Metaphysics, once known by the ancients as the Queen of Science and suddenly, the music of its truth lit a fire within my being. It taught me that we are all born with a great purpose etched into our essence and that this journey called "Life" beckons us inward to activate that exceptional within. It gave me the secret of emotions and how they are the tools of creation and form the paths along which our consciousness can run. It taught me that we can only create along the frequency we chose to align with. It taught me that we are all here to experience the wonderment and excitement of expanding the truth of our Self and in the process become a beacon that others who are trapped in the dark can use as a guiding light back to their own authentic truth. At the age of 35 I finally decided to become the author, the auto-biographer of my own life. I could no longer let anyone else write the chapters of my future. One of my most favourite writers wrote what was on my heart far more eloquently than I ever could.

"I hope you will go out and let stories, that is life, happen to you, and that you will work with these stories... water them with your blood and tears and your laughter till they bloom, till you yourself burst into bloom." Clarissa Pinkola Estés, Women Who Run with the Wolves: Myths and Stories of the Wild Woman Archetype
It was my own journey that gave me the understanding and deep empathy for the words written throughout this book. Life gave me the gift of walking in their shoes and the discernment to hear the message of hope and courage contained within each chapter.

What an honour to be asked to write the forward of this amazing compilation of women of substance. These Wild Woman, fearless in their rawness. Vicki's own experiences shines through as each life step prepared her and honed her determination, shored up her credibility and gave her the ability to lift others so they can be counted amongst the difference makers of this world.

Each person generously shares their vulnerability as they courageously bare their souls so that others can see that it is not your circumstances that determine who you are. They reveal to us how you can use those circumstance to find the reserve of gold within your depths to create a path that leads you out of the dark into the glorious light of truth. The beautiful cross section of all walks of life contained in these pages shows us we can all be heroes, whether we take on the difficult heroic task of being a stay at home mum or we are out there running a multi - million-dollar company. Life is not about what you get from it, it is what you bring to it. The measure of your life force is not in what you do but who you choose to be in that doing.

It was the title of Vicki's book that first spoke to me. "Dance in the Fire of Life". It deeply resonated in me as a metaphor for the very first alchemical process that takes place along the Hero's Quest. Known as "Calcination" the refining fire that burnt off the dross of old beliefs, limitations and restrictions that bind us in our own self-imposed prison of fear and lack of self-trust. Cleansing us of all that seeks to keep us powerless so that we, like the phoenix, can rise from the ashes of our past, glorious in the freedom of our ability to soar above what was and delight in the prospect of what will be. The power of our life's myth with its struggles, pains, mythical demons and ultimate triumphs ignites desire in all those who dare to venture beyond the beliefs we took on early in life. A time when our cognitive wherewithal was defenceless against what I call "GOOP" The Good Opinion of Other People.

As you read these life journeys let these stories speak to your soul. Ask yourself "Where is their story mirroring back my reality?" "How does their triumph light the path for the next step in my journey?" Maybe their story is your story – get out there and share your triumph. The world needs everyday heroes. Become the extraordinary in your own life. Celebrate the unique contribution you bring to the world. Can you remember a harsh period of your life, what deeper self-knowledge did it gift you? Don't play small as you never know the difference your story may make in another person's life. This is a book for all people, women and men who burn to know the truth of themselves and to make a contribution by just turning up as, their true selves.

I want to congratulate 29 beacons of Light who grasped Vicki's vision and helped build a collaboration of difference makers. But most of all, I want to honour Vicki for having the guts to stand up and announce to the world "This is ME" and put the call out to women everywhere to become a part of a worldwide movement SheRises Global.

Dr Rosemary McCallum

Understanding people, and what drives them, is Dr. Rosemary McCallum's passion.

For over 25 years she has worked with thousands of people unleashing their potential.

By utilizing her unique blend of science, people become empowered to express who they are through what they do.

Impactful, funny and practical Rosemary will delight, challenge and teach you how to take control of your own life by implementing a proven success formula. A formula that you can use immediately to activate your own unique attributes through the power of emotional intelligence.

Rosemary has a PhD in metaphysics and extensive experience in Behavioural Science. She is a sort after Keynote Speaker, Published Author and an Authority in the field of Human development.

Dance In The Fire of Life!

Introduction.

This book is about stories. Simply put, life is an accumulation of stories. In every moment and every day, our stories are being created and often we do not give them a second thought. Pivotal life moments are rarely given too much attention until such time as our focus is taken to them. This is exactly what I encountered when I put the call out to find my 26 co-authors for this unique opportunity to inspire hope in others with our stories.

One hundred and fifty-seven women from all over the globe responded within twenty-four hours. I was overwhelmed, surprised and humbled that my vision and intention for this beautiful book had resonated so quickly and with so many. What surprised me even more, however, was that most of these women did not believe they had a story and an accompanying message to share that anyone would be interested in reading, however, the pull to explore this opportunity further and respond to my call was far too strong.

As this was the first time I had put a book together with twenty-six other women from so many different time zones, I decided early on that this book was not going to be rushed and that it needed my full attention and dedication. I focused totally on creating a space where these beautiful women would feel safe in having deep discussions about their lives and I initiated many thought-provoking conversations within the group and individually, taking them to places in their minds they never thought possible. This was the key. Our fortnightly Masterclasses were where my co-authors discovered their superpowers, their individual brilliance and their courage to stand up and acknowledge that they have a story, in fact, stories within stories were unveiled, what they stood for and who they have come into the world to BE was uncovered and transformation took place in many parts of their lives.

Far too many women these days are confused about who they are and who others want them to be. Our lives are noisy, jammed packed with responsibilities and social media is putting a lot of pressure on women to look, be and act a certain way. The world, as it is today, even though it is 2019, is very disempowering for most women.

For the past 18 years, I have worked as a Holistic Therapist with hundreds of people, men, women and teenagers, many of whom were feeling despondent, lacking hope and vision for their life. During their sessions, they would share with me the letters they had written for their loved ones as they were contemplating taking their own life.

The common theme among the women coming to see me in this state, was that they felt the world took notice and made them feel visible when it came to the way they looked, their size, their body, their features and other superficial aspects of their physicality and yet, they felt the world took little notice of their mind, their intellect, their personal and professional achievements, their aspirations and their opinions. They felt they had become invisible to what matters and had resorted to believing they had no value and nothing to look forward to.

In working with these women, I found the KEY to helping them transform. Together, we were able to light up a path to fulfilment and joy, and at the same time place the path to suicide into a permanent 'black-out', never to be found again. All I had to do was to ensure that within the deep transformational work we did together they re-discovered who they were and, often, discovered for the first time their brilliance, their feminine power and their ferocious feminine courage. This is what I termed their own, unique 'Devine Soul Wisdom' that had yet to be accessed and lay buried deep inside their psyche, never having seen the light of day.

Once they unveiled their brilliance, they went from total despondency and devastating melancholy to an awakening of who they had come into the world to BE. The spark of love for their life was now re-ignited and as they continued to explore their relationship with themselves on the deepest possible level, their light in the world expanded.

Each woman's' discovery of her feminine mystique and the unequivocal feminine wisdom resulted in her ability to stand in her own power and purpose and follow her unique inner guidance. This resulted in each woman experiencing her life through a fiercely empowered state of mind. She could not help but have her newfound feminine confidence become visible for all to see and, for her vision of who she has come into this life to BE infused within every cell of their being. This made it impossible for her to ever get lost in the cancerous growth in our world that is born out of the superficiality, fakeness, pressure to look ageless, destructive limiting self-beliefs, all coming from a low self-worth and a low self-belief which as a result always ends up in the dark land of melancholy and despair.

"To meet one's own spirit is to search in the depths of one's soul where the pearl of divine wisdom awaits to adorn us with its glowing brilliance, forever encircling us in this human experience and igniting deep curiosity in others to do the same."
Vicki Gotsis Ceraso

My mission is to lead women into fearlessly unveiling their greatness to the world and confidently stepping into their feminine power to become the influence the world is crying out for.

The book, Dance In The Fire Of Life was an idea sparked from all the work and interactions with my clients over the years. This spark ignited an insatiable need to create something that will help women ignite their light and unveil their Devine Wisdom. I could not bear to see another woman stumble upon that dark path of despondency and deep melancholy which ultimately takes away her desire to BE who she has come into this life to BE!!

Each of my awe-inspiring co-authors has dug deep, uncovered her stories, her messages and her reason for being a light in this world. Each woman has trusted me to ghostwrite her chapter alongside her when necessary, ensuring her message is clear and her unique spirit is weaved within every page. I will forever be grateful for their trust and understanding. All I have ever wanted for these women is to witness them standing in their power, shining brightly and expanding their light so they can touch, inspire and pass on the beacon of hope to all women. They have not let me down.

If you are reading this Introduction and enjoy our beautiful book, consider if there is a call within your heart and soul to explore who you have come into this life to BE and to expand your unique light out into the world.

Reach out to me and I will help you write your own contributing chapter to one of my up and coming Anthologies, or, your very own Book, Workbook, Course, Keynote Talks, TED talk, and more.

Rest assured that under my watch you will not be producing something superficial in content and message as so many are doing these days. I am not interested in producing 30,000-word business cards. I'm interested in infusing each of my authors words with heart, soul, integrity and purpose.
I will help you unveil your brilliance and together, we will let the world understand clearly what it is that you have come into this world to offer through who you have come into this world to BE.

Join me in this rousing, inspirational and emotional united march of the Feminine Rising!!!

Together we can take measured and purposeful steps to catapult our individual lives as WOMEN RISING and ultimately transform the happiness and success destiny for the next generation of WOMEN RISING HIGHER!

My Cherished Soul Sister

Within YOU is the ability to bear the next generation
Within YOU is the ability to love insatiably
Within YOU is the knowledge that love is more powerful than greed, more powerful than hate
Within YOU burns the desire to show the world how profoundly judicious and necessary your sacred teachings and practices have become

For YOU are the vessel that holds wisdom generously bestowed upon it by generations of women who came before you
YOU are the vessel that will generously pour her wisdom into generations of women who have yet to come from you
Without YOU, humanity cannot exist, therefore, YOU are as vital and as essential as any man can be
If this is so, if this is true, then why is it that society is determined to keep YOU down?
Why is it that YOU are often downtrodden, disrespected, tortured, both emotionally and physically, for your intellect, for your beauty and for your wisdom and foresight?

Why is it that when YOU speak up, you are told to sit down?
Why is it that when YOU achieve great success, you are told to be humble?
Why is that when YOU stand for what's right, you're told it's not your place?
Why?
Why is it so?

HOW does a man who has a wife, a mother, a sister or a daughter come to the conclusion that it is perfectly acceptable to disparage, to demoralise and to dispirit the female psyche to the point of eradicating and annihilating any trace of self-confidence, self-esteem and self-regard?
HOW does that happen?

Women, do not let anyone put out YOUR glowing feminine light.
Fan those burning embers and re-ignite YOUR passions, YOUR purpose and YOUR life!
YOU are of value.

YOU are a precious gem whose shine should not and will not be taken from her
Whose value will not be allowed to diminish and whose existence here on earth is
more than just to offer pleasure and sustenance to those around her.

YOU are the strength behind your family
YOU can endure and overcome anything
YOU can create
YOU can think and YOU can negotiate
YOU can cure yourself of illness and you recognise how valuable and magical
your kiss and your hug can be to those you care about.
YOU are gentle, yet resilient.

Your only flaw is that YOU forget your OWN WORTH which is the very thing
that gives power to your oppressors and those who are intimidated by YOUR
incredible feminine power.

Re-discover and unveil the powerful, intelligent and confident parts of YOUR
psyche.
Fearlessly step into YOUR power and pass this down to the next generation of
women who will also become the influence the world is crying out for.

THIS is how we begin to change the world!

Vicki Gotsis Ceraso
SheRises Global

Melbourne, Australia

*Written for International Women's Day, 2018 and shared hundreds of times on various social
media platforms, read to 2000 women in Africa and also to hundreds of women in the USA*

"

To meet one's own spirit is to search in the depths of one's soul where the pearl of divine wisdom awaits to adorn us with its glowing brilliance, forever encircling us in this human experience and igniting deep curiosity in others to do the same."

~VICKI GOTSIS CERASO

Re-Ignite The Embers Of Your Life
Fearlessly Ignite a Relationship with Your Soul and Watch Your Light Expand
by Vicki Gotsis Ceraso

"To meet one's own spirit is to search in the depths of one's soul where the pearl of divine wisdom awaits to adorn us with its glowing brilliance, forever encircling us in this human experience and igniting deep curiosity in others to do the same."
~Vicki Gotsis Ceraso

Dear Cherished Soul Sister,

I have a calling deep inside my soul to share with you the wisdom I have accumulated along my journey in life. Yes, I have accumulated wisdom in the form of valuable lessons throughout my life and yet, I do not profess to be wise. My hope is that my sharing will encourage you to go deeper in search of your own divine internal wisdom and ignite within you curiosity and a passion for life that may have eluded you up until now.

I am a true believer that as a result of our life experiences, there is a brilliance that shines through in a unique way for each one of us to discover, and this very brilliance itself is subtly weaved throughout the essence of who we are on a spiritual level. This brilliance is OUR unique light. It is a reflection of our unique soul and therefore each light shines in a way that is comparable to our unique fingerprint and becomes our unique signature, created only for us. This light is also a reflection of the accumulated wisdom we have collected, understood and embraced. The more we learn from our life experiences, the brighter and more expansive our light becomes so it can reach out to all who need to draw healing energy, insight and guidance from it.

Our LIGHT is our SOUL. It is the essence of every experience we have ever had and represents our authentic, true self.

People today have an unquenchable thirst to find their purpose in life as if to not be successful in that quest is an inexcusable failing on their part. The truth, how-

ever, is that our only life purpose is to be a LIGHT. That's it. Our life purpose is nothing more and it is nothing less.

"What do you mean by our only purpose in life is to be a LIGHT?" I hear you ask. Our purpose is to spread love, kindness, forgiveness and empathy throughout the world and we do that by purposefully raising our vibration so high and so bright simply by changing the way we think. When we no longer allow ourselves to entertain thoughts of hate, envy, fear and regret, our vibration transforms into one of such deep love and deep understanding of ourselves, of the human condition and of every other human being on the planet.

When YOUR light shines brightly, people feel better by simply being in your presence. Never underestimate that the biggest impact we have on another is the feeling we leave them with after spending time with them. We actually have a choice in what energy we are putting out there and the effect we have on other people and on situations. We have so much more control over our lives than we allow ourselves to understand and acknowledge. Think back to recent interactions you have had and how these people made you feel within those interactions. Whenever you think of them, the first thing that 'pops' up is that very feeling you experienced during that interaction, much quicker than the memory of the conversation itself. You will remember the way they made you feel.

We are all so concerned with leaving behind a legacy and yet, we fail to realise that our true legacy is in the brilliance of our light that will linger in the hearts and minds of all those whose lives we touch.

> *"I've learned that people will forget what you said, people will forget what you did, but people will never forget how you made them feel."*
> ~~ *MAYA ANGELOU*

So if being a light in this world is our purpose, our enjoyment of life is in the pursuit of finding what sets our soul on fire. In other words, it is the journey towards the discovery of our passions that deserves to be fully explored, experienced and digested so that we get the most joy out of our life. If we are to be a light in this world and to enjoy the journey of our experience, then we need to bring both light and passion together as one. To pursue and then live our passions whilst being the light for all around us, is a fulfilment so deep and so vast that it cannot be emulated anywhere else in our life.

So, dear cherished soul sister, unearthing who we are on a deeper level is one of my greatest passions. This is where MY unique light shines ever so brightly. Helping people to understand that they have VALUE and what they have to say IS important enough for them to speak their truth at all times, is a labour of love for me. Transforming people from self-doubt and limiting self-beliefs to fearless and unfathomable confidence is the first of many steps I lead people to in order to find their VOICE and what they STAND FOR in life… Who they have come here to BE. I help people to understand that in order to have a VOICE, they need to have a MESSAGE and in order to have a message, they must understand their STORY and it is within that story that their brilliance, their SUPERPOWER is unleashed. It is in this discovery of what their life experience has taught them and the lessons it has gifted them, that they can share their message, have their voice heard and allow their light to expand and shine brightly. What better way to do that than to learn how to access all of who they are meant to be and share it in the form of a book, a course, a talk/speech. I help people ignite the spark and then expand its light as far as they can. When you experience your life and yourself in that way, you will live in irrefutable bliss every day!

So, indulge me if you will as I share with you parts of my story and the corresponding wisdom I discovered along the way.

I have found that situations, people and experiences come into our lives for many reasons. One of those reasons, I believe, is to help remind and guide us towards our magnificence, so as to live the life we have only quietly dreamed of. After all, our dreams and our yearnings could very well be markers we have placed along our life-path before we entered this world to remind ourselves of what it is we have come here to accomplish and to experience.

My life has gifted me with numerous opportunities to explore and discover this divine, empowered wisdom, I call my Inner Guidance System, within me. As I travel through my life, often trying desperately to avoid the experiences, lessons and responsibility these challenges bring forth, I have realized that my life's challenges were hiding valuable gems within them. They have provided me with growth, deep understanding and empowerment.

During one of my earliest challenges, I clearly remember my father encouraging, and therefore empowering me at a very young age with the belief that I was capable of anything I could imagine for my life. In parallel, I also recall another significantly influential person tell me I would not amount to much at all, and, actually went on to suggest that it would be best for me to stop dreaming big because to do so, would only set myself up for disappointment. These two totally polar opposite experiences, I believe, were instrumental in influencing my pursuit of discovering within me the resilience and courage necessary to face challenges later in my life. My greatest wish is to inspire and empower you with the same belief. I want you to understand that your life challenges were not meant to be burdens to internalize and be defined by. Rather, they were meant to be valuable lessons that have you living from your all-powerful state of mind.

There is nothing more valuable that I can think of gifting you than the unequivocal wisdom that every woman has come equipped with ALL of the necessary sacred tools she requires to overcome ALL of the challenges she has chosen for herself - from a time now long forgotten. These sacred tools are a part of the feminine mystique that supports every woman to stand in her own power and purpose and follow her unique inner guidance, resulting in experiencing her life through a fiercely empowered state of mind.

I want your state of mind to be so full of certitude that you believe you can do anything and seek to create BIG goals and dreams for yourself. I want you and every woman on the planet to have choice!

My precious soul sister, as you travel through your life, you may encounter challenges and perhaps, at times, even adversity. Understanding that you have within you a pearl of divine wisdom which when unlocked, will directly connect you with your ability to stand powerfully, to discover your inner guidance and unveil your empowered state of mind, is what will enable you to live a joyful life.

It is within your robustly confident state of mind, dear soul-sister, that your unique 'sacred tools' can be found. Some of these may be Courage, Resilience, Compassion, Faith, Strength, Intellect, Power, Empathy, Trust, Creativity, Authenticity, Integrity, Being Your Word... and so much more. Please remember that these tools are at your disposal to tap into whenever you are guided to do so.

My darling, this all-powerful state of mind, once unlocked, will sustain you throughout your entire life. It will nourish your soul and birth a state of lasting empowerment within you. You will not have to live your life feeling disempowered by crippling fear and self-doubt, as I have endured at times.

I want you, in times of doubt, angst or at times where you find yourself sliding into disempowerment, to reach into the deepest part of your soul and pull out those valuable gems, those sacred tools you have come into this life with, and Rise Up and INTO your unique power!

Avoiding and hiding from life is tragic as you take away the opportunity to experience all that you have come into this life to experience and learn. If you are numb to life's experiences and all that comes with these, you will end up trudging through life aimlessly, feeling empty of all significance and relevance. A life that is evaded and anesthetized, is a life wasted!

Alternatively, as long as you are present in your life and allow yourself to be fully immersed in the experience of living, your life, just like mine, will provide you ample opportunity to discover your greatness along with your unique purpose and calling.

It will enable you to fearlessly pursue what sets your soul on fire!

For me, the experience as a child of taking on the 'imagined responsibility' of being the glue in my parents' relationship, forged my creativity, my intellect, my sense of humour and my resilience.

Another pivotal moment in my life came with motherhood. While the experience of being a mother to three beautiful sons before I had turned 30 years of age was neither unique nor of great significance, coming to the realization that my son, Rick, was not developing at the same pace as other children his age, however, had a monumental impact on me.
Initially, it brought me to my knees. In my struggle to get off the floor, breathe and do everything in my power to not allow myself to drown in the sea of tears which I had shed, I stood up, stepped into my power and came face to face with a side of me I had never seen before. There she was, standing right before me and gently inhabiting my soul, the 'Ferocious Feminine Mama Warrior' and I wanted to understand it all!

I immersed myself in studying everything I could get my hands on to work out what was wrong with my precious boy; despite the medical professionals' resistance and lack of acknowledgment that there were any problems with Rick's development. In fact, the doctors believed the problem lay with me; and tried to diagnose me with Munchausen syndrome by proxy: a psychological disorder where the mother or caregiver fabricates illnesses in her child in order to be the centre of attention. This was completely devastating to me, and I felt so shocked and totally disempowered.

Vindication and a bittersweet relief came when Rick was finally diagnosed as autistic. I rose up and acknowledged to myself that I had the power to take back control of my life and that of my son's.

In looking for answers and in searching for ways to ensure that I, as a young mother who was strong in her opinions and her personal self-belief, was not dismissed and overlooked, I made an invaluable discovery. This discovery continues to serve me powerfully and I am sure will do so for the rest of my life. I share this with you here as it is unfathomable for me to keep it to myself knowing how much it has helped me in my life and how much it can help you.

I fumbled my way and stumbled upon my own INNER GUIDANCE SYSTEM and this discovery led me to have a steady, slow flow of guidance and wisdom whenever I need it. It gave me the confidence to allow resilience, tenacity, unbreakable self-belief and new-found confidence to come out of the shadows and SOAR!

Suddenly, I had power!
Suddenly, I had choice!

Together with this endless stream of inner guidance, I enabled myself to become my son's advocate, my son's voice! I have never, ever doubted myself since.

Tapping into that endless source of guidance that is patiently waiting for us to unlock and access, is possibly THE most enlightening experience we will ever have as it is a bottomless vessel that holds the answers to all the questions we seek to find answers to. This Inner Guidance System is what accompanied us into this lifetime, but all too often we forget it is right there beside us, as obvious as our shadow and over time, just as forgettable.

I wish I could tell you that the discovery of my inner guidance was as a result of some intelligent, wisdom filled and purposeful intention on my part. I wish I could tell you that there was a purpose-driven search which was smooth, elegant and respectable like a beautifully orchestrated ballet - to do so, however, would be untruthful.

Please understand that when I say I 'fumbled my way and stumbled upon my inner guidance', I don't use that phrase fleetingly. I want you to understand that I actually DID fumble like a woman frantically searching in pitch black darkness for something, anything she could get her hands on, to help her and in turn, help her son so that he gets the best chance possible to reach his potential and have a joyous life. Not only did I not know what I was frantically and blindly searching for, when I did stumble across my Sacred Inner Guidance System, I was just like a drunken sailor trying to keep her balance on a ship in the middle of the ocean, in the midst of a ferocious storm, void of any resemblance of finesse and respectability whatsoever!

If anyone tells you, my dear soul-sister, that their own spiritual awakening to their inner guidance was smooth, easy, beautiful and emotionally painless, you can, of course, choose to believe them. However, I'm more inclined to believe that they have forgotten the pain, much like giving birth. The pain and trauma of giving birth is for the most part forgotten once the baby has arrived so the mother can bond with and nurture her child… and is not afraid to do it all over again.

If your experience of internal and spiritual awakening is similar to mine, rest assured that we are not alone and the surprise discovery of our own unique inner guidance is worth it all! Our own unique Inner Guidance System embodies all of the sacred tools we came into this life with. It is these Sacred Tools that are patiently waiting to be called upon to help deal with all of the challenges we have chosen for ourselves. Remember, we do not come into this life with more than we can handle. My biggest realization and among the most valuable lessons I've learned along my journey thus far has been that once my sacred tools were recognized, unpacked and acknowledged, that toolbox - and it's well-earned contents- are forever available to me.

See, my darling, you may never go through anything as difficult nor as challenging as what I have experienced - nor will I have likely endured what you have; and comparing is unnecessary. That said, in the event that you do, please know, unequivocally, that you, just like me, have everything you need to propel you to greater heights in your life and get you through anything. You cannot be destroyed by anything in life unless you let it!

You may never experience crippling financial loss as I have - and understand that such an experience has the power to ignite in you, as it did for me, a powerful drive and determination – a determination kept alive by unfathomable courage, uncompromising self-belief and the will to bounce back up and resume your life path with grace and incredibly deserving feminine pride.

I can share with you, without any doubt in my mind, that everything that happens in your life, happens for a reason. Often, you become frustrated because you do not understand why some things happen to you but with a little patience and willing insight, the lessons that come from your experiences are always revealed at the perfect time.

I am at a point in my life where I am in the privileged position of being able to look back over fifty plus years and identify and reflect upon the many pivotal life-moments that, in hindsight, highlight how important it was for me to keep my mind positive and empowered. I cannot imagine what my life would have been like if I had not. If I had to guess, I would say, it would likely have been a life of total disempowerment, crowded with limiting self-belief and somewhat void of love and happiness. I would have given up so many times on myself and on my life. I can't imagine dying with my music still inside me, never been expressed!

"When you change the way you look at your life, your life will change!"
WAYNE DYER

The only thing that is ever holding you back is YOU. You have the ability to utilize your mind just as you wish. When you achieve this goal of taking responsibility for your thoughts, that's when your entire life shifts into becoming a powerful manifesting machine! You become conscious of your own input and the effect that has on your life. You then become ignited with taking charge of yourself, which is when you start to make your goals and dreams a reality!

I hope you can see, through my sharing with you, the importance of believing that you can achieve ALL of your goals, overcome ALL of your challenges and foster an empowered and fearless way of looking at your life.

You have come into this life to shine brightly and step into your greatness. Never, ever forget that. If you choose to, you can be the possibility of the inspiration of love, greatness, and ferocious feminine fearlessness in this world and take on an integrity-rich and authentic way of living your life!

My Cherished Soul Sister,
I close with a poem I wrote as my heartfelt gift to you in the hope that you may take the wisdom within its words with you on your travels in this experience we chose to call LIFE:

As you travel through your unique life-journey, thank your past for the lessons
Put your future on notice that you're ready to take your awe-inspired dreams with you
Choose to step into the life you crave to create but,
Do not forget to turn your dreams of today into the plans of tomorrow

When contemplating all the things you love and value
Please ensure to include yourself
For self-love is nourishment to your souls' stirring
And the forgiveness of your futile pursuit of approval

Do not take that which appears easy to you for granted
For these are your divine virtues disguised as gifts and talents
They were borne out of a longing to follow the luminous threads in the tapestry of your life
And deserve to be acknowledged and used in service to humanity

Understand, when you experience a breakdown
It will always follow with a breakthrough
When you stand face to face in front of an extraordinary challenge
Choose to see unexpected opportunities instead of imminent obstacles

Take time to breathe, to heal and become re-acquainted with yourself
Discover your voice, speak your truth and reclaim your life
Jump into your fears, set yourself free of all limitation and,
Create possibilities that have you giddy with unimaginable excitement and joy to be alive!

All My Love,
Vicki Gotsis-Ceraso

Dance In The Fire of Life!

Author
Vicki Gotsis Ceraso

Vicki Gotsis Ceraso wears many hats.
She is the Founder and CEO of SheRises Global, VGC Publishing, Together We Rise Magazine, Co-Founder of WiN -World Influencers Network and AWN Global.

Vicki is also a Holistic Integrated Behaviour Practitioner, a Life Strategy Consultant, an Australian Feminine Leader and International Speaker with proud Greek migrant roots, stating that her biggest achievement is her family. Married to the love of her life for 33 years, together, they have three young adult sons whom she often refers to as her 'greatest life–teachers', particularly Rick who is on the Autism Spectrum. Vicki's extensive experience in the study of Personal Development and Human Behaviour led her to create Ultimate Life School & Mind Insights, offering women powerfully transformative courses.

Through supportive leadership, Vicki helps women fearlessly explore the reasons they have not connected to their vision for their life nor identified their authentic self by teaching them strategies to do so and guide them to step into their purpose and dream future.

Vicki's vision is to lead women into unveiling their greatness to the world and fearlessly step into their power to become the influence the world is crying out for.

Her unquenchable thirst for knowledge has led her to become proficient in a multitude of areas over the past 20 years. Her professional specialty areas include:
Strategy Consultant, Coach, Counselling, EFT and NLP, Hypnotherapy, Educational Trainer and Assessor, Life Enhancement Coach-PTSD, Speaker, Author, Poet, Workshop Facilitator & more recently, Global Anthology Creator/Compiler and Retreats Facilitator.

She is passionate about helping women get from feeling stuck and not evolving, into a space where they are ever-expanding and achieving whatever it is their heart yearns for.

*Vicki has recently created quite a buzz initiating a powerful **Global Feminine Movement** called **SheRises Global**, bringing together women to discover and follow the call in their heart and become a part of the collective feminine voice the world is **craving** to hear.*

*One way that Vicki is fulfilling her vision and mission to Raise Women on a Global level is to create collaborative, heart centred Anthologies. The intention and purpose of her **SheRises Global** Series of books is to blend our stories and experiences together, as women, and initiate thought-provoking conversations which will inspire, empower and elevate the hopes and dreams of women all over the world.*
*Vicki believes we are ALL created for greatness and she has searched and discovered greatness in her own life and in the lives of hundreds of women. She is a great believer that every life experience can be used to inspire people to hold on to their dreams and **RISE**!*
*The SheRises Global series of books create a loving, non-judgemental platform for women who have overcome obstacles and triumphed from the lessons learned, to share their compelling stories, with the direct aim to empower and inspire other women all over the world to **RISE** and celebrate their brilliance*
-all the while, embracing women everywhere and at the exact place, they are at right now.

Vicki's books all have one BIG theme and that is that every book she creates will have was she calls a 'Legacy Theme' woven within it. Vicki believes that the best way for authors to share themselves, their story, their message and their gifts is to include the intricacies of their life story which is a form of storytelling and yet it is also the most complex form of writing as it requires the author to delve deep and take a personal journey of discovery.

The complexity of this style of writing involves not only emerging themes, and narrative flow, but also re-creating stories and even dialogue from memory.

Vicki has a gift when it comes to helping her authors get all of their Story, their Message and their Superpower on the written page, articulated in a clear and precise way so to inspire, touch and enlighten the reader in a profound way. She helps her authors accomplish this by using Legacy Themes to direct them in capturing and unveiling their Pearls of Wisdom which are longing to sparkle their brilliance in the light of day.

These are some of the book themes women are joining with Vicki to become Global Co-Authors and/or Authors in their own right:

Sliding Doors
• *Arriving at the Crossroads of Your Life*
• *I am who I am due to my family history*
• *My Life's Work, My point of Genius*
• *What is the Male-Female Equation all about?*
• *Parenting a Child with Special Needs*
• *The meaning of Life - musings*
• *Life after Death*
• *Success is the Willingness to Fail*
• *My Legacy Letter (to my daughter/son)*
• *Strategising and Meeting Life Goals*

Some Titles:
*Dance In The Fire OF Life (Men's Version)
*Ignite The Embers Of Your Life
*Wisdom Whisperings
...and many more titles to come.
**Vicki features her co-authors in quality, Global Magazines, Podcasts and Videos to get their message out into the world!!!

"The collective Feminine Spirit **RISES** *so much higher when women who choose to dance through the fire of life leave sparks of light wherever they go, illuminating the path for the future generation of women to come.*

Dance In The Fire Of Life is a vessel which holds enthralling, thought-provoking and wisdom filled stories generously bestowed upon it by 27 awe-inspiring women from all over the world." is how Vicki described her globally acclaimed Anthology **Dane In The Fire Of Life**.

https://business.facebook.com/vicki.ceraso
www.sherisesglobal.com
www.vickiceraso.com
www.vickigotsisceraso.com
https://www.facebook.com/vicki.ceraso
Twitter: @cerasovicki
instagram.com/vicki.ceraso
LinkedIn: Vicki Ceraso
Email: vicki@sherisesglobal.com
Book In: https://calendly.com/vickiceraso/virtual-coffee-chat
Aurthor Page: amazon.com/author/vickigotsisceraso

Dance In The Fire Of Life *is a vessel which holds enthralling, thought-provoking and wisdom filled stories generously bestowed upon it by 27 awe-inspiring women from all over the world.*

"

What I believe and know for sure, is that by being true to myself, listening to the guiding voice within, has remarkably shifted my perception of who I was meant to be. I recognise that I have all that it takes to be ME!"

~ALL MY LOVE MARY

At The End of Nature's Illuminated Path,
I Discovered My Wings and Stepped Into My TRUTH!
by Marica (Mary) Grahovac

My precious one. From the moment you took your first breath, you were destined to shine. You are a gift the world has been waiting for, just as you are. *I just wish I could tell you without question, that I truly believe this within myself. The truth is, I often don't.*

What I can tell you for sure is that the paths set before you are many, and the ones you choose to follow will always be the right ones, even though at times it may not seem that way.

Your curious youthful nature will be enticed by the spectacular splendour and beauty of the world as she unfolds before you, which may lead you far away from the securities of a life you have come accustomed to. Your journey through life will be filled with adventure, yet not without the lessons learnt along the way.

Learn from Mother Nature. You will be drawn into her intoxicating fragrance and colours as she reveals to you her virtues of simplicity, gentleness, harmony and strength. Trust her my love for she is a reflection of you. When the winds carry your wings to places of unfamiliar ground, know that you are not alone. Listen closely to her voice. It's the sounds coming from the pits of your belly, and you may feel her in the pounding of your chest. She will guide you and tell you if you are off course. Trust her voice, my love, for she speaks the truth and the truth is within you.

For the past 25 years, I've dedicated my life to my family and farming. For 10 of those years, my family and I have lived off the grid, tending to our goats and selling my produce at local markets. It was during these years l learnt to live alongside nature. In a small isolated village 800m high in the mountain region of Croatia, my respect for every fundamental element of life took on a whole new meaning. For the first time in my life, I recognised the beauty in how everything on this mountain is connected. I want you to understand that I learnt to rely on mother nature and allowed her to be my guide because my survival on the mountain depended upon it. I knew when it was time to plough, to sow and plant, time to harvest and time to rest. When she revealed her extreme forces l was vulnerable and was at her mercy. I learned never to underestimate her, anyone nor anything, including myself. From the experiences I have shared with you here, I want nothing less than for you to believe beyond a shadow of a doubt that everything you need is already inside of you. You do not need to live on a mountain to come to this realisation as I did.

The day will arrive when you too will fall in love and how spectacular that day will be!
You will fall in love with his passion, his determination and his want to change the world. In turn, he will recognise the butterfly in you, free-spirited in spreading your wings and trusting the wind to carry you wherever you need to go.
He will fall in love with your spirit that is also craving to nest and create a loving family to call your own.

All of this is what he will fall in love with.
Whatever you do, commit to a man that you get to know well. Commit to a man whose life is not in pieces that you will eventually have to pick up off the floor and put back together again because, in doing so, you are committing to HIS life and HIS dreams instead of your own.

Choose your partner wisely. Chose a man who will equally commit to YOU. Choose a man who will not turn all the things he loved about you into his own insecurities and fears which will, in turn, compel him to control you.

Heed my advice because If you're not careful, those breathtakingly beautiful wings will feel the very first snip of the scissors and the guilt, the shame and the humiliation will begin to be your constant companion. Your memories of the free-spirited life you had before will become the 'never spoken about again' experiences and you will find yourself standing in silence, uttering HIS words as if they are your own. He will speak FOR you and Snip! Snip! Your wings will start to look pretty shabby!

It is when you forget to sing and you forget to dance that you will begin to lose yourself and your voice and it is when you lose the desire for self-recognition and respect that you hear even louder the Snip! Snip! of those once, breathtakingly beautiful wings falling to the ground with an all mighty THUMP!

If you allow your values to be abused, your thoughts to be second-guessed and your parenting skills to be mapped out for you, then you will discover angry parts within yourself that you never knew existed and you will begin to hate everything about the woman you have allowed yourself to become. I don't want you to hear the Snip of the scissors disheveling those precious wings and destroying their ability to take flight again.

I don't want you to suppress parts of yourself to satisfy other's expectations of you and your life.

Don't allow yourself to fade away. Don't let anyone cut your wings.
Love brings with it the sweet nectar that we crave to taste but beware of that sweet nectar that seeps from the words of the mouths of those wishing to lure you into the confined spaces of deception.

Don't reach that day in your life where you are painfully looking at your reflection and seeing a shadow of a woman you barely recognise.

Don't reach that day when you find yourself holding your voice back, stop it from being heard, and allowing your words to be twisted and twirled. Those who chose to live their own lies may cause you to become a part of a facade, masking and veiling your true self.

What causes us to do this to ourselves? What is it that allows us to give permission to others to treat us in this way?

It is this imaginary uninvited companion which we call 'fear' and only exists in our overactive imagination that is the culprit. Fear is something we create in our minds. We chose its existence for various reasons and avoid any personal control and responsibility for it. You can choose to pretend and deny the truth and fade away amongst the shadows of deceit. Or, you can stand tall with all that you are, with all your virtues and values and trust everything that exists within you. You have the capacity to draw on self-love so fiercely and share it so generously that you will become empowered yourself and discover your capacity to empower others to do the same.

So, let not fear to befriend your mind, for it will rob you of self-respect and the respect of others. It will lure you into the depths of its shadows and deny you the opportunity to taste the flavours of life. If you allow it to, your fear can fixate you, separating you from the rhythm of nature's calling making it an unpleasant and unnatural place to be.

When your awakening begins, you break away from your silent withdrawal and your yearning for change takes hold. That is when your voice screams out to be heard. That is when your instinct, that feeling of churning and twisting is prompt-

ing you to embrace change. You must listen to your gut instinct. You must trust it.

Treading water for too long and not moving forward feels like you are drowning in your own self- defeating mental state convincing yourself that better days are ahead but deep down, knowing that they won't be coming unless you do something about today. You must always deal with the day at hand. Live in the now in order to enjoy tomorrow.

You did not come into this world to live without out change, without challenges without a sound, and without the potential for growth. To stand still, do nothing, say nothing, you give permission to this false sense of being. Do not allow your values to be compromised, eventuating in becoming consumed by helplessness and despair, until you are grasping to the heavens above and pleading with it to free you from its clutches.

Many a time you will fall short of your expectations. It's alright to feel the pain and sadness that comes from this disappointment. It's alright to grant yourself permission to make all the mistakes you will need to make in life, for perfection does not exist and you are ENOUGH just as you are. Relieve yourself of burden, fault, blame and the ghost of shame. Allow yourself to submit to your weaknesses, in time, they will become your strongest armour, your biggest lessons.

Your lessons learnt will be your truth., It's all the wisdom you will ever need., and it is all within you.

Tomorrow brings unexpected new things. The harshest of storms can thicken the air, blinding your view. The ground may tremble beneath your feet. You will shed the parts of yourself that no longer serve you and sway, bend and break in the process. As you cry to the moon and the sun with tears that wash away the dust from your eyes, only to notice that you are still standing, be in awe of what you are capable of!
Be in awe of who you truly are!

Your roots are deep and wide and when your eyes can still see the sky, you have survived! Your kind, gentle, loving nature, embraces forgiveness and you become a river that flows and moves on in the inevitable direction that it is pulled toward. You have the capacity to heal the wounds of all that is broken and deserve to wear your scars with honour and pride.

You should feel free to paint the world with the colours you possess in your soul and decorate the world with your divine authenticity. Fly high my love, spread your wings for all to see, your colours are truly yours.

The biggest discovery I have had throughout my entire life is the inborn ability we have as women to stand in our power. To stand in, and have power is about being true to yourself, loving who you are, the way you are and discovering what you stand for.

Curiously though, as women, we all suffer the same affliction; as soon as we think about our own needs and wants, we either make ourselves feel shameful and guilty, or, we allow others to do this to us. We then lose confidence in every aspect of our life, from making decisions to identifying with who we are. It is when we allow this debilitating experience of limiting self-worth and self-belief to take hold of us that the world outside our threshold overtime gets bigger and bigger and we become smaller and smaller. We are no longer seen, let alone heard and ultimately, we become insignificant in our own lives.

The antidote for this affliction is to always search out opportunities of solitude so you can explore in your heart the qualities you believe are true and valuable to your life. Notice when your thoughts go to the importance of every other human being, for it is then that you need to awaken the desire and importance to re-discover your own self-importance, your own self-respect and more importantly, over and above anything else, the love that you deserve for yourself.

In closing, I would like to leave you with my analogy of the lessons life has taught me and please feel free to apply this to your life as and where you see fit.

I am who I believe I am. I believe I was a good, loyal, hardworking human being. I never complained about the challenges that came with the life I chose to follow. My justification for that has always been that I alone chose this life, therefore, I take full responsibility for making the very best out of it.

I always tried to be calm, patient and brave as I waited for the rains to fall and quench the parched soil which filled the wells with water. I had disciplined my senses to hear, to smell and to notice all of nature surrounding me and I respected her absolute prerogative to bring forth her will as her motives are never without reason. As time passed, I began to understand how she nurtures all who reside upon her and the way she cradles the essence of life. The hope of new life, growth and then, ultimately, death. I felt a connection to her as if I was an extension of her, nurturing my family, my home and my farm animals, and I taught myself how to bring forth sustenance sculptured by my hands. I never complained, no matter how cold or hot it got, or how tired my body became. I tolerated the loneliness and the isolation, the floods and droughts and never blamed her for her powers and her will. Even more so, I admired her strength and resilience. Inadvertently, I started to mirror and embody her strength by standing in MY own power and in doing so, I realised that alongside her, I had lived and I had survived all these years. Mother Nature prompted me to recognise my qualities for they are my virtues, and they are a part of me I had not recognised, all along.

Oh, how my heart yearns that we all could understand that we are also a part of this magical symphony called Mother Nature. If we soften our hearts and be willing to learn that we are all important to one another, we would grow, mature and become who we are meant to be.

What I know for sure is that we need to BE TRUE TO OURSELVES. If you are feeling stuck in life, l guarantee that by listening to your inner voice, you will shift your energy and opportunities WILL appear. The impossible WILL become possible.
Through all your challenges, your lessons and hardships, you owe it to yourself to pursue your goals, dreams, and desires.

I do not claim to have provided you with any remarkably profound words of wisdom here, wise l have yet to become. I can only speak of feelings that surface from the depths of my soul. I have learnt to listen and trust my inner voice, l am reclaiming my abandoned dreams and my identity. I know I'm on the right path because for the first time in years, l like the person l see in the mirror. As l am discovering myself, I am excited! I finally have a choice! I have the choice to be ME and I love the woman I have become!

My BIG wish is this:
Let's decorate the world with our individual colours, thus paving the path for a better tomorrow for generations of women to come!

Co-Author
Marica (Mary) Grahovac

Marica has an Associate Diploma in Business Studies and Marketing.
During her young adult life, Marica spent most of her time working in hotels, exclusive restaurants and food service departments for institutes such as hospitals and rehabilitation centres. She spent over twelve months backpacking across the world and ended up in the country of her parent's birth, Croatia.

Marica married in Croatia and became a mother to three sons whom she adores. Her life changed dramatically. She found herself becoming very passionately involved in agriculture and farming where she managed and farmed her family property in the mountain region where the scarcity of water challenged the survival of her own and her families' survival every day.

Marica discovered the incredibly resourceful side to her nature and produced not only food but was also butcher, baker and believe it or not, a candlestick maker. Marica is currently working in the Hotel industry again, managing, training others and completing everyday tasks. She is also tutoring English to young children and is now also consulting as an advisor to a Bed and Breakfast lodgings.

In her free time, Marica enjoys her role as senior vocalist in a youth choir and has a love of crafts and meditates whilst yarning wool so as I can create fabulous woollen garments, for winter.

I have recently, through the opportunity to be in this magical book, discovered a new tool and it's MY VOICE which I am able to express through the written word. I have re-discovered ME

Facebook: Marica Grahovac
Email: marica.grahovac1@gmail.com

66

Women alive in the 21st century have the privilege to be born at a time where, more than any other time in history, we have the means, support, access and resources to contribute our voices and perspectives to impact others globally. ”

~LAURIE VALLAS

The Real Heroine Epidemic
by Laurie Vallas

To Every Beloved Child –

As in nature, women's bodies are divinely designed to create, cultivate and nurture growth, and thrive when all is in harmonious balance. Additionally, it is important to consider the environmental influences and multisensory components that either cause or contribute to atrophy; disrupting the equilibrium within that sacred container. Silencing and censoring of ourselves and one another, are aspects of social atrophy that threaten to compromise the health and well-being of future generations. My intention is to both remind and encourage every woman to stoke the embers and fan the flames of each other's voices so that it protects, preserves and restores the balance our world so desperately requires.

~ ~ ~

There was a time when I felt I had little to contribute to the 'cause of raising voices'; as I expected to be busy raising children. My path towards motherhood didn't begin the way I had 'expected' and, perhaps, you too may share a similar experience of 'expecting' your life to unfold according to your 'Plan'; only to realize that 'your Plan' never existed in the first place. What a shocker, huh? Some believe their lives are in the hands of 'God's Plan' - others, a result of 'Divine Intervention'. As I have evolved, so has the understanding of my message, its narrative, and the sobering acceptance that 'my Plan' meant that my much-needed role and responsibility in contributing to the raising, nurturing, and mothering of children – everywhere – required something completely different from what I had 'expected'.

For many years, I didn't realize the genesis of this path originated from parental anecdotes; each of whom consistently shared their guiding principles with me as a young girl. My mother's is, "Stand for something, or you'll fall for anything." My father's, "He who angers me, conquers me." Without a lot of life-experience, clarification, or context, each of these statements and their implied responsibilities, landed on my little shoulders like two enormous boulders. I didn't understand how to interpret or navigate them either. To be honest, I didn't want to – because the risk of 'getting it wrong' felt quite daunting. I just wanted to be liked, accepted – as well as acceptable. I desperately wanted to be considered a *good girl*. The thought of taking either a stand for or voicing beliefs that my family or friends may have opposed, absolutely petrified me. Any wrong 'stand' could brand me an outcast – rejected, not respected; my insights not worthy or valued. Or, worse, I could be shamed. Not knowing who, or how, to ask for clarification – all of my doubts were promptly concealed; on went the armor.

Despite the physical pain I experienced keeping my young, yet big-spirit restrained in constant, bridled censorship – my doubts and fears remained hidden for years; decades even. I subsequently developed a habit of apologizing for just about everything. 'I'm sorry' became a staple prefix to most of my sentences.

This chronic, self-censored way of living eventually manifested into exhausting anger; an anger that attempted to conceal my intense hurt and immobilizing shame. I resented that my capacity to love and to be loved, was indeed being conquered. Many years passed before I could grasp, articulate and forgive the cost of wasting a regrettable amount of time and energy in quiet, polite, yet burning rage. I felt deep bitterness that the anger, and the weight of the armor I embodied to contain it, had prevailed over my desire to be vulnerable, connected and accepted as I am. Like a self-fulfilling prophecy, my inability to take a stand for myself eventually resulted in years of recurring, debilitating knee injuries. I deflected that physical pain by rationalizing that 'conceivably' the best remedy to heal my body and the past would be to raise my children differently (which arrogantly translated into 'better'). I fantasized that 'when' they arrived, I would ensure my children would always know they were fully supported to express their ebullient, authentic selves. My children would know, deep in their bones, that they could stand, encouraged and empowered to make an enduring and meaningful contribution to the world.

And then, in a moment of crushing disbelief, the day came when I realized that children were not intended to come through me. Initially, I didn't understand. Why? With a heart full of love and a soul equipped to nurture, defend, protect, and teach – why not a mother – at *all*?

I recall feeling utterly immobilized in denial, wondering if I was so deeply impaired by fear and shame that it contaminated the 'whole-istically' fertile container necessary to create, and safely nurture a child? Numbed by the prospect that a strong, subconscious belief that, '*I may get this mothering-thing wrong*' potentially contributed to rendering my body – incapable; left me in total panic. Surely this was a mistake? When I miscarried – again – I wailed into my pillow; my mind desperate for answers on how to 'fix' this. *Fix me*. I was convinced there must be a way I could think, wish or rationalize 'a cure' and figure out how to make my <u>body</u> become a sustainable and safe haven to carry my beloved child into the world? It wasn't supposed to happen this way… and not to me.

I grieved deeply – but purposefully.

Through my grieving process, I realized that all of my maternal instincts – combined with capacity, in the form of resources, time, energy, and love – meant my 'mothering' was still needed. Still relevant. My heart was required – not my ego. In my core, I knew there was something else to learn… something more. But… what?

What emerged was a recognition, understanding, and acceptance of the expanded role as a still-relevant woman. This realization pioneered a pathway towards freedom, towards courage, and woke a new willingness to support the parenting of the next generation in a way I had neither previously imagined, nor considered. Part of monogramming that process required me to redefine parenting into a context I could relate to, and then ultimately contribute to, deeper, unmapped aspects of motherhood. This clarification would occur at a very intimate level – requiring me to trust that I also understood unconditional love at a level where I previously believed only 'a mother's love' was capable of knowing.

In preparing for this deep-dive, I became aware of the necessity to navigate towards, and connect into, an ancestral taproot. Once reunited, the inevitable and necessary excavation would require persistent, consistent courage to face and overcome the stubborn, equally hard-wired childhood belief that I was neither good – nor worthy. However, to create the capacity and understanding of loving and trusting unconditionally in a deep, meaningful way, required me to encourage and empower that emerging mother – outside of the long-established societal definition, I was taught.

While I had not birthed children, it was important to acknowledge where I have created from deep passion and breathed ideas and imagination to life. I recognize how the female body can absorb and create like no other creature, and I understand that women hold the unique and singular capacity to take in and transform – miraculously taking an 'if' and nurturing it into a 'when.' Where healing is required, I know from experience that women's bodies can repair themselves by connecting with a body-wisdom only the feminine matrix comprehends.

The questions came flooding in, "…and what do you know about all this?" "Where would you even begin to illustrate and illuminate the pathway towards encouragement or - 'in-couragement'?" "What does that even mean?" "How do

you achieve this, when you are accustomed to being crippled in an arrested state of development by your own relentless self-censorship?" These answers, of course, were not something I could Google.

Where and how to source a way forward into these uncharted depths of myself required the very thing I was most reluctant to do: seeing, and speaking, with un-bridled, uncensored courage. I began with the following:

• To no longer ask for permission, or approval, and proudly stand for my authentic self to reassure the 'self-doubting me'. To no longer cower, or hide behind the fear of rejection and judgement. To know, and believe, that I am worthy of being seen.

• Refuse to be conquered into silence, but to name, transform and re-purpose the source of my frustration and anger into love; a passion for truth and justice.

To achieve this, it was essential to both excavate and translate my innermost dialogue. I would need to alchemize existing words and transform the associated sounds. I was stunned to discover the plethora of words, feelings, and beliefs that could benefit from new explanations.

This is when I recognized that by literally deconstructing and reshaping words – they became re-defined. I suddenly realized that all those years ago, each of my parents had given me an extraordinary gift embedded in those anecdotes. Those words of wisdom were never intended to be heavy, insurmountable boulders meant to weigh me down. I misunderstood myself. The message was, be bolder. The lesson: Be 'bold-HER'.

Further lessons and methods of communication began to re-weave themselves into my vocabulary in ways that continue to surprise me. I began to listen and hear everything in a completely new way; and what I heard began to shape, inform and illustrate a whole new way of experiencing language. Inertia set in, and I felt in my bones I was on to something.

As a young girl, and to this day, one of my favorite allegories is *"The Emperor's New Clothes."* In this timeless tale, we are reminded that we witness a similar 'mass censorship by way of shame' – daily. Shame is a powerful tool of suppression. Shame <u>silences</u>; it prevents us from saying what we are seeing - our truth. The fear of being shamed prevents us from acknowledging when we see the 'naked' Emperors and Empresses, amongst us. In this story, because of fear and shame, no one took a stand for what they knew in their hearts was the truth; all except one boy. When the boy spoke his truth, he spoke the truth of many. As a child, I admired and identified with the boy. How ironic to discover that as an adult woman, oftentimes my behavior was likened more to that of the fearful Emperor, whilst I longed to be more courageous like the boy! All of those years spent in foolish angst, in excruciating, suffocating silence was quite the paradox.

No more.

As courage is the antidote to fear and shame, I gradually began to take incremental risks to express myself more authentically. I shared my grief, my disappointment, and yes, my anger. By every means possible, I began to remove layers of protective armor and open my heart's mouth in all its raw, uninhibited expression – and guess what? No one ran. No one told me to be quiet. Some thanked me, and some wished I had shared sooner. Others said, "Me too – and this is my story…"

Years of energy expended in fear of either being judged or misunderstood had all been an unnecessary distraction, but a necessary process. Galvanized into vigilant urgency, I remember the surge of frustration and self-judgement rise again. However, this time, I could transform it into a passion for purpose. Upon awakening to the responsibility that I no longer had time to squander, the energy that now swelled within me was intrepid boldness. There was much to heal, but much more to accomplish – and much courage was required. Just because I'd lost or broken my compass, didn't mean I was. I could borrow, or even share one until I found my way again.

Let me take a moment to pause and ask: are you unsure of your next step – or daunted by the numerous choices of roads presented before you? Do you have a compass – and do you trust it? Or, do you meander through life, as I have done, trying to find your way? It took me years to understand our hearts are our compasses – our True North; and it's important to share this remarkable navigational tool with others. We need many compasses, aligned, for our journey ahead.

The next step in the excavation of a new leadership model is to explore language and phonetics; highlighting that it can be confusing when written and spoken words generate double-entendres. An appropriate example of phonology I recently observed in mainstream media, occurred wherever the word 'heroine' was used – and misused – to subversively embed two sinister notions:

> • A Heroin Epidemic: a substance, despite its capacity to alleviate pain if used responsibly, it produces more pain to an already hurting world plagued by emotional, psychological, and physical suffering. The suffer-

ing is so crippling that it has created a starvation of epidemic proportions for a craving of naturally occurring, euphoric joy – whereas relief can be obtained only by artificial means.

• A Heroine Epidemic: implying that it would be dangerous, if not catastrophic if there were an uprising of powerful, brave, loving, competent, and courageous women leading across the world.

Women alive in the 21st century have the privilege to be born at a time where, more than any other time in history, we have the means, support, access and resources to contribute our voices and perspectives to impact others globally. We change lives with our 'No' and with our 'Yes.' There is an important purpose for you being here – right now – and your contribution is required.

Another furtive phonetic word is: 'Confidence'. Something said in confidence is a secret. Please do not confuse keeping yourself hidden by convincing yourself you 'lack confidence'. You and your exquisite message are not meant to remain a secret. The world cannot afford the risk of you remaining hidden. If you knew you were truly supported to stand for something, what revolution could you create? What injustice would persist if you kept silent? What would it require for you to take your place within the circle of your community of other, wise women? Women must *'re-member'* and gather our *'support-HERS'*!

Further examination and excavation of words such as 'create' and 'courage' revealed:
- Cre-; sounds like: croí - the Irish word for 'heart'
- Cor-; Latin for 'heart': sounds like 'core', center
- Grá - the Irish word for 'love' - and the prefix of '**gra**titude'
- Neart - spelled similarly to 'heart', is the Irish word for 'strength'

This inquiry reminded me of a statement a friend once shared that her Grandmother used to say,

"Anger in women is a passion for justice"

What if all of this really boils down to:
- Core = what pertains to the heart
- Rage = passion

The signs are all there, buried in HER-story.

What I am calling for is that you, and other women, claim your place in your communities and begin to accept yourselves as leaders - because you already are. Stand up for what you believe in and reveal what is unjust with courage; with heart. Brave women are known as heroines. While in today's world, that is a rather indelicate, if not an unpopular identity to claim. I believe it's only when women reclaim and re-define their leadership language; a language I believe to be inaccurately articulated at present – will the ambiguity and resistance towards both accepting and embracing women as leaders begin to shift. After all, what do we hear when we say the word, *'lead-HER-ship'* out loud? Yes. It's in there. You are 'allowed' to speak 'aloud' and become aware of, and comfortable with, hearing what your words are really communicating.

I ask that you do not squander your remarkable, important, and critical contribution with the illusion that 'you have time.' You do not. We do not. We have been waiting for women like you for *gen-HER-ations*. Please do not misinterpret any setback to mean that 'you cannot'. You can. Women are *create-HERS*, if you are not sure of the 'what', consider and explore all your options. Ask for help, for *'re-mind-HERS'*. Please help each other – and include your brothers. Excluding our brothers would contradict what it means to co-create, and remember (*'re-member'*), inclusivity and balance are essential in this process. Collaboration is an integral part of the emerging female leadership discourse.

As a 21st century woman – all is possible. You have access to resources, I call *'SHE-sources'*, and they are unlimited. Emerging and evolving technologies will continue to enable women to connect with their 3.5bn sisters around the globe. All that is required is for each of you to speak your sacred message. We are here – and 'hear' you. Do not ask for permission – or forgiveness. Do not wait or hesitate in politeness, expecting an invitation. You are not invited – you are expected. We are necessary – YOU are necessary. The world is out of balance – and without our leadership, the disease of atrophy persists.

With every woman who waits with glorious anticipation for her unborn children to arrive into this confused and frightened world, she whispers her most tender prayer with the steadfast expectation that they will arrive – and arrive safely. It is safe for you to come. We are all expecting your arrival at the table – the circle – the stage, to lead your sisters and brothers in their communities. We expect everyone to gather around these tables and be included in these circles, to create the platform from which everyone can speak their most heartfelt dreams and wishes. At this table – everyone will be served.

I have since accepted that I did not need to burden my children with what I was afraid to express myself. I needed to invoke the courage myself, to face the dread

of rejection and speak my truth – demonstrating to many, particularly women, that it can be done – especially in the 21st century. We may be scorned – but we will not be burned. We may face disagreement, but we will not face death. We are the *protect-HERS*. There are too many ways to deconstruct and dismantle the institutions, organizations and systems that have silenced and separated us in the past. We are now able to gather – globally.

Looking both back – and ahead, had I stopped – had I held back just because events didn't go as I had expected, I wouldn't have arrived where I am now. Had I allowed my 'when' to interfere with what was destined – I risked misinterpreting my role and my inner heroine would have remained forever invisible. Silenced. On my knees. Armored Conquered.

This is a rally call for ALL women to gather and join with other dynamic *innovate-HERS*; to replace your armor with **amour**, and genuinely support each other in transforming from vict-hims to '*vict-HERS*'.

What if you are holding the compass – and are the one to direct us towards the solutions we have been seeking, to unlock the answers we are longing to know and the matters we need to resolve? Your voice must be heard.

For you to truly encourage others, you must be willing to 'in-courage' yourself. Your future will be shaped by the choices you make now – next – and in every moment of your unlimited, unbridled life. Your choices will impact others because, you are, and will always be, extraordinarily relevant.

If you are a woman reading this; your experience as female contains powerful and potent wisdom. Do not dismiss sharing your story because it may require you to be bold, to redefine, or let go of how you 'expected' life to turn out. It will be important to cultivate the courage to share yourself on your own terms, so you can leave your own, unique legacy that is necessary for the edification and elevation of the next generation. Let your story begin with, "With her courageous, heroic, bold and loving heart, she went out into the world to…"

"…and we ALL lived *pow-HER-fully* ever after."

Beloved child, thank you for showing up to this conversation. It is time to claim our narrative. The time is ripe to create the words required to inform the dialogue that will become the foundation of an inclusive leadership model; one that is needed to heal the past, the present, and the future.

I in-courage you to stay in this important moment and open up with curiosity, with vulnerability, with trust; trust in yourself, and in others. My hope is that that by sharing, you have been inspired with a 'me too' moment of your own and opening up will come easier to you. I look forward to you also shedding your armor; freeing you to lead with love and witnessing your own awe-inspiring alchemy and all the beauty you will conjure and create – both with, and for, others. As you do so, please keep this in mind, as a woman, you are a natural gatherer. Therefore, you are naturally equipped 'to gather'. Together, we must 'gather', and reach out, 'TO-GET-HER.'

What does your heart's passion burn for? Because yes, I am in-couraging you to claim your place in *The Real Heroine Epidemic™*...

With GRA-titude and gen-HER-osity,

Your M'Other

Co-Author
Laurie Vallas

Laurie is a multi-passionate connector, heart-ist and voracious wordsmith whose creativity emerges in the vespertine hours. Curious about everything, she loves facilitating the excavation of stories and is drawn to projects that create meaningful legacies. Current plans and projects are updated on Facebook: Laurie Vallas – Author and please join the @theheartifacts movement on Instagram.

"

*What became so obvious to this **young girl** as she emerged as a grown woman, was how much more satisfying it is to appreciate human beings for the traits they least like about themselves, their flaws. "*

~JENNY BAINI

Don't Wait For 'Something'
To Shake You Up In order To Wake You Up
by Jenny Baini

Welcome to the 1970's Melbourne, Australia!

The music of choice was the *Bay City Rollers* and *Abba*, the preferred drink was chocolate *Big M's* and *VFL football*, not AFL, consisted of 12 teams playing on a muddy oval on a Saturday afternoon, the mighty *MCG* being the highlight game. Yes, this was an incredible time to be growing up!

The epitome of the *"True Blue Australian Culture"*...right?

Yer, right! Now, let's add to that true blue Aussie upbringing, with migrant parents who were constantly having to adjust to a very different way of life, and giving birth to children who were finding themselves living a *"double life"*.. as *"Aussie"* as they could be at school and to then go home and be, what is commonly known as a *"wog"*, an Australian term for people who have migrated from other parts of the world. Where the music of choice was listening to songs which required subtitles, the drinks AND foods all consisted of something *"garlicky"* and the preferred sport was, yes, football, but the kind of football slightly foreign to the streets of any city in Australia, where men bounced a ball off their heads and the average score was 2 goals, a game we refer to as *'soccer'*.

As dizzy and, at times, as complicated as this life appeared to be, it was, in actual fact, the most enjoyable, wonderfully confusing and life grounding preparation for this place of immense opportunity known as The Great Southern Land.

Living this life was comparatively normal for this young girl, aside from all of the differences and similarities to her family and friends, she chose a life of blending in and the idea of standing out was not an option to be explored. What would the world think of her if they knew she had *"another side?"*

What would the world think of this girl, the same girl who was playing jump rope with her friends at school, getting great marks and going home to a house of profound love and care, was also the same girl who had characteristic traits she was afraid to share with others. This was a side to her she was not about to risk sharing? After all, what would the repercussions be?

On hindsight, I have often asked myself, how does a young girl who found herself having a creative streak from the tender age of 8 years, writing her first song lyrics that were based on having feelings of love in her heart, a field she knew nothing about, but put it down to countless hours watching episodes of '*Days Of Our Lives*' with her mother pre-primary school days, haha.

Was this indeed a phase or was it something more than that? If it is a phase, is it possible that it has lasted over thirty-five years though? So many questions!

Then there was this feeling of constant deja vu, but she wasn't imagining she had seen or heard what was happening around her, she knew, unequivocally, she'd seen and heard so much of it when she was sleeping. That in itself, from a very young age, as far back as the age of four or five years, the universe chose to impose on her a gift, or as she sometimes put it, an imposition of allowing her to foresee much of what would occur in the lives of others, and in world events. How could that be?

She did not know any other child, nor an adult who could hear and see what she was experiencing therefore, there was no set precedence for her to be guided by. So she did what felt best for her. She allowed herself to become lost in the lyrics she wrote and herself in this safe environment. Her way of SUPpressing was to seek comfort in other ways, such as isolating herself in her room or comfort eating, but what she realised was these were all short term fixes, how could this be sustained for the long haul?

Moving through the years, these forms of expression and suppression remained with her. However, by the time her late teens to early '20s came about, a wonderful thing occurred for her...she began to open up, to trust others enough by revealing her true identity and her shame of feeling less than others and/or different, had completely dispersed.

As she peeled away all these layers she had bubble wrapped for so long, she began to attract the energy she had always craved, because she was no longer afraid of herself. That darkness she lived in started to become just a dimmed light which then turned into complete brightness.

She began to find herself in like-minded company. "Wow, there really are so many "me's" in this world..why did I waste so much time mistreating myself?" she would often say to herself.

Then, something happened to this girl..she had finally found the courage to turn her life around. Where once she would ask herself "why me?", she now posed the question, "why NOT me?" And so...her power kicked in! She had decided to use her universal bestowment to help others, and so it goes.....

She had officially given encouraging energy to this "healing" side of herself, with the: "if I can't beat them, I'll join them" attitude. When once as a child, she would plead to her creator to take away these visions of seeing the futures of others, and feeling their pains, she now asked for it to be given to her as strongly as it could be. The irony...she found herself healing complete strangers, family and friends, and more and more was opening up for her.

What became the biggest surprise of all, was the healing SHE received, and continues to receive, in healing and helping others..in her world, it is known as 'coming full circle'.

That's not to say, in this new found epiphany, there wouldn't be obstacles, there were, and continue to be. However, what had altered was her perception, and in turn, from this, a much better way of facing the realities of life.

And then there were the critics....the naysayers, the non-believers and sometimes, they were just plain negatives. These negative people just couldn't understand the concept of stepping out of their own bias, or getting past their own fears, that possibly, just maybe, there was more to life than meets the eye.

What became so obvious to this young girl as she emerged as a grown woman, was how much more satisfying it is to appreciate human beings for the traits they least like about themselves, their flaws. We all have fears, self-doubt and insecurities and knowing that every single person on this planet has been, is now, and/or will be in this predicament fills me with joy! The joy I feel is due to the fact that these people will now have the opportunity, if they take it, to live their lives in the fullness of the purpose-filled intention of it.

For her, the uncovering and the subsequent discovery of the deepest truth a human being's soul holds is exhilarating!

 To know that someone who appears, on the surface as shallow, rude, angry or withdrawn, is really just someone who is hurting, is an incredible insight. It is actually a blessing for both, us and them.. When you can take a step back and empathise or sympathise, nothing may change with who they are, but what does change, and should change, is the way they appear to YOU and the way you respond to THEM.

Having an "aerial" perspective of life, i.e. viewing the world from a more 'soulful' level rather than a "ground" level, can, at times, have its challenges. There are common questions this type of person will constantly ask themselves. When people understand that living from a more spiritual and philosophical understanding of our lives, this is when the best version of US shows up. It is in this space that we finally break the cycle of needing to build ourselves up by tearing others down?"

These challenges and others like it continue to plague her but in the midst of all this, and throughout the years, this soul found her humour! It is this sense of humour that has given her the opportunity to sit back, relax and just be able to enjoy the lighter side of life. Of course, she wastes no time in telling others just how funny she really is, even using her creative streak to make up her own jokes, just another way for her to observe the complexities of human behaviour, including her own!

Observation is also one of those funny things..trying to figure out why each person that crosses our path, actually needs to do so? What is the reason for this? Based on my own observation, it has become very clear that the answer is simple..at any given moment, on any day of the week, we are either a student or teacher. That is, we are here to learn from someone else, or we are placed in that moment to teach others. The most profound moments are when we get to experience both.

There's an understanding that the process of learning has a starting point, which is birth, and the only stopping, in earth time, is when we no longer have a physical life.

It is from this experience, that what has sparked my interest, is the notion that a common thread binds us all, a type of umbilical cord that connects every single human being. Unfortunately, all too often, it takes extreme tragedy or disaster for us to unite as fellow human beings We all band together to help our fellow brothers and sisters, lending emotional, physical and financial support when these things happen. However, why can't we be aware of the fact that this is the way we should always be rather than waiting for a disaster to strike for us to become one with our fellow human beings.

This young girl now stands before you as a woman. This woman has accepted that her life ultimately only has ONE path that is fulfilling and steeped with an insatiable need to serve others. Trust me when I tell you I have tried to live this life differently and it ultimately becomes lost on me. I feel like I have no choice but to use the gifts I have come into this life with -as weird as they often seem to others and even to myself- and intuitively accept I have chosen this life for myself. This chosen path is not always smooth and often is bumpy and uncomfortable to walk on but I have made peace with it and am ready and willing to dedicate my life to helping others understand that life is more about what we don't know and what we don't see, and less about our visible human experience.

Aside from all the seriousness in my story, there really is humour to be found in just about every possible scenario. Imagine riding on public transport in the city, only to suddenly find yourself performing a spiritual healing on a heavily pregnant woman on a crowded tram who is suffering extreme nausea and this woman hugs you so tightly because she is overwhelmed by the help of a complete stranger does not scream normality by any stretch of the imagination...particularly to the onlookers.

Then there are all those times, as a Beauty Therapist, that a client is in the middle of having hair pulled out from their nether regions, legs up in the air, and they're asking you whether or not to pursue "that guy" because they know the first thing you're going to tell them is: "well, you could, but be mindful, he is a Leo and you are a Pisces, and we've discussed how fire and water can clash". It's a daily laugh fest as a healer. The universe makes these decisions to thrust you into comical situations that others can only read about, but that your family and friends can also laugh at because they know that these things "can only happen to you!"
That combination of healer/empath and creative songwriter really does require humour, otherwise, you will find yourself healing, feeling and writing in a negative manner. It's not the worse thing you can do for yourself...laughing at your own complexities and that of others. In fact, speaking from an experienced voice, it is imperative to do so.

Oh, and once you have built up a repertoire of stories, and people begin to identify you as "that person", they start to analyse anything and everything that you say or do. You ask a friend: "how's your mum and dad?", purely out of interest from your end, but from their end: "why, what did you dream about? What are you feeling? Are they going to die of some horrid flesh eating disease? Just tell me, I need to be prepared!" The healer's/empath's response: "whoa! No, of course not, I'm just asking cause your parents are such lovely people, please relax".
Then there are the times when, in a dream state, the empath 's fears have actually become reality. Seeing deaths of people, the dates they will pass away, the way in which they will pass, that is all very heavy. But on the flip side, when you can warn a friend to drive down an alternate route so as to avoid a car accident, or reassure a woman who is desperately wanting to conceive a child that she will and it will be a beautiful healthy baby, even revealing gender and name, that kind of balances it all out.

Yep! It is an endless tug of war with yourself when you are a creative, healing empathic person. There is no doubt about it. However, the rewards are endless. Why go through life just "existing" when you can really live! Whether you are aware of your healing qualities or not, they are within us all. It is highly recommended you tap into it, go on, give it a go! Allow yourself to be vulnerable, and step outside your comfort area of shielding yourself from emotion, your own and that of others. See what happens!

Keeping in mind, with all this, it is essential and, even, mandatory, to shield yourself. Something that has been learned through experience. Times when one feels "not quite themselves", drained or exhausted, is not always "your stuff", quite often, knowingly and unknowingly, we place ourselves in a toxic energetic environment. This can be daily for many, from the workplace to family and friends who are lovely, but you find yourself constantly tired or cranky because they offload verbally and/or energetically.

Think about it; If your energy supply is being depleted by others, what's left for you? Subconsciously, surround yourself with a protective light, say a prayer or mantra, or you could carry stones and crystals. Find what works, and use it.
If only this had been learned earlier in life, a great deal of the heartache experienced could have been spared for me.

Learn, really learn to trust what you feel within. Don't palm off anything as coincidence or your imagination, trust that the universe is sending you messages to grow. Like it or not, you've just got to be thankful for every occurrence, whether it sends a river of tears or a smile that would make Luna Park envious.
It's called LIFE! A stream of endless possibilities with the only limitations being the ones we place on ourselves.

Life is not an exact science, we kind of make it up as we go along. It's similar to following a recipe..sure, you have the required amounts of ingredients to produce the end product, but who's to say you can't add or subtract those ingredients to create your own version of the desired result? Add a cup of love, a pinch of self-care and watch it rise...you, as you are right now, have all the qualities to bloom into the "self-raising" flower you have always been destined to become.

And that young girl from the 1970's Melbourne, who was so unsure of herself and what place she could have in this big wide world, whatever happened to her? Well.. you will be happy to know...SHE HAS FOUND HER HOME!

Co-Author
Jenny Baini

Jenny is an Intuitive Energy Healer and a Massage and Beauty Therapist who helps her clients heal, both emotionally and physically. Jenny is currently working under her business name of "White Feather Healing", located at "Anamaya Health Solutions" in Carlton, Melbourne.

Jenny has always enjoyed her work and her favourite part of her job is meeting people from all corners and seeing them at their most vulnerable and "unmasked" selves.

Jenny is a creative person, and she is crazy about music and dogs. The things Jenny loves most are not "things", they are family and friends. She loves to meet people who are both aligned and misaligned with her journey, as she believes: "everybody has a role to play"

Facebook: https://www.facebook.com/jenny.baini.5

"

I commend my own courage and my own bravery to finally share the raw details.
I do this, not from ego, but because I want to show other women that they too CAN be brave and CAN survive. "

~GEORGINA MANTJARIS

Dodging The Fire Balls Of Domestic Violence
And, Dancing Through The Embers Of The Aftermath
by Georgina Mantjaris

"Bruises Fade,
Lacerations Heal.
But Not The Ripping Apart Of My Heart,
Nor The Scars Left Behind On My Soul"
POEM BY VICKI GOTSIS CERASO

One woman's journey from crippling domestic violence to uplifting hope leading her to mirror courageous feminine power to women everywhere.

I'm finding it difficult to decipher if I'm dead or alive or if this is a nightmare I just can't get out of. How long can I possibly endure this pain? I wonder if there really is a God because the God I recognise in my life would not allow this to happen to me. Perhaps there is a lesson to be learnt here, otherwise, what is the point? Please give me a sign as I'm asking for help. It hurts way too much.
I can't bare this anymore and will finish my carefully planned exit from here soon. Love is not meant to hurt!!!

"It's not the bruises on the body that hurt.
It is the wound of the heart and the scars on the mind."
- AISHA MIRZA

The letter I never had the opportunity to send to you:

Tony,
I told you to be careful for what you wished for. Telling me that the kids would be better off living in the real world with YOU and wishing me dead when I had breast cancer....it's amusing to say the least as to how that has worked out.

Who is here today and who is not?

All I can say to you is I hope you were on your knees when you faced GOD asking for forgive-ness - because only GOD can forgive you!

You may have had everyone around us fooled and the reality is, you almost had me fooled as well, telling me at every opportunity that I was worthless and nothing without you. Everything you did -- in hindsight, only served to make me stronger. I'm proud of who I am - no more monster, I can breathe again!
I can now make it on my own. I am now stronger than I have ever been. This strength had eluded me for too long.

The best is yet to come.
For you, I really have no words other than to say, I hope you have learnt the lessons you came here to learn.

I'll just say this "I wish you farewell".

From the mother of your children.

Putting myself back together has been one of the most difficult things I have ever had to do. The physical and emotional pain has been overwhelming. The secret I've kept all these years is now out and some will be shocked while others will enjoy a good gossip over a cup of coffee.

I'm perfectly ok with that!

I commend my own courage and my own bravery to finally share the raw details. I do this, not from ego, but because I want to show other women that they too CAN be brave and CAN survive.

They too can find the courage to share their story which can result in inspiring hope in another woman who is enduring crippling and devastating domestic violence.

For all we know, our stories could save a life.
I'm taking the liberty of speaking for so many other victims that are silenced by shame, guilt and overwhelming, spine-tingling, crippling fear.

My courage stems from the fact that I am no longer touched by the violence and I am proudly stepping up and inspiring people to talk about the severity of our national domestic, sexual harassment and violence that only appears as a headline when another woman is killed.

It is difficult for me to share all the difficult times with you...I guess I would need much more than this chapter to convey everything that has happened to me and my children. However, here are three pivotal moments from my life that are etched in my mind forever:

One

I'm so excited to be finally moving in and setting up our home together. As wonderful as it was living with my parents for a few months after we were married, I longed for my new husband and I to have our independence and really start our life together.

It was a long day moving in and unpacking our wedding presents. I remember it as if it was yesterday. There I was, washing all the kitchenware while staring out the window looking out to the back garden and dreaming of the beautiful life ahead of us.

The love of my life, the man I said "I do" to only a few short months ago, is standing at the door finishing off a cigarette sharing with me his ideas about extending the back of the house, landscaping and building an entertainment area in a couple of years time.

I'm loving the feeling of being in our own home. I'm loving the domesticity that marriage brings with it and, I'm loving our life!

...Suddenly, out of nowhere, stars appeared in front of my eyes as I felt his big masculine fist connect in the most violent way with the side of my head.

Everything began to go black as I felt myself falling to the ground.
As I lay on the cold kitchen slate floor, he gave one last almighty kick with his big, heavy steel work boot straight into my stomach.
That's when it all began and that is when it all ended!
The honeymoon was over!

To this day I still have no answers to the one-word question in my head; WHY?

Two

Friday's rolled around so quickly.
Every Friday, his first priority was stocking the fridge in the garage with his weekly supply of alcohol before he would even walk in and acknowledge his family.
That sinking feeling in my stomach started.

Like every other Friday night, he would end up drunk while listening to music. The music would get louder and louder as the night went on, to the point where it would wake my baby girl up from her sleep crying inconsolably.
When he reached this point, he had no regard for anyone or anything around him.

On this one particular Friday, it had been an exceptionally hot day in Melbourne. There I was, bathing my beautiful baby girl, getting her ready to settle her to bed when I heard the roller door go up.

Yep, that sinking feeling started.

By the time dinner was finished he was on his third beer. I knew it was going to be one of those late nights. Sure enough, a dozen beers later, up goes the music. Baby wakes. He refused to turn down the music and an argument started.

The bond between mother and child is so strong not even a monster can break it. Sounds of my baby girl crying and screaming in her cot from all the noise coming from the open living area petrified her all night.

In excruciating pain, I am unable to reach her as my hands and feet are bound together with cable ties which are securely locked in place with big strong telephone cables normally used for installing phone lines. In this instance, he had become extremely creative and he had used those telephone cables around my torso to tie me to the dining table chair.

The smell of urine all over my face and body made me physically sick.
I felt totally humiliated.

This was just another one of many terrifying experiences I endured throughout my 7 ½ year marriage to this monster.

Three
I arrived home to see his work van unexpectedly early in the driveway. My happy mood from spending time with my mother's group changed very quickly.
A sense of dread overtook my entire being.

All I wanted to do is feed and bath my tired, grumpy, hungry little girl and have an early night myself.

Not long after I walked into the house, he started questioning me. He wanted to know why I wasn't home and where I had been? His mood escalated even more and he started blaming me for our baby girl being grisly and clingy. Nothing I did to calm the situation made any difference.

Heavily pregnant with my son, and holding my baby girl tightly in my arms, I ran to the bedroom taking the phone with me… this had now become something I did all too often.

All I could think to do was to barricade, myself, my unborn child and my infant daughter, so I locked us inside the bathroom ensuite holding onto my baby girl waiting for the police to arrive. I was desperately trying to keep us safe even though I rang and rang begging the police to hurry but it took two hours before I heard the doorbell ring. At this point, I need to point out that fifteen years ago, domestic violence was not taken as seriously as it is today.

At the time, the decision to call the police for help felt like the biggest mistake of my life, because the very next day he was home again and this time he had a frightening determination in his eyes. He was determined to teach me a lesson on keeping my mouth shut.

To keep my baby girl alive from having her throat slashed, I endured the most horrific torture. I took every punch, every kick to my body, screaming at him to not harm our unborn child while he was dragging me around the room by my hair.

I allowed myself to take the brunt of his explosive rage so that my baby girl would not be harmed.

To this end,I succeeded. She was not harmed.
I, on the other hand, was a physical and emotional mess.

"If you want to know what it's like to survive hell and still come out shining brighter than the sun, just look into the eyes of a woman who has survived intense damage and refused to allow it to destroy her softness".
- Nikita Gill

Having shared those three pivotal moments in my life was not easy because as you can imagine, re-living a time I would rather forget is very difficult. It takes me right back and the fear and all the emotions that go with it return.

My escape out of this nightmare was made possible by a single phone call that I received. That phone call was my mother sharing her heartbreaking news that she only had 12 months to live if she didn't receive a liver transplant immediately. As bad as the news was to hear, all I could think of was that this could be my way out of the marriage.

Within a few days, he agreed I could go and visit my sick mother. I packed up as much as I could into the car and drove from Melbourne to Adelaide with my two-year-old daughter and seven-week old son.

It wasn't until I drove past the 'Welcome to South Australia' sign on the side of the road that I physically remember exhaling and bursting into tears all at once. I had such a profound release of emotions that I had to pull the car over.
To finally reach my parents' home was such a relief! I finally felt safe. A feeling I had not felt in over 8 years!

My parents had an idea I was unhappy and weren't overly surprised when I told them I didn't want to be married anymore, however, I found myself having to put my feelings aside as I needed to be present for my mother as she was deteriorating very quickly. I made the decision not to reveal the truth behind why I was leaving him. I felt it was n't necessary for them to know all the gory details of what he had done to their little girl.

I must say, I am eternally grateful to the family who was experiencing their own grief of loss and yet found it in their hearts, four months later, to gift their loved one's liver to my mother who became a donor recipient and got her life back.

Hanging up the phone from telling him, " the marriage is over" was merely the beginning of getting my life back. There I was, the realisation of saying those four words to him, those very four words I never thought I would find the courage to utter, was like an out-of-body experience.

My head was rapidly spinning around with what next? What I had just done brought on a whole new level of fear but breaking the marriage and stopping the violence towards me and the threat to my children gave me the grit I needed.

It's really insidious how domestic violence affects you.

Impacting on my mental health and well-being continued way beyond the relationship ended. The psychological impact was far greater than the physical injuries I suffered at the hands of my husband. I struggled to function daily. I struggled to nurture my children, feeling ashamed at how I allowed him to abuse me, isolating myself, not participating in social activities and struggling financially.

Research shows that for many women, an array of psychosomatic illnesses, eating disorders, inability to hold down a job, insomnia and devastating mental health problems like post-traumatic stress disorder (PTSD) are just some of the symptoms that have long term effects after the relationship has ended.

The psychological impact of domestic violence can creep up ever so quietly. It is scary enough to make the courageous decision to get out of there that by the time you realise you MUST leave, you've been disempowered, broken by being degraded, you just don't know HOW. You don't see it clearly until you are really safe, and it has taken many years to see exactly how extreme the abuse was. Mine was extreme. He convinced me that I was not loveable to anyone; not to my family, not to my friends and not even to my precious babies.

He repeatedly told me that I was a nobody without him. He even tried to convince me that the reason I was unable to breastfeed my little ones was their way of telling me they didn't love me. He would tell me how lucky I was to have him and that he was the only one who could love me. I was so brainwashed to believe all the crap that he told me that I found myself consoling him after he abused me for how bad HE felt for hurting ME!!!.

Can you believe that?

It's amazing how you can love someone for hurting you. Remorse is part of the pattern of violence. He never took full responsibility for his behaviour. After months of pleading, he finally agreed to attend a marriage counselling session with me. By the time we both walked out of the room, he had narcissistically manipulated the professional believing through his try-hard childlike performance we had a loving, beautiful relationship showing me affection with his arm around me and a confused look on his face as to why he needed to actively work on changing HIS behaviour?

It was in this moment that any hope I had of 'fixing' our issues and stopping the violence just disintegrated into an invisible mess left forever on the floor of the counsellor's office, all opportunity of re-connecting to it forever gone.

Coming out of the marriage, one of the biggest lessons I learnt was that I WAS NOT THE WOMAN HE TOLD ME I WAS.

He was so afraid of losing his power and his hold over me that in his sick delusional way, this is how he showed his love for me.

Expectations placed on him as a young man allowed him to be the way that he was and perhaps even speak to the cultural expectations of a husband being seen

as the head of his household. Domestic violence has long been perceived as a consequence of a patriarchal culture where men feel that they can do whatever they like to women. This needs to change!

Violence is about control over a person or situation. It occurs when someone decides to use physical, sexual, emotional and/or spiritual abuse to get their way. It has been well documented that most of the men who perpetuate this type of behaviour, are not violent or controlling outside the home. This was so true in my situation! Nobody would have guessed or even been able to imagine the level of violence that he was capable of dishing out.

To this day I can still picture myself in that marriage. It's like having an out-of-body experience as if the abuse was only an hour ago and I am desperately afraid for my life. I never ever thought that I would be THAT kind of woman... So, that brings me to my next question; what does an abused woman look like? People judged me because, in their mind, THEY would NEVER date an abuser.

If you are going through anything that is in the slightest way similar to my experience, let me hold your hand and let you know that I understand.

I know you are scared, you probably feel trapped and making the decision to leave is hard but you need to drop the 'shame game', put the ego to sleep and muster up as much courage as you can and get help! Help is out there for you when you're ready.

I want you to be a survivor, not a statistic, not another woman whose life was taken from her from an abusive husband/partner.

I know what it is like to be so overwhelmed and so used to being the victim that you can not possibly use the word 'survivor' in any context let alone believe that you can come out of this nightmare...ever!

In the meantime, until you are ready to leave, you need to keep yourself and your children safe.

This is what I wish someone had told me when I was going through the abuse:

Know your abuser's red flags and be alert.
Identify safe areas of the house, establish a code word or signal to let others know you are in trouble.
Be ready to leave at a moment's notice and practise escaping quickly & safely whenever you get the opportunity to do so.

If you are reading my story and you have not been abused yourself, but you're wanting to help someone in a similar situation and have no idea how then what I suggest to you is to:

- Ask her if she would like to talk about it
- Respect what she is going through
- Highlight that domestic violence is not ok
- Reassure her that you will be there for her and that she is not deserving of the violence
- Encourage her to have an 'EB'- Emergency Bag ready: clothes, toiletries, a set of clean sheets, copies of important documents, an envelope with cash plus telephone numbers for emergency assistance
- Suggest you hold onto the EB for her
- Help her establish an Emergency Exit Plan

Some days you'll find coping is a moment by moment process and other days it will be easier. However it looks for you is fine, - don't make it wrong! Remember the new path of independence is important to learn to live your own life. On days when your identity feels consumed by the victim mentality, try to see yourself as a strong, powerful unstoppable survivor and if you can't see it yet, that's ok. I will hold that survivor strength in my heart for you and when you are ready, I am here to give it back to you. xo

Abuse comes in all forms, when you have to wear a 'mask' in public because you're afraid of letting people in and you're afraid of what he will think, say or do to you and/or your children THAT is abuse. That is abusive TO YOU!

It's been more than 15 years since I left my dangerous and abusive husband, and I'm now recovered enough to speak up.

It's time for me to have a VOICE. A universal voice for all women. I have an insatiable need to ensure no woman is ever dependant on her partner to meet her basic needs, removing one of the barriers against leaving an abusive partner.
I will speak for all the women who remain in compromising lives and I intend on campaigning publicly to raise awareness and advocate for social change.

My aim is to continue on from all the amazing work Rosie Batty (an Australian victim of family violence) who has so bravely advocated from the very first day she lost her precious son; I want to influence on national public initiatives and funding, support services, police and legal procedures in Australia.

I have a new found passion for *right over wrong*, being heard over *suppression* and *survival* over *death*, all of which resonate deep to my core. I hope through continuing to bring light to this subject I can help stop yet another story from appearing as a headline because these stories have the same theme every time, just a different face.

So, with this fire in my belly, and an insatiable hunger to raise my voice on domestic violence, I have made a promise to myself to spread awareness and break down the barriers and I will be doing that the best way I know how. I am holding a sacred space to co-create a life of magic that YOU and I deserve. Together, I can lead you to self-love, health and wellbeing, bring joy and happiness to yourself and your children...just like I am doing for my own family, in a beautiful new home I have called '*BodyConnect*'. The more I grow, the more I want to share with you.

Co-Author
Georgina Mantjaris

Georgina has an extensive background in Recruitment where she worked for 22 years and reached General Manager. She is a devoted mother, a carer for her elderly parents and a global business owner who lives in Adelaide, South Australia.

The things she loves most in life are hanging out with her teenage children, walking along the beach while watching sunrises and sunsets and sitting around a table enjoying great conversation with dear friends while indulging in delicious food and wine.

Over the past couple of years, Georgina has developed a passion for health and well-being and has found a solution to help manage her stress and her sadness and rebuild the foundation for wellness after her bout with breast cancer. She has since become the Creator & Founder of **BodyConnect.**

In her newfound business, Georgina helps women release the shackles of both physical and financial pain and is keen to work with survivors and victims of Family Violence.

"Freedom to have choice and live a life of self-design which leads to self-love, health and wellbeing ultimately brings joy and happiness. My mission to help women who still remain in compromising lives because they have not yet uncovered, like I have, that it is possible to be released from being imprisoned in their own fear is what drives me to campaign publically to raise awareness and advocate for social change."

Facebook: *https://www.facebook.com/georgina.mantjaris*
Facebook: *https://www.facebook.com/groups/1974126686141544/hhttps:// www.instagram.com/georginamantjaris/*

"

*I am passionate about our
potential to change our lives
so that we not only survive
the hard times but grow to
become better people from
the knowledge and wisdom
we have gained from our
experiences along the way
as we 'dance through the
firestorms'
and rise from the ashes. "*

~DANIELLE AITKEN

Dare to Believe
by Danielle Aitken

This is a story of possibility and potential, of belief, faith and hope. This story is mine but it could be yours if you believe it can be. It's a story about change and personal transformation, thus I will start at the beginning so I can express to you my journey from there to here.

As I start to write this chapter, I find myself sitting on an airplane travelling from Melbourne to Brisbane trying to make the best use of my time, because this is what I always do. I am acutely aware that I am a product of my life's experiences as we all are, and all of my experiences to date, have led me to this very pivotal moment. As I reflect on some of those pivotal experiences and some of those pivotal people, I am fondly reminded of my Grandmother. She was the matriarch and a much beloved member of our family. To say she had a massive influence on my life is quite the understatement. My grandparents, along with my Mother, were focal in my developing life choices, beliefs and value systems. The women in my family are strong and I grew up heavily influenced by this fact. My Grandmother, having survived a war and a depression was very keen to educate us how best to survive this life. She instilled in us the importance of security, and for security we needed to be able to rely upon ourselves. This meant we had to have a career that would allow that to happen, a career that would always keep us in work and so it was that I became a nurse and my sister a chef. Two wonderfully pleasing choices according to my Grandmother, because people always need to eat and they always get sick, not necessarily in that order but nonetheless , we were set.

Nursing for me was a wonderful career. I learnt, I studied, I became a midwife and I studied some more. Women's health became my specialty from pre conception to delivery and beyond, and thirty years later I was sitting comfortably in a very good career as an IVF patient coordinator in a private practice connected to one of the most prestigious IVF centres in Australia. I had job and financial security and a wealth of knowledge amassed from over 30 years of study and experience. My grandmother would have been very happy. But there was something else I was doing, that at the time I was completely unaware of. I was sitting fair and square in the middle of my comfort zone, the exact same comfort zone I had been sitting in for many years. I knew what I knew and I didn't even have to think too hard about it. My job was exciting and at times I was working at the cutting edge of scientific IVF work. Life was good so why would I ever want to change? But there was something stirring inside of me, something that was telling me there were things yet to be discovered.

My transition began during my years in IVF as I found myself more and more having to attempt to assist women to deal with enormous emotional issues when time after time their treatments were not successful. The nurses were at the front line. We were the patient's advocates, unofficial counsellors and often their life lines. After many years of carrying this heavy emotional burden which was a part of my job, I once again decided to embark upon a course of study that for me was to be pivotal. IVF was a difficult journey for many and I became a counsellor to arm myself with more tools to help me to assist couples and women in particular, to survive this emotional roller-coaster. Little did I know at the time that this was also to be the beginning of a life changing journey for me.

When I became a counsellor I began to discover the potential we all have when we learn how to take control of, and change our thoughts. I was excited by this potential and wanted to learn more. I soon became a clinical hypnotherapist and embarked on a journey of learning and discovery that would span many years. I was like a sponge, reading all I could read on the potential of mind body medicine and this has changed my life forever.

It was at this time that I decided to take my own leap of faith as I ventured out of the safety, security and comfort of a career that I had spent my entire professional life and over thirty long years mastering. This purposeful leap of faith, which would take me right out of my comfort zone and directly into the frightening uncertainty of the unknown, was until this point of my life something I would never have done. For me it would have been something akin to jumping out of a perfectly good plane without a parachute, but with faith and self-belief I did just that, and I have never looked back.

I chose to trust in my vision to create something special and worthwhile that would help many people including myself. I had a vision and I chose not to be influenced by those who questioned what I was doing and those who thought I was going completely mad for leaving my privileged career and moving into the unknown. Being a Senior Nurse, Midwife and IVF Nurse Patient Coordinator was how I, and others, defined myself. So the task was set, I needed to completely recreate the image of who and what I was.

My learning over this time allowed me to discover the massive potential we have to not only change our outcomes, but to change our mindset and achieve states of happiness and acceptance that are often missing in the lives of so many. The mechanisms of these processes are steeped in quantum physics and my scientific mind grabbed hold of these principles and allowed me to transform them into something understandable. I now know, understand and trust, in the immense power of belief to transform our lives.

For my personal journey, I began to visualise what I wanted and exactly how I wanted it and one by one things just started to fall into place. My now successful private practice was dreamed into existence through my constant focus of attention. As I deliberately set my focus on what it was I wanted to create, I simultaneously set aside the negative thoughts and the what if's that would quickly derail my vision and keep me stuck in inertia should I choose to listen to them.

The process of choosing which thoughts to listen to and which thoughts to ignore was a practice that developed over time. I continued to notice the ever present negative chatter in my head and all the "what if I fail"… negative thoughts, but in order to move forward I knew I needed to constantly challenge these negative thoughts and negative self-beliefs. This was essential for me if I was to move from where I was to where I wanted to be.

The key and pivotal lesson for me at this time was the understanding that as soon as I became aware of these thoughts and feelings, I always had a choice; To listen to the self-limiting thoughts or not to listen, to feel anxiety or to choose to focus on something else. I had learned many years before that fear and anxiety changes nothing at all, but it effects everything. It effects what you do, It effects what you don't do and it effects how you experience this moment, here and now when the very thing you are worrying about is probably not happening at all. I chose to be aware of those thoughts that could potentially hold me back and I chose to challenge them by asking myself; Is this an old thought? Whose words are these? Do they belong to me or someone else? Is this thought true or is it a fear? Will this thought help or hinder me if I listen to it? One by one I chose to release those negative thoughts and negative feelings as I chose to recognize them for what they were, just thoughts and just feelings, nothing more, nothing less.

In my practice I now see so many women who are stuck in outdated patterns of thinking, and feelings that keep them attached to old yet familiar outcomes. I now educate and empower women to challenge their faulty beliefs and self-limiting

thoughts, and in doing so create new and often spectacular outcomes by letting go of the traumas of the past. Right now we all know more than we have ever known at any other time in our lives and that knowledge comes from experience. Every experience gained from life's adversities can be transformed into a gift of wisdom that can only be gained from such experiences. When women discover how to release the negative emotions connected to these experiences, which would otherwise continue to damage them by leading them straight back to the same repetitive negative self-thoughts, anxieties or low self-esteem that brings them to seek therapy in the first place, the results can be extraordinary.

The principles to create the changes we seek are available to us all because they are based in human potential. These principals allow us to create change, physically, emotionally and socially. So many women feel disempowered as though they have no ability to change their situations, but I would say to them, as soon as you become aware of something you do not like or do not want, be it thoughts, feelings or situations you always get to choose what you do from there. Very often we cannot change what is happening in a given moment, but we always get to choose how to react or respond to that situation.

I believe the solution to disempowerment is trust and self-belief and an ability to embrace the possibility that life can be something else. When women not only begin to see the solution, but when they can really imagine it in every way; how it will feel , how it will look and what exactly it is that has made the difference, they really can begin to step toward those changes day by day, thought by thought and feeling by feeling. It is important to remember that the powerful potential of the mind and body does not discriminate between a good outcome and a bad outcome, it just presents you with outcomes directly connected to your powerful thoughts, feelings and beliefs on which you focus. It therefore becomes a matter of prime importance; be very careful what you focus your attention on.

When I was ready for my next challenge, utilizing all of my knowledge, experience and wisdom, I set about dreaming into existence a story about transformation and personal growth. A story designed to empower women to find value in even the most painful experiences and transform their pain into precious wisdom so that they could rise up out of the despair of unexpected trauma and create something new and valuable. Before I did this, however, I had to once again lose my own negative self-talk and my own negative self-belief that told me that I couldn't! I was a poor speller and I was never great at English at school so how on earth could I write a book?

Once again I became very aware of the negative chatter in my own head that threatened to hold me back and instead of giving those thoughts power, I chose to imagine my completed book. A book I truly imagined would be a best seller and I even imagined they would make a movie out of it. I chose to believe this for several reasons; my book, Sarah's Story, was a story that needed to be told. A story that was specifically designed to empower women to seek new destinations when all hope was seemingly lost. A story that could not be told until I was ready, until I myself had learnt what I needed to learn and that was firstly the power and potential of my own thoughts, and secondly, that you and I always have a choice. My book is now completed just as I imagined it would be and what's more, it is a wonderful story of triumph over adversity that stands as a metaphor for anyone struggling with life's difficulties. A book I know is only a reality because I chose to believe in myself against the odds. Sarah's Story has now been sent to the publishers and I fully expect, trust and believe that it will be a bestseller .

When I was first introduced to the Dance In The Fire Of Life project, I was well on my way to creating Sarah's Story and I was amazed to discover that my book was so aligned with the Dance In The Fire Of Life philosophy that I felt I must be a part of this amazing collection of women from around the globe as a part of my journey too. Again I had to marvel at the powerful universal force of attraction at work as like continued to attract like.

It is my desire through my work and through my writing to educate, assist and empower women to discover and trust in their own true potential as they dare to believe in their ability to be all that they can be. This very same ability and potential that can just as easily work against you by holding you back or weighing you down with self-doubt or limiting beliefs, when used in the right way, can be liberating and transforming. When women begin to understand how to connect to this very powerful force in the right way… they can and do, change their worlds. I'm sure you know what is wrong or not working in your life. Perhaps you spend a great deal of time focusing on those problems. You may even notice that the more you focus on these things the worse they appear to be. Now I will ask you to consider something else instead; What is it that you want? What makes you happy? What gives you joy? What do you want in life and how will you know when you have it? What will it look like? What will it feel like?

The powerful subconscious mind that has the ability to cause your body to immediately respond chemically and physically to every thought you have, when focused in the right way, can create the most amazingly spectacular results. When you bring to mind what it is you truly want and when you imagine it "as though"

you already have it , that powerful part of your mind will begin to respond to those thoughts as though it is already real and so I say to you, focus on what you want, only on what you want . Imagine it vividly and in detail and focus on it often. Your imagination is like a GPS. Unless you put in the right coordinates, you really have no hope of reaching your destination. When you know what it is you truly want and when you really focus your attention on it you can begin to bring it closer and closer, almost in direct proportion to the amount of time you spend focusing on your goal.

The powerful force that has the ability to create great unhappiness or disease can also lead you directly to your bliss, to that which brings you joy and happiness. Trust and believe in your ability to create it. When you want it to happen and when you truly expect it WILL happen you may be delighted to discover it manifesting before your eyes.

I have learned over the years that we all have our story. A chapter that defines us, that makes our experience unique from anyone else. For some, this is a story of pain and despair, for others it is a story of hope and courage, but it's only when we learn to take the valuable lessons from our experiences and release the negative emotions that may have previously weighed us down, that we really get to create something new and unexpected.

I truly believe that nothing is ever wasted and nothing is ever lost. Every experience, the good and the bad gives us valuable lessons and valuable insight from which to learn and move on from as the canvas of our life's tapestry is constantly enriched by our lessons and discoveries that when all placed together create our bigger picture.

This chapter is designed to inspire, and to encourage women to take their own leap of faith and follow their dreams as I did. My life's work is now dedicated to assisting people to be the best they can be and as a result of that, I have come to truly believe in the immense power and potential of the human mind. I know beyond a shadow of doubt that within each individual is a God-given ability to achieve the desires of their heart and soul.

I am passionate about our potential to change our lives; so that we not only survive the hard times but grow to become better people from the knowledge and wisdom we have gained from our experiences along the way as we "dance through the firestorms" and rise from the ashes.

I now not only live the life I was born to live, but I also have the joy and the privilege of helping others do the same.

If I could leave you with one final message it would be to let go of fear and trust and believe in your potential as you discover the power of your exceptional mind to create the changes you seek.

So it is that I do what I do so that I can be what I choose to be, an author today, and tomorrow ….. Who knows?

The sky's the limit, when you believe it is.

Co-Author
Danielle Aitken

As a highly experienced nurse and midwife, I spent over twenty years working at the cutting edge of IVF in Australia. Now a counsellor and clinical hypnotherapist running a successful private practice in rural Victoria, I assist people to move through trauma and crisis by helping them to discover their inner strengths.

I'm passionate about empowering people to achieve their goals and reach their true potential by working with the principals that I discuss in my chapter of Dance in the Fire of Life; Dare to Believe. Author of Sarah's Story life after IVF, it is my desire is to inspire people through the power of the written word.

Website: https://www.naturaltherapypages.com.au/connect/daitkencounselling/about_us/about_us
Facebook and Instagram: Danielle Aitken Clinical Hypnotherapy and Counselling
Author website: https://www.danielleaitkenauthor.com.au/

"

Without a strong sense of self-identity, it's hard to live a happy life.
I have always been fascinated with how to develop self-identity.
Why? *I was born an identical twin.*
Identical does not mean the same.
Suffice to say, trying to forge my own identity has been a challenge in a world that generally thinks people who look the same have the same likes, personality, behavior and goals."

~Carol Davies

My Journey to Self-Identity
by Carol Davies

You are whoever you want yourself to be. You are here to create. You are here to create your world in any way you want. Without a strong sense of self-identity, it's hard to live a happy life. The inconsistency of conduct makes it difficult for others to comprehend you. I have always been fascinated with how to develop self-identity. Why? I was born an identical twin. Identical does not mean the same. I will get into my story a bit later. Suffice to say, trying to forge my own identity has been a challenge in a world that generally thinks people who look the same have the same likes, personality, behavior and goals.

What do we mean by self-identity? Who you are is the basis of Self-Identity. It's the way you see yourself and your relationship to the world. Understanding this, enables you to look at your identity and more critically makes you who you need to be. A sense of identity develops the essential qualities that direct the decisions we make (e.g., connections, profession). These decisions reflect our character and what we esteem.

Our life journey can have quite varied paths. Mine certainly did. Little did I realize when I was very young where I would end up as an adult. My journey took me to a place of isolation and sadness from which I was unable to escape for many years. I used to feel I was one half of a whole, never truly whole within myself. Duality in any form is hard enough for adults to make sense of. It's rare to be part of a natural dyad, or a group of two people, the smallest possible social group. As a large portion of us know, character, autonomy, and independence are fundamental to a person's emotional well-being.

A youngster's feeling of self and individuation is shaped early. For twins, the procedure is convoluted by the need to isolate from the parent, as well as be independent of her/his twin sibling. This is much more troublesome for identical twins who are frequently confused for each other by companions and even family. Twins at a young age hence may not find a way to endeavor to individuate from each other.

From our earliest existence, our encounters begin to weave our feeling of character. Incalculable things guide this point of view. As far back as the minute we're conceived, we're finding out about connections, what we need to do and how we need to act with a specific end goal to get our necessities met and feel secure. We figure out how we are seen by our families and caretakers, not simply through what they say to us, but rather through their demeanors and micro-expressions, their tone, their accessibility or deficiency in that department. We witness how our parents and families treat themselves as well as other people, disguising more than we can intentionally envision.

Our identities develop not simply by reflecting what we see but rather from responding to it. Our brains are intended to recall the excruciating and alarming encounters, the extensive and little injuries that showed us the exercises of who we should have been to survive. We make mental barriers to protect ourselves or so-called psychological defenses. These guards can go ahead to impose blocks on our most genuine self, impacting us to act and take part in progression that can hurt and point to confinement in us later in our lives.

These impacts fit together, making a feeling of self-personality. We appear on the scene with our own one of a kind hereditary qualities and personality, the possibility to build up our very own autonomous feeling character, in view of the things that light us up and give our life meaning. Our constructive relational encounters can enable us to create kind states of mind toward ourselves as well as other people. Notwithstanding, our negative encounters frame an establishment for our basic inward voice. Like an interior mentor, scrutinizing and baiting us promote from our genuine selves, this internal voice is our actual foe.

Again, for the duration of our lives, this *"voice"* is there to characterize us, reveal to us what we should or shouldn't do, how we must carry on. It is the unwelcome domineering part who supposes it knows us superior to any other individual. It's that reverberating serenade in the back of our heads that is stating, *"You're excessively poor/narrow-minded/appalling/moronic/tenacious to have what you need."* It mentors us to stay with our guards. "Try not to request anything. Deal with yourself first. Never let him excessively close. Ensure she won't dismiss you. Act naturally adequate. Act as you couldn't care less. Try not to be helpless. Never surrender control. You're uncommon; you merit better."

My twin sister and I were dependable with each other while growing up. It was just when we got to college that we began spreading out. My sister was more outgoing and had a larger group of companions; I was standoffish. I wanted to remain quiet about myself and participated with her friends when I felt like it.

We split into different subjects for our college degrees – I studied Spanish and she studied French. I think it helped us develop as separate people. We were still almost constantly together at that point. However, still being close, we both had more certainty to go and accomplish something all alone on the off chance that we expected to.

I was never worried about why I was so reserved compared to my more outgoing sister. However, I generally felt out of balance going and endeavoring to make new friends. We were so close to the point that I never felt I required any other individual. Completely through my undergraduate years, I thought, "Well, as of now, I have the dearest companion I'm ever going to discover. I don't have any holes that need filling."

As I mentioned earlier, being an identical twin, I was raised with no real sense of myself as an individual person. My mother dressed us the same. The family and friends always referred to us as "the twins". My sister and I shared friends. We did not have separate special or best friends. We were in the same classroom all the way through school. Even teachers had a hard time telling us apart. I accepted this as normal until the age of 18 when I went to the same university as my sister. By that time, I was tired of not being accepted for myself, and I desperately wanted MY talents and special characteristics to be known and recognized. However, I didn't have a clue about how to go about individuating myself. I started by dressing differently finally. It was a joy to pick out my own outfits and not to have to agree on something and then hope there were two of the items in the same size. One advantage of my sister and I wearing different clothes was that we had a much larger wardrobe selection as we shared a big closet. Of course, I ran the risk that she would decide to wear the item I wanted to at the very same time. Anyone who has a sister she shared clothes with can probably agree that was frustrating. Also, at university, I was finally in some classes completely on my own and I enjoyed that so much. It was unique for me to feel like an individual for the first time.

It was comical sometimes that people I did not know would greet me when passing by, and there was no opportunity to tell them I was "*the other one*". Sometimes, it was just easier to smile and nod and wonder who the person was. Once in a while, my sister would be ill or not want to attend her class for some reason. If I could, I attended a class for her and few people ever noticed the difference. I knew what she was studying as we often helped each other with essays or other research. So, it was very interesting that during university I was learning to be an individual but taking baby steps. I had the full-time support of my sister being around. I still had my very best friend for love and assistance, in the safe world of the dyad. On the other hand, having control and ownership of what I was doing allowed me to be more motivated and confident.

One's feeling of personhood and personality encounters another boost in the teen years. This is a period where an individual attempts to isolate further from her/his family, home, and childhood. She/he is scrutinizing the qualities and goals with which she/he was raised. By endeavoring to make sense of which of those she/he will keep, and which will be disposed of, the person may discover comfort in lining up with an associate gathering or coterie.

I never truly developed my separate social circle or friends while attending university. It was safer to stick with friends I knew previously and who also knew my sister. I did not like to take chances or stand out from the crowd. That was not the way I was raised. Taking risks or being different was discouraged in my family. It was part of the family dynamic of how I was raised. I knew nothing different, so I accepted this as normal. My parents were excellent and loving people. They protected my sister and I as best they could from the hardships of life that they had experienced. Also, they had no training on the best way to raise twin daughters, so we all learned as we went on.

I became rather perfectionistic, critical and negative about myself. That was part of the family behavioral dynamic. I ended up feeling worthless, incapable, and fearful about most any situation. I believe I became a perfectionist because of the underlying belief that I would only be loved and accepted if I got everything right. I put on a brave outer mask to hide behind. I projected a certain confidence about myself that just wasn't true.

In **Things Will Be Different for My Daughter: A Practical Guide to Building Her Self-Esteem and Self-Reliance**, creators Mindy Bingham and Sandy Stryker portray how in youth, belonging to a peer group beats singular personality. They take note of that "[t]here is wellbeing and security in the gathering way of life as [adolescents] move from who their folks need them to be and battle to discover their identity." This fundamental procedure is confused in twins who, for the most part, have trouble finding their unitary personality since they see themselves as a component of a couple. Regardless of whether they, as a set, have isolated from their family, despite everything, they have not shaped their unitary personality since they have not isolated from each other.

Even though I had academic success, I never felt I was a success. My family often commented on my appearance, implying I was overweight and ate too much. I secretly felt sad and ugly. Who would love or want to be friends with a fat child? Years later, I saw pictures of myself with my sister and we weren't overweight at all!! I don't know why people made those comments. My sister and I were pretty girls who looked of normal weight in most pictures. I certainly never felt pretty as a child. When things were good, they weren't good enough, and disaster might be around the next corner. When things were bad, it was a confirmation of what I knew would happen. I dreaded just about everything.

I finished university after obtaining a graduate degree. My sister had finished a couple of years earlier and was working full-time in the city where we grew up. We were still living together with our family. I still had my best friend and in-built support system – my sister. Now, everything was about to change. I was unable to get a job in my native city and had to move for a job in another city 8 hours away. Also, I was getting married in a couple of months. What tremendous life shocks and stress I had at the same time. If you check the renowned Holmes and Rahe scale life stress inventory, I underwent 4 major life shocks all at the same time.

These included getting married, moving residences, starting a new job, and losing a family member. I felt disconnected, quite anxious and little self-confidence. In the past when I had felt that way, I automatically had my built-in support and cheering section – my twin sister. Of all the major life shocks I endured, not having my sister around produced almost unendurable psychic agony. I experienced a profound change in the most important emotional relationship I had ever had.

Suddenly, I was no longer part of that supportive dyad I had always had. I was on my own and woefully ill-prepared to function on my own. I did pretty well in the new job, I got married to a pleasant man and I enjoyed my new home and city. Inside, I felt like a scared, abandoned young child, alone and unprotected in a strange new world. I was finally on my own. I thought I always wanted to be on my own and have my own identity. I had no concept of how to be a fully functioning adult. I changed jobs a few times, I lived in other countries and I had outward success. Inside, I was still that frightened small child who had lost her guide and best friend.

I tried many years of counseling, therapy, inner exploration, spiritual studies, medications, nutritionals, self-help seminars, personal growth seminars, infomercial packages… you get the idea. However, after doing so much work, my issues about not being good enough, fearful to stand out and low self-confidence were not resolved. After all this I had endured 2 unhappy marriages, not being in the right jobs and had put on a lot of weight I could never seem to lose. I had spent many thousands of dollars and years of my life to try to get to the place where I could have a nice adjusted life. None of this changed the fact that I was living in a terrible prison of hidden unhappy feelings, thoughts, and beliefs. No one was able to get past my mask and ways that I automatically protected myself. I was always so tired of all the pretences. I just didn't know any other way to be.

About 10 years ago I was doing training to become a life coach. I found out about an intriguing energy healing modality called Tapping or EFT (Emotional Freedom Technique). I had some sessions with an excellent practitioner. I gained clarity and understanding of the root cause of my fears and low self-confidence. What an awakening as years of inner guilt, shame and never feeling good enough diminished. I felt like I was seeing the world through new eyes. My negative thoughts, feelings, anxiety and need to be perfectionistic were hugely diminished. I felt light and free.

I was so excited about Tapping that I decided to add it to my skills as a coach. My niche and my focus were now centred on holistic coaching, working with the body, mind and spirit aspects of clients. I finally realized that I had come into my true self-identity. I knew my purpose and why I was here on earth. I was no longer just a half of a whole. I was finally a complete masterpiece.

I finally felt capable to build the life I had always wanted, to carry on with the existence I should have lived. The ability to succeed now is a core belief I have developed.

At the point when a client reveals to me they need to be more successful, I realize that character issues will surface for them as emotional blocks. These issues - who will I be, who is the new and improved version of myself, the end result for the old me - undermine lasting change inside ourselves and our clients, basically because we are extending ourselves and don't feel comfortable with our identity as it is. Our customary ranges of familiarity are tested when we push ahead, regardless of whether we started or looked for the change.

Figuring out how to address the enthusiastic difficulties that accompany developing and winding up more effective can drastically improve your long-term success. Fortunately, personality issues and clashes can without much of a stretch be tended to and neutralized with EFT tapping when you realize what to search for in yourself or in your clients.

Every dread about changing can be linked to a particular past event. On the off chance that you feel anxious to change, where does that dread originate from? What occurred in your past that set you up for this dread? What has happened in the past to color your experience?

When we begin to perceive that we are transforming, we generally have a "*personality struggle*" that surfaces. This implies, who am I now that I never again have this issue?

Without a strong sense of self, it's difficult to have solid connections. The irregularity of conduct makes it difficult for others to comprehend you. Also, on the off chance that you do not have a feeling of your identity, it's conceivable you battle with trust. Your dread would be that on the off chance that you let individuals close they will eventually reject you.

I wish I could tell you it was easy, I wish I could tell you that all you could desire is within your reach – and it can be. However, there is some work involved. Not the heavy lifting kind, no. For some, it may be considered heavy lifting if you've never done any work on the interior on yourself. For now, let's just say that learning how to have a strong sense of your identity requires courage to get clear on who you are.

Co-Author
Carol Davies

Davies is a lifestyle success strategist who helps busy, stressed entrepreneurs discover where they really want to be in life, then find out what excites and motivates them to change and grow with her notable SPIRAL (Success Program Investing in Revitalized Achievement in your Life) program. She uses holistic modalities such as life coaching, NLP, EFT Tapping, crystals and Reiki with her clients.

If your mindset isn't right your life doesn't work. You need to find your passion, Carol believes. Carol's favorite mottos are "Just DO it!" and "Live your best life now!"

In 2007 Carol came back to Canada after a successful 22 year career with the United Nations in New York and Geneva. She founded her own coaching business to help clients needing help in life/career transitions and stress-management. She's a writer, life-long student, cat-lover and based in Ontario, Canada. The things she loves most in life are her dear twin sister, travelling, and volunteering. She's been a professional coach for 12 years, and really loves it.

Website: www.thepassionmotivator.com
Facebook: www.facebook.com/caroldaviescoach or
www.facebook.com/Caroldaviesthepassionmotivator/ or
https://www.facebook.com/groups/159714244716403/
LinkedIn:www.linkedin.com/in/caroldaviesthepassionmotivator/
Twitter: www.twitter.com/freeyourspirit

Dear Anne

Enjoy the flight!!

with love

Linda xxx

"

*I know that when I have **fear**
I am on the brink of doing
something wonderfully
amazing for me.
I'm a much happier person
and a work in progress
because there is still so much
for me to explore and enjoy."*

~LINDA CURTIS

Fear Crippled Me...
But not any MORE!
by Linda Curtis

You're about to read about a *miracle*. If you think you can find a credible excuse not to become all you are capable of becoming then please think again; all the 'reasons' for avoiding living your life to the full have been taken because it was me that created the Encyclopaedia of Excuses and the Catalogue of Coping Strategies; furthermore, I became the master of my craft.

First, let me ask, have you ever been all geared up to be somewhere, to do something new or to meet someone and have been so overcome with fear or nerves to be frightened off? Yes, so have I. In fact, I have been so consumed with fear, I have avoided and literally run away from so many events, it became my norm.

In this chapter, I'll give you a glimpse of how fear crippled me; kept me from myself in this exciting, amazingly adventurous and unpredictable world. I'll show you what my life is like now and more importantly, if any of my story resonates with you, you might see what keeps you in that almighty uncomfortable comfort zone and what steps get you on the path out to freedom.

For as long as I can remember I lived in a state of fear; fear of the unknown, fear of upsetting someone, fear of getting things wrong, fear of getting something right, fear of getting in the way, fear of challenging the status quo; fear of being abandoned and more so fear of being rejected. The list was endless and maybe you have a few of your own.

Possibly having been labelled by the midwife in the first few moments of life as being a 'nervous baby' had something to do with how I lived my life for a very long time, who knows? Either way, it became a role I lived to absolute perfection until in my fifties. Coupled to this was my absolute belief in the perilous threats if I disobeyed whomsoever in command: don't eat that you'll be sick; don't run, climb or you'll fall; you won't like that; we the family don't be, do, have or go to .... fill the blank!

Consequently, not only did I develop fears of just about everything, but I was also confused by the outcome; so eating a sausage when someone didn't want me to would make me sick yet if it was my dinner, I had to eat the sausage. How does that work? The 'don't or you'll fall' order from my mother echoed full blast when a battle axe of a head teacher Miss Cooke at my first school bellowed at me for not climbing on the frame, usually out of bounds to first-year infants. I can hear my five year old me trying to pull from her grasp saying in obedience and unconvincingly, 'I'm not allowed'.

Looking back, the climbing frame incident was the first time I felt what I can only describe as a kaleidoscope of terror that dominated my life from then on; each facet of fear shifting in importance and significance gaining force through the years. I am only five and yet I feel hated. All my classmates are looking at me crying in shame and embarrassment; they are all waiting for me and now I just want to run away and hide.

It did look a fun thing to do but I didn't know how to engage and interact with the others and of course, I feared the physical pain of falling my mother taught me would happen. I have subsequently realised that I never learned how to play with others. I recall sitting alone at my desk on my first day at school waiting for permission to join my contemporaries at the toys and games and form new friendships and relationships. Although I did have permission on that fateful occasion, the fear of my mother's impending wrath won the day and Miss Cooke's yellow stained, tombstone teeth snarling her lack of compassion was somehow easier to live with.

It was an awful sickening episode and the first time I recall giving up something I really wanted and instead, suffering by being obedient. By doing right, I was doing wrong; the seeds of a confused existence sown. Incidentally, no one did fall, so I learned on the one hand that it must be just me under the threat of doom and disaster. While on the other hand, to avoid impending catastrophe the result was shame and humiliation. From then on my home was made in the shadow of fear and uncertainty and in my growing up years I learned to be submissive and pretty much all choice was made for me. It was as if I subconsciously relinquished any possibility of making my own decisions in, and for, my life. How sad is that but unfortunately very familiar to many, particularly women, at various stages during their lives.

This mental chaos stayed with me because the order of the day at home was "don't question me", so I didn't. I was dutiful to my mother's words. Don't get me wrong I was just as naughty as the next child with siblings, vying for love, attention and approval. It appeared a loveless and harsh upbringing and I became adept at knowing what not to do through punishment but sifting out what I could do was more difficult and far too risky. My parents virtually controlled my friendships, what I did, where I went and I mostly obeyed although not without a tantrum or two.

I developed the belief that questioning was a personal threat to authority hence my two-dimensional education and dread of school. My interpretation of questioning a teacher in my lack of knowledge or misunderstanding was undermining the teacher's ability to teach and, carrying with me from the climbing frame incident, fear of being stigmatised as rebellious, sullen and unapproachable. What else was there but to believe it was my fault when I didn't learn, didn't understand or when things went wrong which can still be my Achilles heel.

The final nail in the coffin of my self-esteem came about when my parents separated and my thoughts of living with my dad was the better option. We looked at several cottages together and one place, in particular, appealed to me. I remember so clearly the evening sun shining through the low window into a bedroom that I felt was mine. The mirror over the pale green wash basin in the corner catching the light which, in my heart of hearts, was the room I thought my dad would choose. When I told my dad which room I preferred he turned away and said 'I wasn't planning on you coming with me, I thought you would marry your boyfriend'.

I stood in the empty room feeling the familiar shame, embarrassment, humiliation; rejected, unwanted, unquestioningly speechless being unceremoniously jolted out of the nest. I didn't feel unloved because I didn't really know what that was but I did feel hurt and very much alone; in that consummate aloneness, I was too stunned and sad to cry.

Being the obedient little girl, less than eighteen months later I married my boyfriend on my twentieth birthday. Having rarely made a life decision until then, I was suddenly thrust into a very adult world and two years later I became a Mum.

I didn't know about postnatal depression but I had this constant internal battle trying to be someone competent, important, worthy while being completely exhausted. I was clueless as a new Mum to this beautiful little girl, my daughter. I can admit now that I struggled; I had no one to help me. It wasn't in my consciousness to ask for help because I thought, if I did, it would confirm I was useless and a failure; a naïve adult pretending to be grown up. Needless to say with that start and who we both were, the marriage didn't last. This is probably where my blasé faking started.

What I've concluded through endless self-searching is that I didn't know how to

be responsible and take responsibility for me, my behaviour, how I felt, how to choose. I turned to others for my happiness, contentment and self-worth as I struggled to not only find value in myself but to see who I really was. Time and life seemed to run away with me; I constantly juggled trying to be something to people while living on my nerves edge and this is how my life as wife and mother evolved. My communication was clumsy and tactless at times; my world was dark and lonely, false and fearful. I felt a fraud.

Added to this was the guilt for encouraging my two gorgeous, willing and able daughters to do the things I worked hard at to sidestep. I didn't want them to miss out on life because of me. The sad thing is I thought that was it; my life path stretched before me, the hand I'd been dealt and nothing could change. The reality being, I was just too afraid to consider anything else, ever, because that would mean me confronting the fears I had put so much time, energy and effort to avoid.

For simplicity, I clumped and compartmentalised my fears into fear of people, places, public transport and food otherwise my head was stuffed, swamped, overrun, overwhelmed by the vast number of threats that appeared to accompany me every waking moment of every day, every week, every month, every year that made up my entire life until I reached the age of 51. I missed so many moments, minutes, hours caught up with the consequences I carefully and deliberately calculated, or as I see now, miscalculated, living in my fearful world.

I had successfully created my Encyclopaedia of Excuses and Catalogue of Coping Strategies to instantly find a way of dealing with the dread as well as to be convincing; my behaviour was so realistic that other people also used to find an explanation for me and my actions however bizarre they were.

The urgency to avoid both familiar and unfamiliar experiences was so strong while I was in the panic mode that I became oblivious to anything but the need to escape. Once I had taken some kind of avoidance action I felt no better, in fact, I felt worse. Moreover, in those moments of 'Linda, you've done it again' in order to restore some essence of internal calm I normalised my behaviour. My abnormal behaviour was my normal because I was so well practised and could instantaneously manufacture some plausible reason for my actions. I became a master of deceit; deceiving everyone, including myself. It worked. It never became apparent to me that anyone ever suspected the fear, terror and panic I felt that overwhelmed me to take, quite often, drastic evasive action.

From my first day at school observations, other people seemed to have so much more of a clue how to live and behave without anxiety or fear, doing everyday things without a second thought. Their world didn't appear to be hostile and threatening. On the contrary, it was ordinary, yet exciting and daring. For me, accepting invitations meant tactical calculations of where to sit to have a clear run at the exit; assessing what to eat because food had become the enemy. In the end, I physically couldn't eat in public and because of that experience, now I can easily spot an eating disorder a mile away. Thinking what to say at the school gate so I didn't reveal what an uneducated and ignorant impostor I was, became an energy drainer, as did rationalising how to travel; if I couldn't drive or be a front seat passenger I didn't go, so inevitably flying was out. I doubt these 'others' felt the guilt and shame of letting people down when they didn't turn up with no explanation or apology, as I did.

I tried to model myself on my sisters but that seriously backfired. They, like these 'other people', appeared happy and carefree. Maybe this was how they saw me because I had become a master of my craft, living with the underlying belief that I didn't know how to be spontaneous, to be daring and adventurous.

One of my greatest successes was getting straight on to a waiting bus from a train. I'd paid my fare and realised the enormity of doing just that; looking at my ticket marvelling at this achievement. Many moons ago, on a previous bus journey, I panicked and had to escape and rush off the bus at the next stop, I then had to walk six miles home and make yet another excuse for being late. You see, for someone who had avoided using public transport for years this **spontaneity**, no forethought or planning my exit route, was my success. I was elated at my accomplishment! That I got on the wrong bus and had to walk quite a distance in the rain is neither here nor there.

There have been thousands of episodes where I have panicked, lost my nerve and taken avoidance action and ***now my life couldn't be more different***. Without a doubt, I have experienced a personal miracle. The contrast is that while I still have a real fear of the unknowns, I know that fear is almost always excitement in another coat. I know that when I have a fear I am on the brink of doing something wonderfully amazing for me. I'm a much happier person and work in progress because there is still so much for me to explore and enjoy.

So, you ask, how did I manage to change every aspect of my life from living in fear of people, places, public transport and food to be enjoying a life full of adventure and ordinary stuff? Well, the answer is simple: I got honest; I owned up to myself.

You've probably realised there was more to it than that and you're right, there was a crisis point where I was on the threshold of lying to one of my dearest friends

when in December 2002 she asked me to an event that would encompass all of my fears. As I was on the phone accepting her invitation I was already running a script that told me I would get out my old faithful Encyclopaedia of Excuses or Catalogue of Coping Strategies. When I put the phone down the truth hit me; I was instinctively saying yes and, at the same time, subconsciously planning not to go while knowing I really didn't have any reason or excuse not to. This was my friend and I didn't like what was about to happen, with this realisation, I simply couldn't muster up the energy to find a credible enough excuse to cheat. I had got so weary and fed up with bending the truth, of lying that I just fell to pieces; it was my rock bottom moment. Strangely, in my aching, pitiful sobbing, there was a calm and a gap in time allowing me to make a choice. If I resorted to my dog eared Encyclopaedia of Excuses or Catalogue of Coping Strategies the time gap would seamlessly close and no one would be any the wiser, or, I could step forward into truth and honesty. I knew there was only one way out, and I took it. I just wanted out of the pain, lies and subterfuge.

As a complete physical and mental wreck, I blurted the whole story in one long stream of garbled words and sobs and, thankfully, I was too emotionally exhausted to reject the help offered. Once I had made up my mind to deal with my fears it took maybe just three or four hours to get my head straight and to work out a strategy; it felt so good to purge, at long last, the poison of my imagined fear.

The solution is simply that together, my co-strategist and I planned the occasion to every last detail. In my mind I walked through the event from leaving my house for the fifty mile journey knowing, one way or another, I could not fail; I would arrive late enough for the 'dreaded seats' to be taken but not so late to attract attention, I had already chosen the kind of thing to eat so looking at the Indian menu was merely play acting. I mingled with my friends and their friends and I really did have a truly enjoyable time. My security was my in-built exit strategy; if I felt overwhelmed I would excuse myself and purposely take time out to calm down without calling it running away. That never happened.

I know I nervously chatted past my usual bedtime at my friend's house, I couldn't even clean my teeth (yuk) and was probably awake for most of the night but hey, I had survived the previous evening. I had done it; I had met my fears, and no one knew. Back home I was encouraged to talk through every aspect of the event in detail and to recognise the significance of why I went, what I achieved and how I did it and to celebrate all the positives. Also to imagine what if I hadn't have gone. THAT event became my benchmark and my watershed.

After that the magic really started to happen; by creating a strategy for what I thought was a one-off event, when other opportunities came up the fears started to evaporate until they eventually they fell like dominoes. How it works I can't really explain here but I didn't need to go through my winning formula again with such precision. The following April I can't say I didn't hesitate when my daughter, who at this time knew nothing of my fearful life, asked me if I'd like a holiday with her to Rome but my accelerating forward momentum wouldn't allow me to say 'no.' That trip is a story in itself and if patience was needed on my first EVER flightseeing the Alps poking through the clouds and making commentary on every peak, my daughter won the prize. The same year I flew to Barbados, December it was Prague with my other daughter.

I continue to travel the world and have a place in the sun with the love of my life; I've also travelled alone east and west to the other side of this planet; I love using public transport and have recently taken two cruises and sailed in my man's yacht. I eat all kinds of foods, occasionally in the finest restaurants, and am now known to be the one to try the unusual; I have studied and am a Bachelor of Arts; I am a well-qualified teacher, coach and mentor; I'm living my life BEING, DOING and HAVING what I want on life's roller coaster. I say 'Yes' to opportunities because I can.

The events I feared, that governed my being, are now in the realm of my normalness. Fear no longer cripples me or my creativity. Yes, I still hold back sometimes and get the collywobbles and it is in these moments that I put on my Big Girl Pants and bring my mantras into play, What is the worst thing that can happen, Linda? and Why not, Linda? and If not now, when, Linda?

I live an incredible life now and absolutely love my transformational story from fear of people places, public transport and food to being who I am today. Do I have regrets about the opportunities I missed? Of course I do, but it is more sadness than regret. I became embroiled in a vicious cycle and as the fears got deeper and more complex I couldn't ever contemplate either the risk of revealing what I saw as weakness and failure to seek help or even the possibility of living in a better way. I believe now if I had access to the wealth of experience, inspiration and purpose within Dance In The Fire Of Life when I was in the clutch of crippling fear of whatever my unknowns were, I think I would have been able to step out of my shadows of fear much sooner, knowing I wasn't alone with my feelings of secrecy, shame and embarrassment.

I know on the other side of fear, without a shadow of a doubt, is the most amazing feeling of achievement; I always acknowledge, applaud and celebrate the accomplishment of every new, different or difficult experience. I cannot go back now and, because I'm no longer in the stranglehold of fear, I feel free; if I can do it then

anyone can. I still have to deal with the ordinary and the extraordinary stuff that happens to everyone but a true miracle happened for me and it can happen for you.

I have a gift for YOU in the form of a message to share; I'm feeling my fear, knowing those well-kept secrets are being lovingly revealed so that you will know you're not alone. If any of my story resonates with you, dear reader, I am reaching out to you and for you.

Living my truly amazing life, laughing every day together and having fun; travelling, doing what we do and literally planning what's next, a postscript explodes in this story that requires me now to bring into play everything I've shown you to deal with the ordinary, the extraordinary and the downright excruciatingly painful. Less than two months ago sadly and tragically my man had a sudden, catastrophic brain bleed from which he didn't recover. In a matter of a few hours, he went from being my happy and funny life partner to being an organ donor. It is the shock of him no longer being around and the unrelenting sense of loss I'm feeling in the turbulent ebb and flow of grief, because a part of me has died too; the person I could only be, with and because of my man, has gone and I'm missing that part of me, also.

In these early up and down days of aloneness, I have a choice. I can sink into a tumultuous black hole or I can, given time, become reborn and create who I want to be, plan my future and be open to new opportunities; to live my life in the best possible way, just as my man would expect of me, **and I will, because I can.**

I'll drop by again sometime and let you know how I'm getting on.

Co-Author
Linda Curtis

Linda Curtis, the creator of **SixtyPlusSuccess**, knows if you're heading towards sixty or sixty plus, you have a great future ahead of you.

Linda's special 'thing' is transforming lives, quite simply, by the power of changing the way you think; she is proof that it is never too late to turn your life around.

As a Master Coach, Trainer, Teacher, Speaker and Writer, but most of all as a **'life unleashed'** Mentor, Linda has inspired countless people, through her holistic approach and by her own story of crippling fear, to explore those hidden talents and ideas to become the best version of **your SELF**.

Linda is the proud Mum to her amazing daughters. She now loves to travel, is a regular spectator of live sport and music, enjoys authentic cookery and fine food and writes short stories.

"Fear is just excitement in another cloak" – Linda Curtis

Business Name – SixtyPlusSuccess
Twitter: https://twitter.com/plus_sixty
Instagram: https://www.instagram.com/sixtyplussuccess/
Facebook: https://www.facebook.com/Sixtyplussuccess-385952461839732/
Linkedin: https://www.linkedin.com/in/linda-curtis-822662a/
Website: www.sixtyplussuccess.co.uk

Dance In The Fire of Life!

"

I am sinking.

I want out but I dare not move.

I'm trying to understand why I'm

here and why my body and mind are

moving in different directions.

I'm angry, I want to scream.

I open my mouth but nothing comes

out, only silence.

I stare on in silence as fear takes

over once again.

And so I stay just a little bit longer.

I know how to defend myself

around here."

~Eleni Ikon

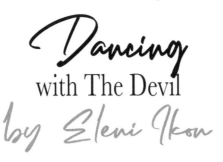

Dancing
with The Devil
by Eleni Ikon

I can see a faint light of hope in the distance. I can see all that is wrong in my life, all that I want to be different and all that I want to change. Yet, I still cannot take a step forward or speak my truth. So here I am, standing in what feels like quicksand, desperately trying to make sense of what brought me here and yet, getting nowhere, feeling trapped, tangled in a web of lies, that are dragging me down by my feet.

I am sinking. I want out but I dare not move. I'm trying to understand why I'm here and why my body and mind are moving in different directions. I'm angry, I want to scream. I open my mouth but nothing comes out, only silence. I stare on in silence as fear takes over once again. And so I stay just a little bit longer. I know how to defend myself around here.

"I never dreamt of getting married. The whole white picket fences thing, the family with the 2.5 kids did not appeal to me. I always dreamt of being on my own with my little girl. Things didn't go as planned…. At the age of 17, I made a decision that changed the course of my life forever. The choices we make can and will dictate what happens next.

So, my dance with the devil begins.

It's 1987 I'm 21 and pregnant. My first instinct is to terminate the pregnancy. Something tells me he will not want it.

My feeling was right. He instantly orders me to have it terminated. I get angry, how dare he tell me what to do with my body and try to control me! I leave but make it clear to him that I will be going ahead with the pregnancy and that I don't need him. I can do it on my own.

Shortly after, he arrives at my parent's house which in turn alerts them that I am pregnant. I fought so hard because I did not want to get married. However, coming from a strict Greek background, my parents would not hear of it, especially my mother. Her words still ring in my ears "No bastard will be born in this family!"

Why did I allow my mother to push me into a marriage I did not want. All we

have done since we got married is argue followed by beatings whenever I try to stand up for myself and challenge him.

Close to the end of my first pregnancy we got into a fight, things escalated and he grabbed me by my hair and slammed my head into the wall. I was crying from the pain but had no emotion. As I looked at him, I thought, what am I doing here? I hate you! A couple of weeks later in January 1988, my baby girl was born.

It's now 1991. I am pregnant again. He didn't want this child either. He threatened that if this child was another girl, he would kick the three of us out of the house. We're still arguing and fighting constantly. Then one day, he pushed me through a glass door! Crying violently, I began swearing at him as I struggled to clean up the glass off the carpet, blinded by the tears that were streaming down my face! He panicked and left the house. I was crying and stressed out and in my mind, I thought about how much I loathed him for what he was putting me through. I thought of my daughter who was asleep in the other room and I thanked God for small mercies.

During the night I had a sudden urge to go to the toilet, but I couldn't. I was up and down all night, my bladder was so full, but nothing was coming out. In the morning when he returned from God knows where I asked him to take me to the doctors. They admitted me and I went straight in for a procedure where they discovered my uterus had tilted back and they had to reposition it. In my mind, I knew that the previous days beating had caused this but I was too afraid to tell anyone. When I came to, I was bleeding heavily and the nurses were tending to me, I was bedridden in the hospital for a week, and during this week, my worst nightmare came to life! I felt like someone with an iron fist punched me in my stomach and then I went into labour! My baby girl was stillborn. I named her Christie Maree, as she was born on Christmas Day. This plunged me into a deep dark hole. I was not able to function, so much so that the hospital organised her burial for me. I went to my babies funeral with one friend. He did not attend.

It's 1992 and I am pregnant for the third time. The physical and emotional abuse continues throughout this pregnancy as well. Yet again, I fear for this unborn child's life. God help me if I do not give him a boy. I wanted a girl because I wanted to replace Christie. I never wanted to give him a son. I hated him so much. I questioned God, why is this happening to me? What had I done to deserve this? In February 1993 I gave birth to a healthy baby boy.

I have no feelings. He broke me, I can't function as a normal person, I am a robot walking on eggshells. I'm just going through the motions. Every day is busy, it's what keeps me going. I don't have a minute to myself from working full time, driving my kids to school and to their extracurricular activities and keeping my home in order. I have OCD. Everything has to be done the right way, at the right time and it has to be my way. The clock runs my life. It's my only way of coping.

I lost faith in God and stopped believing completely. I felt he had abandoned me, so I abandoned him. I had been waiting for God to take this pain away and make things better. I did not realise at the time it was all in my own hands. I DID have a choice.

It's now 1994 and we were arguing over him going out all the time. I feel like a single mum. Many times he doesn't come home for days, sometimes weeks. He's never home anymore but when he is, he causes arguments and beats me up just to get out of the house and go visit with his girlfriend, unbeknownst to me, he was having an affair.

On Christmas night he wanted to leave at midnight. We argued and I asked him where he's going on Christmas night. He got angry that I questioned him and that I demanded that he doesn't leave the house. The fighting started, he went into the bedroom and in his rage, he ripped off the end of the wooden bed, pulled it out with his bare hands! He punched me, hit my head against the wall, things went flying everywhere. I grabbed him by the back of his leg to stop him from leaving. He dragged me along the floor as I was crying. He left anyway, leaving me in a mess once again.

I'm confused and alone, I don't want anyone to know what is going on in my marriage. I have a lot of friends, but nobody knows. I don't dare share any of this with anyone. My upbringing ensured that I was ashamed and afraid to speak my truth. I wouldn't even admit my truth to myself. On many occasions, I would frustratedly wait all night for him to come home. His phone was always switched off. I have lost count of how many times I threw all his clothes out onto the front lawn and then would take our sleeping children from their beds, put them in the car and drive to the top point of the Westgate Bridge only to find I had driven us all back home again. I don't know what possessed me to go there. My intention was to suicide and I wasn't leaving my kids with HIM! What was I thinking??? Yet, I did this time and time again. Once back home, I would put the kids back to bed and put his clothes that were strewn all over the yard away. He would come home and had no idea of what had almost occurred.

Even my parents sent me back to him. So I felt trapped, after all, if my parents wouldn't help me, no one else would so I resided to the fact that this was what I had to endure for the rest of my life.

10 years have passed. I woke up this particular morning and took his phone while

he was sleeping. I got the kids ready for school as usual and jumped in the car to do the drop offs. I had no idea what I was going to do with his phone. I did n't even know what possessed me to take it. Omg, I realize I don't even know how to use it! I stumble with the buttons and manage to get into his message bank. Subconsciously I knew what I was about to discover but I refused to admit it to myself. That would make it all too real and then I would have to deal with it and take action.

The message I heard was from a woman I knew all too well. She was calling him 'babe'... All my suspicions came to light. Somehow, with tears streaming down my face, I managed to get my children to school. Tears for the known and for the unknown. I went into autopilot.

I returned home. I don't know how I got there and went to the bedroom, stood by the bed with his phone in my hand and asked "Why?... What made you do it?" He woke up, looked at me a little confused until he saw the phone in my hand. He knew right at that moment that his secret life had been exposed. He couldn't even look me in the eyes, he answered: "You made me do it!!!"

This was the beginning of the biggest battle of my life. The battle for my sanity, my freedom, my truth, my children, freedom from his physical, emotional, verbal and spiritual abuse. The abuse had been so frequent that I had lost my identity and the only way to cope was to allow myself to go into autopilot and become robotic.

It took 3 months to get him out of the house but not out of my life. The beatings continued, until one day a friend came to visit and saw my body black and blue from the beating a few days earlier. She left, called the police and they came to my house entering through the back gate that she had left open for them. He was ordered by the police to leave and not to return again. He tried many times, but I never let him in.

The next morning I felt weird....Like something was missing. I'm watching my life in replay. In just seconds my life with my abuser flashes right before me. I felt very lost like a limb was missing. Then I realised it had been 24 hours and I had n't been beaten up, that was my moment to step into reality, stop being a spectator in my own life, and start taking charge!

I felt so ashamed that he had an affair and led a double life, I didn't want anybody to know the truth because, in my twisted reality, the facade I had created of the perfect existence and marriage was so far removed from the truth that I believed it myself. I was embarrassed and felt dirty like I was the one cheating. Why do wom-en carry the shame when they have nothing to be ashamed about? After a long period of abuse on every level, I felt worthless. I only existed through my abuser. It was only behind closed doors whilst I was face to face with the devil that I lived in reality and once the moment of abuse was over, I would go back to my fantasy world. The world saw me as a strong woman, however, in reality, I was beaten and broken. He was very careful to never leave evidence in places that were visible. I would help by only wearing clothes that covered up all the bruises.. I was so ashamed.

Leaving wasn't an option. I was his property. My spirit was so broken that I believed I did not exist without him…. I was a broken woman!! I didn't have the courage to leave. If the police had not intervened, I cannot honestly say that I would ever have left. When he finally left, I realized there was more to life without him and that was the beginning of my reconnection with MYSELF!

I wasn't raised around abuse and that's why I did n't recognise it as ABUSE! I didn't know how to express what was going on to myself let alone anyone else, hence my earlier referral to being emotionless. I had no feelings. I was not allowed to feel, let alone speak.

That life I had known, become accustomed to and allowed myself to accept will no longer be! I will not feed the dragon any longer. Not anymore... I'm coming out! The woman hiding behind the abuser. The woman who held this home and family together, the woman that everyone only knew as his wife.

And so the journey of self-discovery begins.....

I want to share with you what I've learned from my experience:

Just say NO! It's NOT ok to let yourself down.
Just one small tiny decision can change the course of your life. Listen to your intuition and trust because it will never misguide you. Have faith in the unknown and follow your path with determination no matter how wrong it may look to others. People will always have something to say. Don't be swayed. The more connected you are to yourself, the less fear will be active in your life.

The universe will never present us with a situation that we are not ready to deal with mentally, emotionally or spiritually. I now allow the universe to lead me. I have no expectations of anyone. My biggest lesson is that if something is not aligning with me, I can now say NO! I found my voice and can now speak up for myself. I have a new found courage in my convictions.

In writing this chapter, I went on a search to breathe life back into my emotions,

allow them to come to the surface and really delve into them. For too long, I only existed from one robotic motion to the next. Every day I lived a lie and every night my thoughts haunted me with the truth. What I discovered on this writing journey, was that I protected myself by not allowing myself to 'feel' any emotion at all. That needed to stop. In order to get through challenging times in life, we must feel the emotions before we can rise above them. The healing is in the recognition.

At the time, I was in hell, however, in hindsight, it paved the way for me to grow, develop strength, self-confidence, honesty, openness, compassion, kindness, integrity and wisdom. From the outside, my life looked perfect. I had a successful business, two beautiful children, someone who seemed perfect, a large group of friends, attended VIP events, dined at the best restaurants, had a lovely house, beautiful clothes...but it was all an illusion. I was miserable, hated myself and my life.

After I left him life became even more challenging. I was absolutely broken in every way imaginable. But I still had two children to raise, guide and nurture while I raised myself out of the ashes and put ME back together. The best part about hitting rock bottom is that I got to choose exactly who I wanted to be and how I wanted to live my life and this time, I did it my way.

I now have three beautiful children, amazing friends who respect, appreciate and accept me for me and more importantly, I love, respect and trust myself.

I have an amazing relationship with my two boys who amaze me every day with their compassion, acceptance and desire to make the world a better place. I love my daughter dearly and I am grateful for the small things in life. I treat myself and my body well. I have no outside expectations. I have learned to surrender and be led by blind faith and I have a new found love for God.

This book and mastermind discussions were the trigger for me stepping into my authenticity and no longer running away. Many decisions were made because I didn't want to disappoint anyone. I now follow my heart, my intuition, love myself and put myself first. If I'm not okay, how can I take care of my children, my business, be a good friend, daughter, mother or partner? I now understand myself on a deeper level. I am satisfied with who and what I am...I am HAPPY!

The damage caused by his abuse lasted for many years after I left him. I have been on a journey of self-discovery since 1997 and only recently have I really come to terms with the impact that his abuse has had on my life. I have just now really come to terms with the fact that I WAS in an abusive marriage.

If you identify yourself in my story, don't waste another moment. Take a step forward right NOW! Stop living in denial and take a leap into your magical truth.

Follow your heart and it will lead you to YOU! The time to live your truth is NOW!!!

My story could be your story or it could be the story of a woman you know. The truth is that these stories belong to all battered women. It is time that we all let go of the emotionless denial and shame which plagues most battered women and begin to put the pieces of our lives back together. We need to talk about domestic violence so as to be the inspiration of hope to other women experiencing these types of experiences right now... it is our responsibility to use our experiences to help other women.

My aim in life is to see women rise above their challenges, learn from their experiences and share what life has taught them with other women who are desperately seeking answers and solutions right NOW.

MY PAIN HAS BECOME MY STORY.....BE TRUE TO YOURSELF, BE AUTHENTICALLY YOU!!

Co-Author
Eleni Ikon

Eleni is a passionate entrepreneur, co-author, hair stylist, inner healing coach and mentor. From hair oil, contouring make-up to inner soul healing, she helps her clients look and feel amazing from the inside out. She has been working closely with people for 38 years and loves witnessing the magical transformations....anywhere from their hair to their inner being.
Eleni is the owner and founder of **Haus of Hair & Beauty** *and* **Motivating Your Soul** *both of which help women from all walks of life feel good about themselves. Over the years her business expanded from hair and beauty to inner soul healing....her true life calling.*

"I am passionate about helping women find their passion and purpose in life, heal their past trauma, find their voice and to know that they matter. I love to watch the process of a wounded soul heal and flourish."
Eleni is a devoted mother and serial entrepreneur from Melbourne, Australia. Her loves in life are God, her children, her friends, the beach, Santorini and her dogs!

Website: www.eleniikon.com and www.eternalfreedom.group
Twitter: https://twitter.com/eleniikon
Instagram: https://www.instagram.com/eleniikon/
Facebook: https://www.facebook.com/eleni.boo

"

*When we experience loss,
we experience autumn in our life.
A season has come to an end.
We need to allow the dropping
of the leaves.
It's time to honour our inner
emotional landscapes."*

~PRASANNA DIANA MANUELA

The Blood Moon

by Prasanna Diana Manuela

The red moon is calling me out of bed to be with her. There she is… up in the sky surrounded by an endless array of stars. When the red moon is in the sky, it is said that night is an auspicious night. Different traditions have their own wisdom they share about it. But for me, I celebrate my newly claimed freedom. I feel a global expansion in my bones. You know when a blossom is nearly ready to pop and it's laying low for just that little bit longer? She rests, cycling through days, nights and perhaps weeks… then when the conditions are favourable… the days are getting just that little bit longer and warmer… tension and pressure builds up some more inside the small little tough shell and then when she can no longer hold back her joy and excitement… the little bud suddenly gives way as the blossom bursts into freedom.

So often in life when we are going through very challenging times, the stress and tension of it all builds up inside of us. Then comes that moment, when we give up fighting… we finally surrender. We don't know what to… but in the end, it's a giving -in to LIFE (Living in Fearless Evolution) itself. After that, we enter the dark night of the soul when we don't see our way forward. We have seemingly lost everything. It's like laying below the earth in the dark cold winter's night. In that moment we have to trust, that in due time, spring will return when the time is right. For that long moment, however, we feel lost, confused, heartbroken and empty. We cannot see our way forward. Just like the blossom inside the tied little shell is hidden away from the light, waiting patiently in the dark.

If we know how to navigate through such times, we emerge new and reborn. But if we don't trust the flow and wisdom of life, we might do what is most devastating to our soul's evolution, and that is holding on to the old. Were the cherry tree to hold on to the leaves in autumn, she would have no spare room or life force to create a new season of fruit.

But let's go back a bit… I wonder how far I should go back for you. One thing is for sure; I have experienced more than the average amount of loss in my life. I could tell you about the story of losing my son or how my mother walked out of my life or how my body was slowly wasting away over years. But I won't go there today. I want to tell you about the final stripping down that happens before the

floodgates of abundance finally break and lets in wealth on all levels… whether it be in your health, relationships, family or the work you do in the world.

I was given a blessing about 2 years ago exactly during one of my Dark Moon Dreamings. It was winter, that's when I hibernate to dream up the next cycle in my life and business. That particular night, I stood on a huge jetty looking out onto the wavy dark water, feeling into where my life was going to take me. Then a message came to me that I am being blessed by the Divine. She qualified herself by saying that a blessing isn't always easy to accept as it entails a falling away of parts of oneself that currently prevents one from fulfilling ones soul's destiny.

I immediately thought of my marriage. "Please not the marriage I hope…" but it was too late. The path was laid out already. I had been with this very special man for nearly 30 years. I had loved him every day of that. And yet our relationship was the only part of my life that wasn't growing or evolving. Every other part of my life had transformed and grown and turned into gold but not my marriage. As much as I wanted it to and worked hard at it, it was frozen in concrete. It occupied such a huge amount of my life-force and yet, it just stayed at the exact same spot. It was the only part of my life that was out of integrity with who I had become. I had awoken to the fact that perhaps, despite all my efforts, this was never going to change.

You see, as a natural wise leader, you need to surrender to your heart's calling. Mine has been calling me to serve on a global level. I know this sounds crazy, especially if you knew how I lived for so long. You can read about my life being surrounded by the beautiful Australian Bush in my book 'Elemental Woman'. But in a nutshell, my greatest joy comes from being totally surrounded and submerged in nature. Just like where I am now, spending the night, glancing through the tall Eucalyptus trees in the hills to admire the blood moon that is blessing the earth right at this moment.

Gradually the bright silver full moon is covered by this magical red light transforming it into what they call a blood moon. During a woman's fertile years, she disappears if she lets herself… just like the moon tonight… into another space, another state during her own moon time and/or Dark Moon. Her sensitivity heightens and so do her spiritual powers. It's her Wise Woman time. Nature has invented natural periods to withdraw from the outward busy, detail oriented material life. Instead… if given the opportunity, it offers a time where whatever she has not dealt with quite yet, will rise to the surface, to be healed. Her deepest wounds can be flipped into bright jewels to be used in her life and work in the world. Woman is blessed with this opportunity each month. In some tribes, it was understood that women would have revolutionary dreams during such times. They would go away together to rest and nurture each other and themselves. The tribe was eagerly looking forward to the women's return sharing their profound insights for the village and the people who lived in it.

As women, we are designed to cycle you see. We are created to experience ourselves in different aspects or dimensions, depending on our time in the cycle. In some ways, the time during Dark Moon and moon time could be described as the winter time, as it draws us inward to rest and replenish. It is in this deep space of rest that we tap into our inner Wise Woman. If you let her, she has profound insights for you, your family, community especially your own work as a healer, artist and conscious entrepreneur.

Sometimes we have bigger life transitions that call us inward for prolonged periods. Can you see the beauty when the leaves of your tree of life are falling? Can you trust just that little bit longer when you are in the dark of a winter's night and you do not see your way forward? Remember, the golden seeds below the earth are ripening as you feed them with your heart's devotion. Just as spring follows winter, so your new life will stir once again.

At the beginning of the year two years ago marked the end of my 29-year relationship. It was then that we left our family property, where we lived with our horses, goat, dog, chickens and rabbits. My partner and I both had separate office spaces to work from on our property. It was divine. We lived 3 min walk from a peaceful bird sanctuary with a creek running through it. We could walk right through it and arrive at the beach with lovely cafés across the water's edge.

The end of my marriage was closely followed by the death of my mother-in-law who had been in my life for 29 years as well. To make things even more challenging, I had a retreat to run right in between her passing and funeral. To be honest, I had no idea how I was even going to turn up to this retreat, it was more me who needed to attend one. But there were women flying in from interstate, and to try to re-organise a group of women, retreat centre, caterer etc., it's basically impossible. So, I decided to give it my best shot and come in my raw and fragile state. The women have always been amazing up to this point. They are the kind of women who take responsibility for their own actions, reflect and are eager to grow and transform. They looked out for one another and they supported each other, including me.

For some reason, the wind was blowing differently right from the beginning of the weekend. By the end of it, I felt as if I'd been ripped apart by a pack of wolves.

If I wasn't heartbroken before arriving at the retreat centre, I certainly was in a million pieces now… the funeral only being on the very next day. The irritations amongst the women went on afterwards, making me responsible for a lot of it and in the state I was in, I was too sensitive to set boundaries and the hungry wolves went on to devour me.

It showed me amongst other things how little loss and death is honoured or even understood in our society. We place unreal expectation upon those who grieve. Death comes in so many different forms. In my case, I lost my love, my home, a lifestyle and my mother-in-law all in a matter of 3 months.

When we experience loss, we experience autumn in our life. A season has come to an end. We need to allow the dropping of the leaves. It's time to honour our inner emotional landscapes. After the disastrous outcome of that retreat, I decided to withdraw from public life for as long as was needed. I cancelled all my upcoming training and I prioritised my own healing.

I love walking at night in the bush being hugged by a blanket of stars. A lot of magic usually unfolds for me here. One of these nights, I suddenly began to communicate with my Cosmic Lover or so I called him, not really knowing what that even meant at that point. This continued for a few days each night. Then there was a message "contact Michael D S." This went on for a few more days.

Then all of a sudden, his name appeared one evening on Facebook, and I sent him a message. What unfolded from here was miraculous. We connected a couple of days later to talk. Within a short period of time, it felt as if two worlds had come together as one, the feminine and masculine aspect of the universe. There was a knowing and familiarity that was uncanny. We shared parts of our life you would only share with someone you actually lived that life with.

I felt totally at ease in his presence and fully trusted him. The biggest gift he gave me was the gift of seeing me, seeing all of who I am. What we discovered was far beyond any romantic relationship, it was Divine Love in human form. I had met my soul twin, the only other being with the same soul code as mine in the entire universe. He totally adored me and reached out to me frequently. When I looked into his eyes, I saw myself. We were connected on levels that only happens once and it far succeeded the physical world.

We had both come out of 29-year relationships, both had two teenage daughters and an older son, we were both grandparents. We had studied the same spiritual teachings… we even blessed our food the same way.. We were living parallel lives, caring for our families and attending to serving in the world. Our hearts rejoiced and thrived in this divine love… until the tide suddenly turned. After living separately for over a year, Michael's wife suddenly wanted to give their marriage one last shot… for three months by undergoing therapy. Like a mantra, he frequently shared with me that he didn't want to go back, but still agreed to her wish even though he had left three times due to emotionally suffocating in their marriage, or so he told me.

At the end of the year we were both speaking at the same event and when I got there, Michael was there with his wife who was dancing to her victory song. Apparently never to be seen in support of his work, this time, however, she made sure she strutted proudly by his side through the conference.

I never forgot the day I found out in a roundabout way that he had moved back into the family home. As he had asked me to I give him some space to complete his affairs with his wife. I was looking forward to seeing him at the planned event. My heart was deeply shattered when I found out what actually happened. "If I could just pay my depth, I would give her the house and start life all over again." Michael so often uttered. His depth plagued him no end and it negatively affected his health and work. Being an empath and feeling deeply for others, I offered to pay off his depth. His intention was to repay me later or so he said like so many things. Being a celebrity in his field of expertise, what he seemed to fear the most was to lose the admiration and respect of his following. What hurt me the most was that he received my support, love and money and it didn't even occur to him to keep me in the loop of his change of plans.

I returned home feeling betrayed and heartbroken. Not having fully emerged from the loss of my marriage and the death of my dearly loved mother-in-law. Losing my twin in this way, was a heavy addition I could hardly bear. The loss of a twin is huge. It feels like parts of you have been ripped out of your heart and soul. Being a five-dimensional relationship, a cosmic relationship, in other words, the loss is deeply felt on a spiritual universal level… and it seems to happen right inside your heart. As deep as my grief was, I knew, that this was all part of a bigger divine plan to strip me down to my raw essence. I knew I was being prepared for a much bigger role in life. What was asked of me was to fully surrender to this purification process.

As I rebranded and reorganised my business to create more space to speak and travel internationally, I also cried, danced and prayed. Profound healing occurred. I was able to forgive the unforgivable and with this, I was diligent to not leave anyone out. My new life had no room for holding grudges or judgements. My life

needed to come from inner freedom; serving from the depth of my heart and soul.

Right when the final pieces of rebranding were coming together, my father-in-law passed away and then shortly after, my daughter-in-law's brother at age 34. We ended up having two funerals within one week. I was a flood of tears for 10 days straight. My father-in-law's death marked the end of my involvement with this family after having been a part of it for 30 years. I used to love seeing Dad every Saturday night for dinner and a movie until he died.

Loch's death affected me very deeply. My heart grieved for Deb, a lioness, advocate and loving mother. I grieved for Chloe, who lost her brother and I grieved for my son Michael who lost his best friend. I cried for me because it could have been me losing a son. It was as if the tears would never stop.

In only 1.5 years, my marriage had ended after 29 years, I had moved house twice, I changed my legal name, don't mention the paperwork! I re-branded and fully restructured my entire business. I had spoken internationally three times and I experienced three deaths in the family. In the middle of it all, I hurt my back and my twin soul betrayed me. Any one of these events could have caused me to collapse or worse, give up. To top it all up, I wrote my first solo book during this very challenging time.

Even though I had a whole cocktail of huge life events all happening at once, by trusting and surrendering one step at a time to the wisdom within my heart and soul, by allowing my life force to navigate through what otherwise would have been a deeply confusing time, I fully emerged in my true essence ready to shine brighter than ever before. And with this, my book 'Elemental Woman' was published and became a #1 International Bestseller within five days of its release date. Around the same time, a man came into my life who celebrates and supports me affectionately and passionately even though I was not looking for a relationship.

Just as the Blood Moon transforms into her bright silver splendour once again, I emerge clean, pure and open. And with this, my heart is singing songs of gratitude. I feel deep gratitude for the support seen and unseen during the last two years. I am stronger, freer and happier than I have ever been before.

One of the biggest transformations I experienced was choosing consciously to release my fear of loss and abandonment. I chose to open up to receiving life in its glorious abundance. I opened my heart to allowing love in… again and again and again. Life truly wants to bless you. Your life absolutely adores you and loves you. It wants to bless you and in fact ravish you. Life is this big wild powerful force that is begging you let it have its way with you. Life is not to be understood, it's to be fully received.

Co-Author
Prasanna Diana Manuela

Prasanna Diana Manuela is an International Speaker, Feminine Prosperity Creatrix and International Bestselling Author of Elemental Woman™. Prasanna works with conscious and creative female entrepreneurs who want to Awaken their Heart's Calling into every detail of their life and business.
Prasanna embraces a rich tapestry of life. She inspires women with her love of beauty, nature, family and the freedom to express all of who she is, joyously and powerfully.

When it comes to creating a business that is 100% aligned to your Heart's calling, Prasanna is exceptional. She offers life-changing events virtually and in person, and travels regularly to share her passion to Awaken a New Generation of Wise Woman Leaders.

Elemental Woman™ experiences gift you the ancient knowing you seek to ignite vitality in life and business.
Elemental Woman™ Awakens your Heart's Calling and opens you to your innate Feminine Creative Force to regenerate from the inside out. This work brings profound self-understanding and connects you with a power that is far greater than you ever imagined.
Prasanna's 2018 book "Elemental Woman" is an International #1 Bestseller and #1 New Release on Amazon.

Author's page: https://www.amazon.com/Prasanna-Diana-Manuela/e/
B07H2MX81F?ref=dbs_p_pbk_r00_abau_000000
Facebook: https://www.facebook.com/prasannadianamanuela
Facebook: https://www.facebook.com/elemental.woman.tm/
Twitter: https://twitter.com/PrasannaDiana
Instagram: https://www.instagram.com/prasannadiana
LinkedIn: https://au.linkedin.com/in/prasanna-diana-manuela-a07533106

> **"**
>
> *Once again I found myself*
> *following an unknown path.*
> *I had not been searching for this;*
> *the opportunity just*
> *showed up*
> *and my intuition told me to go.* **"**
>
> ~Zeffi Laxmi Shakti Devi

Dancing in the Fire with the Goddess
by Zeffi Laxmi Shakti Devi

My life path has led me to a complicated dance with the Goddess. I have moved through my life learning truth upon truth. She has led me, encouraged me and mentored me to be more and more and more. Along the way, I have had many adventures and each adventure has led me to a greater understanding of Her, myself, and my path.

I was born in Athens, Greece to a simple family with a secret that they did not share with me until I was in my 30's. From the beginning of my life, I have had a special spiritual connection which manifested in many ways. By the age of nine, I was reading Tarot cards without any training. I used regular playing cards to make predictions for my mother's friends. I also loved a tiny church devoted to Mother Mary on an island that we frequently visited as a family. I took it upon myself to clean the icons when we visited. I saw it as my spiritual service. Over time I came to realize that this was part of my soul purpose in this birth; to connect with Her to bring her Alive; to wake her up inside of me so that She's alive. In my teens, I appeared much older than my chronological age. When my future husband met me at my aunt's house he thought I was 21. He was a U.S. Navy pilot stationed in Spain. This was my first major experience of following my intuition which told me to marry him, so at the age of sixteen, I married my husband and left Greece to live in Spain. Looking back I can see how instrumental to my life path that decision was to simply follow my intuition. Since the moment I left Greece with my husband, my pathway to the Goddess accelerated, though I didn't fully commit to her until I was 27 years old.

While we were living in Washington, DC. I met a woman who invited me to join a weekly meditation that she was holding. I was reluctant because I thought people who meditated had strange things going on in their minds. I didn't know what kind of people they were and I felt very scared about going to meditate for the first time, but my intuition told me to try it. At my first meditation, I found it was very difficult. I couldn't concentrate and couldn't focus as expected. Though the experience was difficult for me, I found that my body felt really good afterwards. So, I went back. The first three times of meditation were hard for me but during

the fourth one, I was able to calm my mind. I started having feelings, emotions, and visions. Thus I made meditation a part of my life. I encourage others to not be hard on themselves if meditation is difficult at first. It is one of those things that takes time and if you give it time, the rewards far out measure the effort.

My meditation teacher at the time was healing cancer in her body through these group meditations. I discovered that during meditation I could see inside people's bodies. I had visions of my teacher's spirit guides and I saw what was happening in her body. When we focused on another man, I saw his heart jumping out of his chest and saw the veins that were not working right. When I asked his wife about his heart she told me that he was going in for open heart surgery. Back then we didn't know that there was such a thing as medical intuitive. I had no idea that's what I was, that being a medical intuitive was another of my gifts.

One of the most pivotal times of my life occurred during a 6 month period in 1987 when I lost all my money in the stock market, got a divorce, and lost my business which was a nightclub in Washington, DC. I have no idea what I was searching for when I left an incredibly easy marriage, but I was looking for something deeper in my life and in doing so, I found my spirituality. My spiritual path was not easy to discover in 1987 because back then we didn't have the books to guide us. Once again, I simply followed my intuition and moved to New York to work in the fashion industry. Letting go of all that stuff was very, very scary. Being alone in New York was also very scary. But even though it was all so scary, I found that it was also flowing so easily. Sometimes, we just know we have to step out and do the impossible, the unexpected. Sometimes we have to ignore social norms and just do what it is that we just know we have to do. We have to do what feels correct inside, to follow our deep knowing.

I was so heartbroken with having lost everything. I went through a lot of different emotions, and a lot of running away. My family was unable to accept me for letting go of my marriage. Back then divorce was deeply frowned upon. Also, my mom thought I was a witch because I left my marriage and went into the spiritual path. I had lost everything, including my family. I had no communication with my mother for 10 years. Because of the choices that I made I had no one to turn to. The only place I had to go to was me and so I turned inward.

My gift was so big and was waking up so fast, but I still had no idea what was going on. While I was in New York I met my guru who initiated me to the Goddess. He is not very famous but he was an amazing guru for me. Not having a lot of money, I decided to travel with him to India for three months and follow the path. Many people and especially young girls and boys now follow this path, but at the time it was very unusual. Once again I found myself following an unknown path. I had not been searching for this; the opportunity just showed up and my intuition told me to go.

After India, I followed the fashion industry to South Beach Miami. I opened a company providing courier service for the fashion companies flooding into Miami. I still felt lost and was trying to figure out what I wanted to do exactly. I stayed in South Beach for three years and one day this incredible book about Native Americans came into my hands. I love ancient cultures so it was natural that I would love Native American culture. I decided with a friend of mine to move to Arizona with the excuse that I was going to open another company just like in South Beach because the fashion industry was moving into Arizona. I moved to Tucson but it didn't feel right. I went to Phoenix to visit a friend and that didn't feel right. This friend suggested that I take a vacation and go check out Sedona because it is very beautiful and very spiritual, so I packed everything and headed to Sedona.

It was here in Sedona that I found what was hidden deep inside me and my life began unfolding in a very different way than I had thought or expected. Actually, this is how the Goddess works. She leads you into a place that you never thought you would go so that you can have the resources and problems that guide you to do your inner work.

~ ZEFFI LAXMI SHAKTI DEVI

I was amazed by the energy in Sedona. The energy is red and very fiery. It felt like coming home. The locals claim that if you can make it here and she doesn't chew you up and spit you out, that you belong here. So that happened to me – she didn't chew me up. She kept me here for sure for three years without allowing me to go out of Sedona. It was interesting because I had access to leave, but I just couldn't. I would go up to a point on the road towards the highway and I would pull off to cry and then I would just have to turn back.

I knew I needed to heal from everything. I needed to heal from my childhood, I needed to heal from my divorce, I needed to heal from the industry. I needed to heal from everything that had happened in my life up to that point in time. At that time I was 33 years old which holds a very spiritual meaning for me because this is the age that Jesus was when he died. I knew that 33 is the most healing time in our life and also a powerful time for spiritual awakening.

Sedona is an incredible place. The energy in Sedona is very strong and "works you up". It was here in Sedona that I found what was hidden deep inside me and my life began unfolding in a very different way than I had thought or expected. Actually, this is how the Goddess works. She leads you into a place that you never thought you would go so that you can have the resources and problems that guide you to do your inner work. My life after that was very interesting. I had some money because of the company I sold in Miami, but I also needed to get a job so I worked as a concierge at one of the biggest resorts here.

Again, something inside me was screaming but I had no idea what that was. I was meditating, eating healthy, working on myself – everything that everybody does now. I had a couple of people here who were my mentors but I had to discover everything on my own. I started to study and began to reawaken my gifts. I started working as a healer, medical intuitive, and a spiritual teacher. All my life I was guided to new knowledge, segment by segment, but it was in Sedona that everything came together. It was never logical, it was always intuitive.

I had to go through all these trials and had to begin clearing karma and staying strong within myself so I would be ready to invite Her inside of me. It's so important to learn how to embody the Goddess. Inviting her in is the most incredible thing that I have learned in these 30 years of spiritual progress in my life. With Her inside of me, I have learned how to heal myself and to be open with no expectations, allowing this healing energy to find the best way and the best solution inside of me. As a result of embracing healing energy to do what it needs to do into my life, I can now share my talents without holding back.

All my life I was guided to new knowledge, segment by segment, but it was in Sedona that everything came together. It was never logical, it was always intuitive.
It's time now for us to spiritually grow and to heal. Allow yourself to relax and trust this transformation. Trust unconditionally, there's nothing to be lost but everything to gain.

~ZEFFI LAXMI SHAKTI DEVI

The Goddess woke inside of me 30 years ago and demanded that I speak my truth, that I will be my true self 100%. She offers miracles in my life and time for a deeper initiation. She taught me how to stay balanced between my masculine and my feminine energy and how to ground my body which allows me to stay strong and allows me to go with the flow. I also learned how to be a pillar of light so I could burn bright while it burns away everything that doesn't serve me anymore.

In 1997 I travelled back to Greece for my cousin's wedding. My family saw my strength and recognized the path I was on. My mother casually said; "you are like your grandmother" and then she told me the secret that they had kept from me. My mother's line, from my great grandmother all the way down to me have been very intuitive. My grandmother died with that secret. Sometimes we have to step away from our families to do the work necessary to find ourselves. When we are strong in our own self we can return to be accepted in our truth.

The secret of the Divine Feminine is wisdom. I sit with her in meditation and she talks to me. She put me through many initiations so I would stay strong. She has told me not to resist change; to be who I am and not sway because I do not need to be like everybody else. She told me how to speak the truth even if it hurts and to stay strong in my intuition. She taught me to trust and through all these initiations I became whole; our purpose IS to become whole. Through her help and inviting her in, I feel like I rise like the Phoenix. It's time now for us to spiritually grow and to heal. Allow yourself to relax and trust this transformation. Trust unconditionally, there's nothing to be lost but everything to gain.

Fifteen years ago, I realized a new purpose in my life. I recognized that the Goddess ignited me so that I could start helping other women. I needed to start working with women to help them discover who they really are. I serve as a life coach, I counsel women. I have been organizing a yearly gathering of women called **Woman Arising** each November in Sedona, USA. I have begun taking groups on sacred journeys and I also counsel couples. I am helping women to clear their womb, to clear their emotions, and to realize who they truly are.

My spiritual growth has provided me with a deeper insight into the needs of women and men. We have gotten off track on our relationships with each other. We need more love and more understanding. The more I connected with my inner self, the better I could understand others in a significant way. The individual experiences seem different, but the underlying base is the same. The more I worked with myself and situations in my life the more others showed up with similar situations and I was able to help them.

Our earth needs us to become stronger, more in tune with the needs of the world.

Our children need us to be the best we can be so that we can guide them along their path. Our men need a kinder, gentler world and they need us to stop being so angry at them. We need to realize who we truly are and embrace our inner knowing. The more inward we go we discover more strength because we don't rely on the outer world, we discover our own inner power.

Every step along the way I have experienced trials and suffering, but these were experiences for me to build on. What we do with these lessons determines our next step along the path. There is no time for blaming others, there is only time for us to determine what we need to learn and accept responsibility as the creator of our daily life. Know that you are the divine power because the feminine is rising within you to guide you and is there to protect you, trust you, and love you. Step forward into your path. My wish for you is that you learn to dance in the fire with the Goddess.

My spiritual growth has provided me with deeper insight into
the needs of women and men.
We have gotten off track on our relationships with each other.
We need more love and more understanding.
The more I connected with my inner self,
the better I could understand others in a significant way.

~ZEFFI LAXMI SHAKTI DEVI

Co-Author
Zeffi Laxmi Shakti Devi

Zeffi Devi was born and raised in Athens, Greece and is amongst the world's foremost natural empaths and is a highly gifted intuitive.

Based in the ancient and mystical mountains of Sedona, Arizona for the past 25 years, Zeffi has been working with men and women from all over the world, helping them tap into their inner power. Her intuitive spiritual counselling, medical intuitive and healing gifts and workshops will assist her clients on their path to discovering and awakening to their True Self.

Zeffi's lifetime study of the Mystery Schools, the True Yogini path, Tantric Buddhism, and Native American teachings, and her exploration of all of these techniques through her life experience has made her a true healer.

Zeffi Devi focuses her abilities on transforming lives harmed by illness. Yet more than helping clients to return to well-being, she helps them grow by harnessing their own feminine energies. Zeffi's clients come from Europe, Asia and North America. She spends approximately half the year in Greece and half in Sedona, Arizona, where she hosts "**Woman Arising**," an annual festival since 2012 for conscious women who are ready to dive deep into the Devine Feminine.

Facebook: Zeffi Laxmi Shakti Devi or https://www.facebook.com/zeffi.devi

"

Thank goodness for that final wake-up call as it made me sit up and take action, otherwise I would not be here sharing my story and what I have learnt with you. If you are living your life where you are working long hours, always looking after everyone else and not taking care of yourself and you feel that somehow your body will just carry on supporting you regardless, then hopefully my story will inspire you to start seeing things differently."

~SUE RITCHIE

Inner Pearl Diving
Took Me From Mess To Success
by Sue Ritchie

"When you start loving yourself and respecting your time and energy, things will change. Get to know your worth, and your value will go up."
~Germany Kent

There are a number of things that happened to me in my life that resulted ultimately in a big wake- up call with my health that made me make some huge changes. Strangely enough, but also typically for most people, I think there was more than one wake-up call with regards to my health and the way I was living my life. At the time, I chose to ignore those, get back on the treadmill and just continue to live my life in the same old manic way. The truth is I really didn't know at the time that they were wake-up calls and that the universe was trying to tell me something. I thought it was just bad luck that those things had happened to me, as so many of us just tend to do.

Thank goodness for that final wake – up call as it made me sit up and take action otherwise I would not be here sharing my story and what I have learnt with you. If you are living your life where you are working long hours, always looking after everyone else and not taking care of yourself and you feel that somehow your body will just carry on supporting you regardless, then hopefully my story will inspire you to start seeing things differently.

If you were with me on 6th July 2009 you would have seen me in my doctor's surgery, waiting for the results of blood tests. As I sat beside the doctor's desk, she peered over her glasses and said "Susan, the results show that you have Hashimoto's disease. That's an autoimmune disease that affects your thyroid gland and this explains why you have been feeling so tired recently."

I said. "Oh OK I can get my immune system well again and I'll be healthy again." In a very stern voice the doctor replied "Susan, That's impossible. You will be on the medication for the rest of your life."

Her sternness really took me by surprise. I sat there dumbstruck.
All sorts of thoughts started to race through my head as I tried to desperately make sense of what she had just said.

Is that it then?

Am I going to feel the way I do for the rest of my life? Am I now going to have to struggle with brain fog, memory problems, pains in my joints, recurrent cystitis and low energy for the rest of my life, which could be more than 30 years?

Are you joking? I have dreams. I want to travel. There are so many places I want to visit in the world. I love geography and all the amazing landforms on this earth. I love meeting people from different countries and finding out about their way of life and beliefs. I want to be able to run around after my grandchildren - if I have any. I've always been very active. Can this really be the end of those dreams? Is that it? Surely not?

The prognosis was just not acceptable to me.
I walked out of the doctor's surgery that day with a prescription in my hand and a decision that I would do everything I could to get myself well again.

But then 6 years ago I found myself in a place in my life that I can only describe as a black hole. It was like being stuck in a hole where the sides were all slippery and no matter how hard I tried, it was difficult to get any traction. I just kept sliding back down again into the sticky mire. It was a veritable "Slough of Despond". For those of you who may have read John Bunyan's Book the Pilgrim's Progress, you will know what I mean. I was in a terrible place in so many ways.

How did I feel? - Unfulfilled, depressed, fat, sick and tired, and I was hiding away. I had my own direct marketing business that had been successful, but because I was hiding away, the revenue started to dry up and I wasn't earning very much money.

The money thing was huge for me. Since the age of 14 I had worked in the holidays, I worked to put myself through university because my father refused to pay for me, I owned my own house and supported 2 wonderful children for several years as a single parent and was the major breadwinner as well. I still put in all the hours and more working, but it wasn't creating the result I desired. I really valued my financial independence and somehow despite one or two difficult financial times in the past, the universe always supported me and money would show up at just the right time. But this time I was in such a bad place I had lost all trust in anything.

I had never been in a place quite like this before. So how come everything had turned totally pear-shaped? The truth is it had been building probably for most of my life. I never felt any love for myself. My inner critic has always been so vicious! No matter what I did, it or I was never good enough. It would be impossible to count the number of nights sleep lost from me continuously beating myself up. Going for hours and hours on end over why had I done that, why had I not done this, why had I said what I said? I should have said something different. I could have said it so much better. Why was I so stupid? Why couldn't I be more like other people? They always know the right thing to say. What comes out of their mouth is always so eloquent. They always seem to be able to say the right things at the right time... and on and on I continued.

I would always prefer to agree with what people said even though I knew it wasn't correct or I never commented. I hated confrontation and it was so much easier than standing up for what I knew was the truth. I always felt so stupid and in-adequate. I was always scared that I might be wrong even though I really knew intuitively that I wasn't. In many situations, I was just not able to totally trust my own intuition. I guess I was scared of what people might think of me.

And yet, I had a successful corporate marketing career, before setting up my own business. I had reached the heights of being Marketing Director for Europe in a global organisation. So what was this situation all about? This became the start of a journey of huge personal growth, learning and enlightenment.

In March 2013 a friend suggested I attend an event that she thought would help me. I felt that it was right to go so I did.

The speaker was up on the stage. I sat in the front row listening to them telling their story. As I listened the emotion started to build in me. It came from deep down. The tears started to roll down my cheeks. I was in a state of disbelief. How was it possible that someone else could feel the same way about themselves as I did? How could someone else have had such similar experiences to me?

How could it be that they don't feel good enough? Surely, I was the only person in the world who feels like that? The only person who didn't think they were worth anything. The only person who felt no-one liked them. The only person who felt they were unlovable. Can you believe that for forty years I thought I was the only person in the world who felt like that about themselves!

There she is looking amazing, confident, speaking on stage to lots of people. How

could she possibly feel these things about herself? Everything in her life must be wonderful and perfect.

She and her partner shared the details of a programme that they ran and they talked about how it changed people's lives for the better. They would show you how to deal with that negative voice in your head that constantly lies to you. How it prevents you from achieving all the things that you want to achieve in your life because it constantly wants to keep you safe and small.

My heart said, "You really need to do this Sue". My head said, " Sue you can't afford it, you are not really earning anything at the moment". An argument between my head and heart went on for a few minutes, and my heart won. I got my credit card out and I paid the £2,500 for the week's programme. Thank goodness I listened to my heart, because I wouldn't be in the place I am now; living a successful, healthy, energised and fulfilled life where I take care of myself and maintain a good work life balance if I hadn't. Strangely enough, the money came in fairly quickly afterwards to cover the cost.

The programme was exactly what I needed to kick start my ascension out of that black hole. This might have been the first time I listened to my heart and took that action, but it certainly has not been the last. The first time takes courage, but when you see that your heart knows best, it becomes so much easier to take notice and make decisions in your life based on what your heart truly wants.

Someone once told me that the biggest problem human beings have is thinking. We think way too much. We spend too much of our time in our heads, rather than listening to our hearts. I was definitely one of those. One of my best skills is analysis! My brain can analyse situations and things for hours and what a waste of time that can be ultimately! We are always too worried about what other people will think. But they are not the ones who are having to live your life!

The problem is that when we are constantly busy living, pounding away each day on the treadmill of life, we never allow ourselves quiet time. After all, quiet time would just be a waste of time, wouldn't it? You can't just sit and do nothing, can you? Your negative voice will be telling you that you are being lazy. Isn't that true?

I know that was certainly true for me, but then as I started taking 15 minutes each day in the morning to practise meditation, I noticed changes starting to occur. I would start the day in a calm place. If I asked a question before I started my meditation, I began to hear answers. I was tapping into my inner wisdom or my higher self. If challenges came up during the day I would notice that I handled them in my stride. My stress levels went down. I started to sleep better. I started to feel more positive.

I now start the day each morning telling myself how wonderful and amazing I am. It's not easy at first when your natural instinct is to find yourself constantly lacking. But when you make it a regular thing it starts to become so much easier. The more you practise, the better you feel about yourself. As you shift that energy from negative to positive, you will be amazed at how other things in your life start to change for the better.

My daily self-care became my priority. I took time out to walk in nature. I was connecting with the world around me. I was noticing things at a detailed level. I went "pearl diving" every day. I spent time finding the pearls in my life. Focusing on the smaller things to be grateful for each day is not so easy, but taking the time to do that really pays off. The more you see the positive value of the smallest things that happen to you during the day, the more you see the shift in your mind-set and the more you will see things start to shift for the better in your life.

Being grateful and appreciating someone making you a cup of tea, holding open the door for you, for someone thanking you, be thankful for the air that you breathe in, being grateful for just being alive. Taking time to notice and appreciate the little insect that you spot on the wall going about their daily business. They might be tiny and insignificant but they are part of the amazing work of Mother Nature that makes the world go round and we are all interconnected. When I started to appreciate and express my gratitude my whole mindset began to move away from focusing on the negative of my situation and the state of lack to one that was positive about myself and my future.

The biggest change came when I made a decision about what I was going to do with my life, based purely on what was right for me. I had to do what was right for me from now on. It didn't matter what other people thought or said. This wasn't their life. It was mine and I wasn't living. I was just existing. There was very little fun or joy in my life. I had lost connection to the real me.

The big decision I made was to downsize my business in the sense that I would only work with existing customers so that I could create a good work-life balance and take time out to look after and heal myself. I had the difficult decision of making someone who worked for me redundant, but despite feeling uncomfortable with it I went ahead. She very quickly got another job so there was no need to worry.

I guess you are probably thinking that without me putting all those hours in like I did before that the business would shrink. The truth, however, to my surprise as

well at the time, was that the opposite happened and I doubled my turnover and almost doubled my profit in that year. How did that happen? Well, it was a case of having to manage my time better. I set and kept my work time boundaries. You know, it is quite amazing how much more productive we become when we know we only have a fixed time for things to be completed. I realised that I wasted a lot of time in the not urgent and not important box. It's so easy to do when you keep constantly checking emails, and checking social media. You sort of get caught up in it and before long you realise you possibly spent an hour, not being productive.

I learnt to focus on working on the key things that would grow my revenue and profit when I was in my work mode. I focused on working on things that were urgent and important. Then when it was focus on me time, I let go of the work stuff and focused on doing things that made me feel good. The big realisation was that I am a very creative person, but being so busy I had let go of doing the creative things that fed my soul. Photography came back into my life, particularly photographing nature. I also engaged in colouring, painting and singing.

Then one day, after meditating a word popped into my head that told me the root cause of my health issues. Yes, I know that might seem hard to believe, but it is the truth. The word was Candida.

When I researched the symptoms, I couldn't believe how many of the health issues that are signs of a problem with candida and poor gut health I was able to tick off. The root cause of my Hashimoto's disease lay in an out of balance gut microbiome. I found a totally natural way to rebalance my gut microbiome, but it also required me to make some changes to the foods that I was eating. Within 2- 3 weeks my energy started to return and by the end of three months, all the health issues had gone, my memory was back, the brain fog had gone. Amazingly, I also lost 2.5 stone/35 pounds /26 kilos in weight without even trying. Then over the next eighteen months, I was able to cut back on the medication and become medication free and totally recovered from the autoimmune Hashimoto's disease!

In truth, I can say that I hadn't felt that healthy for many, many years. Sue was back!

Having created my own "personal mess to success" I want to help other women, who are in that place I was 6-9 years ago to start living a balanced, healthy, energised, fulfilled and joyful life that flows with ease. So that is what I now do. It's so rewarding doing a job you love and helping others. I just love it.

There are three key lessons I learnt over the years that enabled me to turn my life around. I like to think of these as the three biggest, shiniest Pearls Of Wisdom that life gifted me in order to take notice and make the changes I needed to make so I could gain the life I knew was there for the taking.

In closing my chapter, I will now share my Pearls Of Wisdom with you and I know from my experience that following just these three pearls of wisdom has the potential to change your life as it did mine.

Pearl Of Wisdom 1:

This one was all about taking responsibility for my own health and my own life. It was a case of stepping out of being a victim and taking control of my situation. The big realisation, that I have to say was tough to take on board at first, was that I was responsible for creating everything in my life whether it was good or bad. Yes, I know it's huge and a big pill to swallow.

Through all my negative thoughts and my lack of self-worth and all the worrying about the worst outcomes, I had created that reality. It was only when I started to shift my mindset to being positive and seeing the good and the lessons in the most challenging of situations that I was able to change my life for the better.

Pearl Of Wisdom 2:

This was all about putting myself first. The whole concept of putting the oxygen mask on yourself first as they tell you when you travel by aeroplane is true. It isn't selfish to put yourself first. If you are not healthy and feeling good in yourself, you are not in a place to support others. When you take care of yourself and you feel good, everyone around you benefits and your relationships go from strength to strength. When you are tired, stressed and unhappy, you get grumpy and snappy and it has a negative effect on everyone around you.

Pearl Of Wisdom 3:

Asking for help was the third big lesson. I had been brought up to believe that if I couldn't do everything myself then I was a failure. So I would run myself ragged. How crazy is that? As women, we seem to think we have to do everything, don't we? We put on our Superwoman sparkly big pants and we are invincible! Unfortunately, that isn't true. We are always willing to help others because it makes US feel good. So why are we so selfish in not letting others have that warm, fuzzy feeling by helping us? It was only by accepting help when I was in that black hole 6 years ago that enabled me to start making the changes I needed to make to turn my life around for the better.

So, believe in yourself because you ARE amazing!
"Until you value yourself, you won't value your time. Until you value your time,
you will not do anything with it. "
~M. Scott Peck

Co-Author
Sue Ritchie

Sue Ritchie is passionate about helping stressed out female entrepreneurs and professionals that are busting their guts to re-balance revitalise and re-focus their lives whilst boosting their success.

Sue's previous life involved working long hours under high levels of stress. She was constantly pushing herself to the limit, trying to fit everything in. A big health wake-up call resulted in a decision to create a better work life balance, resulting in one of the most successful years in her business doubling her revenue and profit.

Sue is a coach, speaker and author of an award winning book, Love your Gut: The Practical Guide to Successful Weight Loss from the Inside Out as well as being a co-author in 4 other books. Sue's expert opinion is often sought after on radio and TV shows

Her loves include music, cookery, travel, personal development and socialising. Sue lives with her husband and takes great pride in her grown up son and daughter, not to mention her well-loved crazy cat Bella.

Website: www.sue-ritchie.com
Author's page: https://www.amazon.co.uk/Love-Your-Gut-Practical-Sustainable/dp/1517068673/ref=sr_1_1?s=books&ie=UTF8&qid=1549121283&sr=1-1
Twitter: https://twitter.com/sueritchiecoach
Facebook: https://www.facebook.com/thebusinesswomansmastercoach
Facebook: https://www.facebook.com/sue.ritchie.712
Linkedin: https://www.linkedin.com/in/sue-ritchie/

"

I no longer Fear Death, it is my friend...
I have seen too many unusual things
for there not to be something else after
death. I now call Death a Transition...
a journey to somewhere else.
We never truly leave we, just disappear.
Death is but a door to another life,
another world, another experience."

~JO FULLER

We Never Walk Alone
by Jo Fuller

"Is it the DARKNESS...
The PAIN.....
Or the UNKNOWN.....
That we FEAR....
When DEATH comes to take us home?"
~ JO FULLER

"Daddy please stop you are hurting me! I said", he wasn't listening, his own inner demons were longing to be satisfied. I was sexually abused as a child. The trauma left me with ongoing lifelong self-hate, low self-esteem, weight issues, relationship problems, depression, thoughts of suicide, dying and death. Hence my curious journey to explore the many faces of Death.

I was born and raised in a small country town. My father was an alcoholic and very violent at times. On many occasions, he would hit and even try to strangle my mother. I remember trying to stop him hitting her one night by coming in-between the two of them...I was so little that I just reached his kneecap.

I cannot recall all of the details of the occasions of sexual abuse nor do I need to, however, for the purpose of this chapter, there are two that come to mind which I would like to share. Dad had gone to bed early and from what I can remember, mum had taken me in to kiss him goodnight. He read me a Dick and Jane bedtime story. This particular night after the story had finished he asked me if I knew the difference between boys and girls. He proceeded to tell me that boys have a penis and he showed me his and asked me to touch it. He explained that girls have a vagina and touched mine with his fingers and penetrated me. It hurt. I was confused and really didn't understand. He told me that this was our little *"secret"*. It would be the first of many secrets. I was only 3 years old.

On another occasion, he offered to help mum out by showering me. After the shower, he laid me on a towel on the bathroom floor, laid on top of me and tried to penetrate me with his penis…that really hurt and made me very scared and afraid. For many years I thought it was how Father's loved their daughters.

I found comfort and some sort of normality in country life, riding bikes, fishing, flying kites and in my beloved animals. We always had animals around, chickens, ducks, dogs and cats. I saw baby chicks being hatched, puppies and kittens born. Of course, where there is life there is death. As a small child, I would often try and rescue the dying and ill animals hoping to keep them alive and save them. Even back then I wondered about death, at some level was I trying to save myself or was I being shown my Life's Purpose.

I Often thought of Suicide and wondered what it would be like to die. "How could I ease the pain of the emotions I was feeling…hatred, sadness, helplessness, anger and at times rage"?. Thoughts of death became my companion. Somehow, I found the strength and courage to continue living even when I felt I had no control over my life. I told no-one.

My first powerful experience of death was the loss of my dog, Rusty. He was hit and killed by a car, it was devastating for me. Mum said to me, "Sweetheart, he is now in heaven with the angels and is happy", her statement made me even more curious, "what and where is heaven??". I remember to this day that I drew a picture of him dead with the angels and the sun shining…he was my loyal little friend who comforted me when I cried and was always there for me.

At the age of 11, I experienced the loss of my beloved Grandfather or 'Farve' we use to call him. He died very suddenly from a massive heart attack. I was his little shadow, always watching what he was doing and trying to help. He took the time to show and explain things to me. I remember asking Mum if I could see him and say goodbye, she said, "Honey, you are too young, it would not be nice to see him that way, it would be better for you to remember him alive and happy". To this day I still wish I had the opportunity to say goodbye and tell him how much I loved him. I honour him every day by being the person he could see in me. He still walks beside me and I can feel his love and support when I need it most….it is a knowing, a deep sense of someone's presence.

So what is Death? Is it a beginning or an end? An opportunity or something to be dreaded? Apart from the conventional definition of death, being the end of life. Could it also be the end of a relationship or even an idea? We have been slowing dying since our birth, it is in our nature.

Do we need to make friends with it, as I did and use it as a guide to explore our innermost thoughts, feelings and emotions along with our fears, our guilt and our judgements of ourselves and of others?

So how did I survive?

Often we blame others for our life and the way it has turned out. I spent many years searching for answers to my sexual abuse. It wasn't until I read Louise Hay's Book "You can heal your Life" that I finally realised that it wasn't my fault and I no longer needed to be a victim. Over the years, on and off I have been searching for answers to many questions about my life, "Why me? Why did this happen"? The usual self-destructive victim ideology. In 2010 I came across Linda Howes Book "How to Read the Akashic Records…it saved my life. I started working within the Records on my own personal demons. The Records helped me to understand this trauma that I had experienced which ultimately led to forgiveness of myself and my deceased father, resulting in emotional and Spiritual Healing.

The Akashic Records has proven to me beyond any doubt that something does exist after Death. It cannot be proven in a scientific conventional way, not yet. If I am honest with myself and remember the experiences I have had throughout my life, the proof has always been there. By accessing my own Records, Past Lives and Ancestral Patterns and those of my Clients, I have discovered that we are better able to understand ourselves, particularly why things happen to us, why we have the patterns and behaviours that we do in this lifetime.

A few days before my grandmother passed away I had a strange experience. I was asleep in my bedroom with my dog Cleo on my bed. I was awakened by someone calling my name, it was a soft gentle female voice that said, "Jo, wake up, Jo wake up". At first, I thought it must have been a dream until I realised my dog was at my bedroom door sniffing under the door, her tail wagging. I felt a chill go through my body. I said, "Cleo is there someone in the house?" , hoping that the person might hear me and leave. I hesitantly opened the door but there was no one there. I carefully went from room to room turning on the lights as I went, Cleo was still sniffing and wagging her tail, I was confused and a little afraid.

There was no one in the house at all. I made myself a cup tea to calm my nerves, I didn't think I would be able to go back to sleep, I was trying to make sense of what I had just experienced. "Come on girl," I said to Cleo let's go back to bed, I was about to get back into my bed when I saw a black object the size of a small apple, near my pillow… I stopped dead in my tracks, my heart pounding in my chest and the fear rose from my stomach and stuck in my throat. There on my bed was

the largest Funnel-web spider I had ever seen (one of the deadliest spiders in the world). "Cleo get out, girl" Out!" I yelled. I quickly looked around to see what I could find to kill it, I had to be extremely careful, they are very aggressive and can attack. Lucky for me I still had the broom in my room from cleaning spider webs off the wall earlier that day …you can guess the rest.

So, was the voice my grandmother warning me? It certainly did sound like her voice. Was her spirit part here and partly gone? Was it this state of in-between that gave her the ability to come and warn me or was it her love that protected me? Is Death part of the master plan, our plan, our families plan, a universal plan?? Without Death do we truly value our Lives?

I have myself been to the deepest darkest parts of my soul, the pain so intense that taking my own life seemed the only way out. I wasn't scared, I did not fear to leave…the decision gave me contentment and peace and it is within this moment that I somehow found the strength and courage to live. I have seen many deaths all of which have led me to this place in time where I write this Chapter hoping to inspire others to continue on life's journey even though Death seems like the easy solution.

A few months ago a very wise woman said to me….'it starts with you Jo, always you', your thoughts, the way you speak to yourself, self-love, nurturing, if you love yourself, then others will love you….can it be that simple?

Our partners, friends, lovers and family are all here to trigger us, to help us see in ourselves what needs to be healed….we must truly thank and love them for being our teachers…'Our Guru's… for it is because of them that we awaken and grow spiritually.

In 2010 my ex-partner's brother Adrian came to live with us. He was diagnosed with a Grade 4 Glioblastoma (Brain Tumour) and was told that he only had 6 months to live, he was 37 years old. He was newly married and had a beautiful 3-month-old boy. I had nursing experience and from December 2010 to April 2011 we tried all types of alternative treatments for him, anticancer diets, and supplements. Slowly he became weaker and weaker, and whilst it was a very stressful and sad time we had our moments of laughter.

One day I went out for a few hours, Shannette, his wife and his sisters Debbie and Tracey were left in charge. They sat in the sun drinking wine and beer and everyone was happy. Adrian started to mumble and seemed to be in distress, unable to communicate due to the effects of his tumour. The girls didn't notice at first, but they soon realised that baby Jarryd had been pulling on his Catheter. Soon after this episode, they attempted to get Adrian who was 6'2" tall, out of his wheelchair and back into bed, somehow the wheelchair tipped over and they all ended up on the floor laughing. Even Adrian could find the humour in such a tragedy.

On April 16th, 2011 at 3 am I gave Adrian his last pain relief injection. I had volunteered to sleep in the living room to monitor Adrian in his hospital bed and his wife slept in an armchair beside him. I went back to sleep.

"Hey Jo" the voice called out, I woke suddenly it was 4:10 am. I looked around the room, Shannette was asleep, and there was no one else there. I then realised that Adrian's breathing was shallow and slow, I quickly jumped up. "Hey mate, it's ok, I know it's time to go, you will be ok, we will be ok, I love you" and within seconds he was gone. I knew then that the voice was Adrian's…I just knew it. I woke up his wife and the rest of the family and the final process of grieving had started. I felt then and still do today incredibly honoured and humbled to have been involved in Adrian's transition….his message to me totally changed the way I see and comprehend death.

My Dad passed away at home alone on November 3rd 2011 from a massive heart attack. I was contacted by the local police and told the news. It so happened that I was only a few hours from my home town and was, in fact, going to drop by and visit him on my way back to Adelaide, the timing of his death was perfect in many ways. I have an older brother who has his own mental demons to face and Dad made me the sole executor of his Will. He knew he could trust me in carrying out his last wishes. At the same time, I was studying an Akashic Subject called, "Healing through the Akashic Records"…where one takes their Sacred Wounds and turns them into Sacred Opportunities, what perfect timing to complete my healing process.

I stopped by my childhood home to pick up anything I might need to proceed with Dad's funeral. I was surprised to find his Will in a drawer. Some friends of his dropped by and explained to me that he had been very unwell and in the hospital for a few days. We decided to have a beer from his fridge and a toast to Dad and as we said "Cheers, we hope you are happy where ever you may be", the TV suddenly came on. We all looked at each other, laughed a bit and said where is the remote….it was on the table next to the TV.

The energy in the house was very dense and overwhelming, it felt dark to me…I

knew Dad was there, every cell in my body could sense it. I couldn't stay at the house that night so we stayed at the local caravan park in a cabin. It was the first night in 57 years that I slept with the light on....the dense energy surrounded me like a dark stormy cloud and I felt scared.

My ex-partner and I spent several months renovating the property for sale. It was in very poor condition. We spent a number of months travelling the 12 hrs from Adelaide to N.S.W. back and forth...a 12hr drive. The drive gave me time to think and work on the Akashic Subjects I was studying. I arrived one cold and wet June night around 9 am and drove straight to my cabin. I felt the dark energy again and again I left the light on. The next two weeks I worked at the house renovating, painting, sanding and cleaning. Each day I left by 6 pm unable to stay much longer after nightfall. Towards the end of the two weeks, I had to complete some homework for my Akashic Subject, it included a Pair/Swap Reading for a fellow student in India as well as answering some questions. I was very reluctant to do this as I thought once I entered the Records I would remember all of my childhood experiences which I didn't want to do. I gathered up all of my courage and skyped my friend, I did a Reading for her and she did a Reading for me.

"WOW!!! I couldn't believe it!! Bindiya said that while I was Transforming myself through the Akashic Healing Subject I was also transforming my childhood home and my relationship with my Dad....it was so obvious, staring me right in the face. I then went into my own Records and asked some questions about my sexual abuse. My Records told me that I didn't need to relive my past experiences as it wasn't necessary. My dad came to me during the Reading and we spoke about our life together. He said that he was very proud of me and loved me very much and that we had agreed to a High-Level Soul Contract to play out the parts of our life together and to learn valuable Soul Lessons. I learnt that night my Lesson for this Lifetime was Forgiveness. From that night I felt a love for my Dad that I had never felt before, I finally understood why. That night I made a decision to become an Akashic Teacher and to be of service to others.

Sometimes in life, you question your path and whether you are travelling the right one. I was given a sign.

Recently I was driving home, it was a beautiful evening, crisp and clear, the sky full of stars, almost a full moon. I drove around the bend in the road and there in the middle of the lane was a white Barn Owl. I couldn't swerve in time, it happened so quickly that I hit her with my car. I was devastated. My heart raced, maybe I missed her I thought, or maybe she just broke a wing. I quickly turned the car around and searched for her. I found her lying still beside the road, warm, not moving, her neck was broken. My heart ached as I held her close to my body. "I am sorry my beauty, I didn't mean to hurt you, Universal Spirit take this beautiful soul into your arms, thank you for your wonderful life, and I love you", I said. I bought her home and buried her in the field so she could view the beautiful sunsets we have here. A few days later I wondered if the Barn Owl had been a message for me from the Universe, her death had such an impact….could it possibly be a message?? I grabbed my *World Animal Dreaming* book by Scott Alexander King and there in black and white was my message and I quote, *"Barn Owl is an emissary of change and a harbinger of the inevitabilities of life and death and is therefore also associated with people whose work centres on death. Rather than portraying death as a final destination, however, Barn Owl portrays it as the beginning of a journey rather than an ending."*

I have come to the realisation that my Childhood Trauma was always part of the bigger plan for me, my Life's Pathway. It was meant to be. I feel a divine presence at work and purpose to all that we do. I finally know that my Life's Purpose is to be an Akashic Teacher, End of Life Doula and Animal Chaplin which is truly extraordinary. I feel incredibly humbled to be offered this wonderful opportunity to be of service to those in need, those who are dying and to support their loved ones in this often-difficult time.

I no longer Fear Death, it is my friend… I have seen too many unusual things for there not to be something else after death. I now call Death a Transition….a journey to somewhere else. We never truly leave we just disappear. Death is but a door to another life, another world, another experience.

When our time comes to leave, I know without a shadow of a doubt that regardless of the pain, the suffering or the indignity we may be experiencing in our final moments, that door will open for us and we will take that beautiful journey to the life that awaits us.

I have come to the realisation that my Childhood Trauma was always part of the bigger plan for me, my Life's Pathway. It was meant to be.
I feel a divine presence at work and purpose to all that we do. I finally know that my Life's Purpose is to be an Akashic Teacher, End of Life Doula and Animal Chaplin which is truly extraordinary. I feel incredibly humbled to be offered this wonderful opportunity to be of service to those in need, those who are dying and to support their loved ones in this often-difficult time.

~ JO FULLER

Co-Author
Jo Fuller

Joanne Fuller is an Akashic Records Teacher and Advanced Practitioner and is the Founder of Akashic Studies Australia. She is also an End of Life Doula and is currently studying to become an Animal Chaplin.

Joanne loves Teaching Classes on How to Read the Akashic Records and specialises in Past Lives and Healing through the Records. She has given talks on Discovering the Akashic Records and she has become a sought after one on one Akashic Records Reader.

As an End of Life Doula, Joanne's role is to Facilitate and Support Clients and their families through the stages of Dying and Death.

When asked what drives Joanne to do what she does, she states "I love to help people and animals see their true worth, it is my passion. I believe I have experienced my life so that I can be a voice for those who don't have a voice, stand up for those that cannot stand and awaken those that still sleep."

When Joanne is not working she loves spending time with her pets and taking long walks in nature to re-energise and ground herself.

Website: https://www.akashicstudiesaustralia.com
Twitter: https://twitter.com/ASASoulReadings
Instagram: jo.fuller.315
Facebook: https://www.facebook.com/Akashicstudiesaustralia/

Dance In The Fire of Life!

182

"

In the deepest parts of our souls, we are certain, honest and raw. As life unfolds, it's as though our soul gets covered by layers of protection, which happens each time we face an obstacle or tragedy."

~Kathie Rogers

The Wondrous Magic Of Life
by Kathie K. Rogers

"When you start loving yourself and respecting your time and energy, things will change. Get to know your worth, and your value will go up."
~GERMANY KENT

My wish for you is to believe in yourself so fiercely that you follow your dreams wholeheartedly. Know that others, before you have conquered this quest of life so now YOU too, can hold the belief that you also can, no matter what trials you may face. I truly hope you take something from my personal journey and discovery. I trust that in some way, my words have the ability to jump off this page, and light up your path with encouragement giving you the belief that you have got this! I want you to know that I'm here for you if you need to reach out….

Unveiling Life's Gift
In 2011, Chronic Fatigue Syndrome hit me like a ton of bricks! This illness was thrust upon me out of the blue and forced a myriad of changes upon me. It altered my life and its direction instantaneously. It forced me to slow down, it taught me to say NO! It made me so much more aware of my body and what it was feeling. It forced me to rest. It sorted out my friends for me. It slowed me down so much so that it also challenged me to rethink how I do things and forced me to become more creative and proactive in every aspect of my life.

I researched so much about this illness, tried many things and had so many different treatments, far too many to mention here and I have spent so much money! I felt like time was passing me by. So many pivotal moments in my life were passed by in a haze, my beautiful only daughters' wedding day, the birth of my first grandchild to mention an important few. However, at the same time, "I" was changing, I was growing and I was understanding so much more than I ever did before. Yet I felt like a drifter, a time waster, I thought I was going crazy and that I was lazy. Others had trouble understanding my hidden illness, after all,

I looked fine! For me though, my life was passing me by and I had no idea what was around the corner. I became so emotionally sensitive, I could feel not only what I was going through but…..I found that I could pick up on other people's energies and I could actually feel what others were feeling and experiencing. It was exhausting but eye-opening.

Simply by just making eye-contact, a look, or by passing by them, I felt much of what they were feeling and even thinking. I didn't recognise this as my gift, I thought I was cursed, but that's only because I was so lost at this time of my life. I was in a deep dark place, unfamiliar to me. I saw myself as useless and powerless so how could I possibly unwrap this wondrous gift and discover how to use it?!

I have gone on an internet journey… reading, listening to podcasts, talks on Ted Ex and Youtube, reading blogs, every article I could source, specialists, view and so much more; searching for my own answers. Knowing full well they were deep within me – somewhere! Not quite believing or trusting fully, but I did have that whisper…inside my head 'Kathie, you know you have all the answers to your questions ' it would not subside, in fact, it just kept getting louder and louder… I was struggling against myself, pushing and pulling at the same time, in a state of confusion and without clarity. Not knowing which way to turn.

Recently, I had a call from deep within my heart and soul and I know it was 'Divine Intervention' ….this was my "Magic Moment"! It was just there, the words in my minds eye, and I followed it over and over again … until it ran off my tongue "My own ritual" which, has now become my 'mantra' and it could be yours as well, if it resonates within your soul too: "I know what to do! I know how to help myself! I know how to help others!" I began to believe in myself again, just like that. I wanted to shout it out from the rooftops!

I have always looked for the best, in any given situation. Keeping a positive mind, motivates me and lifts me up, I am the eternal optimist. We are each unique but we all have the same miraculous machine to care for. Our body is merely the shell, not to mention the immaculate computer within, that is designed to be resilient. Our body, steered by our mind knows how to fix itself, heal itself and remove pain. We just need to press the correct buttons.

You have to order it to do what it is you want it to do. You are the master! You are the driver. Honour your body. Be kind to it, respect it and listen to what it is sending out to you and trying to communicate to you.

All is possible in My World and In Yours, if You Believe It Is

The world is - full of possibilities All around us we have supports that we ignore. We need to stand in our own truth and acknowledge when we need help. Try vulnerability on for size., Reach out for help from others and don't limit yourself by people's judgments. Working collaboratively and enjoying the sharing of two minds, - is extremely powerful in helping us find solutions to our problems. - If we put our pride aside and take that step forward it will open new doors and new opportunities. Isn't that exciting?!

Each of us has within us, all that we require to attain what we want in life. We were born with a divine gift that is ever evolving, always growing, and leads us to our purpose in life. When we acquire Emotional Intelligence, we become aware of our capacity to control and express our emotions and to handle interpersonal relationships. Without the use of our emotional intelligence, coupled with our awareness, we do not thrive in any environment. Instead, we stay stuck in our comfort zone, which is not really comfortable, it's just familiar. When you allow your autopilot program to come into play, you weaken your abilities and don't use your brain to its full capacity. You cloud it, and it is never clear as to what you actually want in life. Your brain is in a confused state of mind.

There are no accidents in the universe, we all show up with a purpose. Once we begin paying attention to our thoughts, actions, words and reactions, they provide us with clues that lead to our Emotional Freedom. The freedom to be, to feel, to think and to express ourselves, without holding back.

Notice what your inner dialogue says to you; become an observer of your mind (awareness is the key here). Our thoughts can either empower or disempower us. We can have triggers that set something off within us. At some level, we have self-doubt, which existed well before we were triggered. These triggers can drive the 'Dis-ease' in our bodies and affect our wellbeing.

I discovered, that when we have a negative emotion, we need to express it and let it out, in order to let it go. When we hold ourselves back and don't allow ourselves to experience this – our bodies then notify us that something is amiss and we experience pain, which is the moment that our bodies enter a state of 'dis-ease'.

My Brain, My Ally

Our Brain is a powerful ally. It is the biggest key we possess to unlock the potential to empowerment. We basically live a program, one which is designed to keep us alive…"The survival program" It is a primal program that was instilled in us

at birth. It is an automatic response, (fight, flight or freeze) that is necessary for our survival.

What is important to note here is that the "fight/flight/freeze" response is NOT meant to be on 24/7. It's meant to stop once the stressor, threat, or harmful event is over so we can go back to normal, easy functioning that's less on alert and less on guard. I know from my own experience that when I stay revved up in the fight/flight/freeze response my survival energies, stress hormones, adrenaline and cortisol become depleted and overused. When I get to that point, I am a total mess. Functioning like other people becomes an impossible feat for me, and renders me bedridden for days on end! Reaching the point where I know that I must change something, anything!

We need to look within and release the layers of these enforcing patterns and habits. This is where we find growth and freedom! At times I found this particularly difficult to do, and to power through. Life can be deceptive at times. As my thought process takes me to another place, and I go through the pain of change, like a storm in my life, I am pulled back, into old habits and the comfort of what I know. I wonder what is happening, and if in fact, I believe I am stuck and will never get out of this situation? Then I become aware that it is my bodies way of protecting me from going into the unknown however I also have come to understand that at times like these, my body is not working for me, but against me!

It is a constant push and pull, forward and backward movement, which brings pain and confusion. I was on this ride for a long time, until I understood what was actually happening to me, and that in order to take that step forward rather than stay there, I had to let go of the old ways of thought and old habits. For change to occur, you must keep yourself aware of your thoughts, actions and behaviours. Yes, I know what you're thinking. It's hard work! When you do this repeatedly, it then makes this your new habit. This will then surely become your new comfort zone over time. So, you see if you want to keep progressing and growing you do have your work cut out for you, but the outcome of getting your life back is your reward. You also get Growth and Freedom!

What Does Self-Love Have To Do With IT?
You need to respect and love yourself enough to take this journey of self-discovery and growth, to be uncomfortable in order to move forward and achieve whatever you desire. The more you challenge yourself, the more you discover about your boundaries and your hidden strengths which come to the fore. Respect and love yourself enough to enter this zone in order to achieve more and discover new boundaries, and hidden strengths. Continue to nudge yourself as a reminder that

you survived other events and came out the other end, better and stronger for it! Change the way you think about yourself and your capabilities. Go out of your way to change your internal belief system. Go deep within yourself and you will discover your answers right THERE waiting for you.

Our actions must match our ambitions and our behaviour has to back up our words.

Unrelated changes to our *"goals"* overtime, transform the way we do everything. It is the 'Lead Domino Effect'. It ripples out into the rest of our life. Don't take random actions lightly connect the dots!

If we resist things that we believe are wrong in ourselves it creates suffering. Self-acceptance enables you to make a change in your life. Your "little voice" (internal dialogue) is your compass to life and this is the area you need to work on. Any confusion is the beginning of some sort of message trying to come through and 'change' trying to take place. By recognising our confusion, we are already ahead with our awareness.

The Biggest Mirage in Life is Fear!
Think of it this way – Your problems are just invitations to step through *"Fear"* Fear is just like a mirage. It isn't really there, we imagine it, and take it places within our minds and our imagination. Do not fear failure! Failure is healthy and contains our life lessons. "Failing is just improving the odds of succeeding next time"

We acquire fears throughout our lives, which can make our subconscious associate unrelated things as triggers for these unwelcome feelings and thoughts. The quality of our experiences are dependent on our feelings and when we shut down or suppress our feelings we also shut down our capacity to be fully rational. Thus we are unable to listen to ourselves or be responsive to our deepest needs and our purpose. This results in us becoming closed to the possibility of change and the possibility of discovering resolutions for our issues. Clear your life of collective energy from other sources and people that are not serving you positively, and enable yourself to think more clearly and be able to concentrate on one goal, be it your health, relationships, career etc.

In the deepest parts of our souls, we are certain, honest and raw. As life unfolds, it's as though our soul, gets covered by layers of protection, which happens each time we face an obstacle or tragedy. How does one find oneself through all these layers? Do these layers really serve to protect our souls? How do you find out what you are called to do? Well, the answers lie beneath all these layers which have moulded us into someone other than ourselves, and hence we forget our purpose.

Don't 'Dial' Yourself Down to Fit into the 'Norm'

We tend to "dial" ourselves down to fit into the "norm." Who are you, when no one is looking? Can you be that person all the time? We tend to try to be the person we think we should be, what others expect us to be, but who are we really? Our past continues to influence the present time. The past can, for a time, provide us with the answers to our questions, but do not stay in the past! Do not pack up and reside there because you will carry with you a heavy burden. The pain, regrets and perceived failings will live in your present and stop you from moving into your future.! Flexibility is power, especially with an open mind.

" If you change the emotion you attach to a particular event, you then change the outcome of the event. "

So ... If you change thought, thought can change the outcome.

That is, the conscious mind sets the goal, and the unconscious mind gets it done."

~ DR JOHN BERMAN

Be Open to Both Giving and Receiving

The secret to our happiness is to consistently share our gifts with others, as we only get to keep what we give away. Think about that, the more we share the more we receive. In saying that, we also have to learn the art of receiving, as a lot of us give and do not know how to receive. This was a big lesson I learnt, and at times I still revert back to my old habits, having to remind myself that it is ok for me to receive gracefully. Allow others to care for you, otherwise, you are preventing others from experiencing the gift of giving.

My gift to You! I want to share a precious ritual that came to me almost prophetically. I practised this ritual until it worked for me, and I know in my heart that I am meant to share this with others. I pray that it comforts you as much as it does me.

1. Sit or lie down. Be still. Listen. Really listen to what your mind is telling you about your body. Now feel. Really feel what your body is telling you

2. Tune into your mind...your feelings and then into your emotions. And....whilst listening, thinking and feeling, let your mind guide you to your pain.

3. Sit very still. Identify where you feel this pain. ... tell your pain to leave your body – (follow the script below)

"Leave my body, I have no use for you! Get out! Find the nearest exit and leave from my body"

4. Visualise this pain going to the nearest source of exit via your skin and tell it, speak to it to EXIT your body. Imagine it's a migraine, for example, take that pain and guide it to exit from the tip of your head. Feel this taking place, visualise it.

5. THANK your body for bringing your awareness to it and then state - "Get out, I do not need you any longer!" Now breathe out, exhaling ever so slowly and feel the pain rushing out of your body through your skin and your breath. Be still and calm.

6. Listen again. Locate where the pain was and acknowledge that it has gone.

7. Think of something that makes you happy. Hold that thought. Smile. Tell your body what you want it to do. Be direct. Be very clear. Don't waiver or doubt your own power. After all – it is YOUR mind. Learn to use this power. It is your strongest ally. It will alleviate so much pain, both physical and emotional and many other things that make you feel ill, and put your mind and body in a state of dis-ease.

Your mind is like your computer, you can reprogram it whenever it's necessary to do so. We are not taught this when we are young. We are the ones with the control, but we so often surrender our control to our thoughts. We can take control anytime! We should know this intrinsically, but we don't! We were never ever taught the POWER of our own mind.

In closing, what I would like you to keep in mind is that life doesn't always end up the way we envisaged that it would, no matter how hard we try to change and lead it in a different direction to the way it is going. Often, this causes us to become upset and disillusioned. When we realise that life is stubbornly taking us into a direction we think we don't want, it is always due to the fact that it is in THIS direction that we will discover everything we need and want for our life! Whichever way we look at it, we can try to steer our lives a certain way, we can ignore our instincts and take the wrong road at the fork, but at the end of the day, we are always exactly where we are meant to be!

So, remember, Life is Magic!

" Magic is believing in yourself, and if you can do that,
you can make anything happen"
~Goethe

191

"

How does one find oneself through all these layers? Do these layers really serve to protect our souls? How do you find out what you are called to do? Well, the answers lie beneath all these layers which have moulded us into someone other than ourselves, and hence we forget our purpose."

~ KATHIE ROGERS

Co-Author
Kathie Rogers

Kathie passionately coaches and mentors others and enjoys seeing her clients positively change their lives around. She is the founder of 360 Degrees of Courage, which she began in 2017. Kathie has a natural talent to teach, help and guide others in all areas of life. Her insatiable desire to do good for others directed and led her life to Coaching and to study Counselling.

"People come to me with varying challenges and at different stages of their lives. I feel elated when my clients come back to me as life presents us with new challenges all the time and when they come back to me I know it is because they trust me to help and guide them once again."

Kathie is also a devoted and doting mother and grandmother, a Carer for her elderly mother. and lives in the wonderful city of Melbourne, Australia where she loves the beach, nature, socialising and photography.

Social Media
Facebook: https://facebook.com/kathie.rogers3
Facebook: https://facebook.com/360DegreesofCourage1/
FB Name: Kathie K Rogers
Author Name: Kathie K Rogers
Business Name: 360 Degrees of Courage

Dance In The Fire of Life!

194

"

Who am I? I had absolutely no idea but I
knew I wanted a different life,
a better life ... and here I am, stronger and
more confident than ever!
Change is inevitable, Embrace it!
Change IS growth.
It feeds our soul.
Who Am I? ...
Am I enough?
Yes, I am! ... And so are You!."

~Angie James

Your Time as a Caterpillar has Expired
Your Wings are Ready...
by Angie James

"Come to the edge – we might fall
Come to the edge – it's too high
Come to the edge – and they came, and he pushed
And they flew."
~ CHRISTOPHER LOGUE

Sometimes we wear masks to hide the real us, mould ourselves to be and act as we perceive we should be, what others expect. Why?

Our thoughts drive our behaviours and our actions. Many of our thoughts arrive through our perception of what we see, are told, our cultures and traditions. Often we observe and recognise events in our life incorrectly and these perceptions form our assumptions and beliefs. These then form the stories we tell about who we are. However, we need to be open to reconsider these beliefs, reflect on them and consider changing them. To not do so, can hold us back from finding our purpose and who we really are.

My life, like many of us, has been full of fun memories but also dotted with many unexpected events, scrapes, falls, misfortunes, rocky winding roads, and precarious down-hill slides. Often beaten I wondered … Who am I? Am I enough? Is this my life? Is this the best it can be?

We ask ourselves "Who Am I to be brilliant, gorgeous, talented and fabulous? Actually, Who Are We NOT to be?"
~ MARIANNE WILLIAMSON

My wish is that my words and experience will resonate with you. If you're ready to make a change, to learn, improve yourself, open more avenues and to grow,

please join me as I walk you through my journey where I will share with you how I've learned to stretch myself, understand change as constant and knowing it's OK to fall. If you want to be strong enough, capable enough, hold the skills and resources to move toward your vision and your dreams, through the challenges and changes we meet on our life journey, then I may well be able to help you. Due to the life experiences I encountered on my journey, this has become my specialty and I have helped many to move out of being stuck and unhappy to discovering peace, freedom and utter joy.

Each time I stumbled, fell, failed or got struck down, I felt my self-worth, self-acceptance and self-confidence diminishing. As I struggled with negative thoughts and self-inflicted demons, I searched for an array of self-help books, meditation, personal development programs, affirmations and more. I was on a journey of self-discovery. I used these resources to reflect on the specific situation and my life. Each time, I continued to work on changing my thought patterns and mindset. The process was slow and I took many paths on my journey and each one helped me expand and grow. I just didn't realise it at the time. Life tosses crazy stuff at us! It didn't happen overnight, it 'never' happens overnight, but slowly I raised my persona to one of loving and understanding myself, raising my personal awareness of my strengths so that I could pick myself up. There were "swings and roundabouts". Up I'd go, down I'd come .. thump! One thing I now always do is to catch negative talk and change it. The forward journey had to come from within; it was my motivation to be a better 'Me' that I mustered.

A quick exercise for you:
I invite you right now to draw a line down the middle of a piece of paper, on the left write down what you say to yourself when things go wrong. On the right jot down alternatives to what you're negatively saying to yourself.
For example, you might say "I can't do this, I'm hopeless" .. Change that chatter to "What skills do I need to learn this or who can help me with this"; Change "I'm fat" to "I love myself, I am beautiful"; Change "This is a nightmare" to "This is interesting and an exciting challenge"; Change "What an idiot I am" to "That's interesting, I'll never do that again"; Change "I'm really scared" to "I'm really excited". Can you see how these changes will help?

Years of challenges, changes and endless self-discovery have formed 'Me' … but Who Am I?

It's like peeling an onion, we slowly uncover and unravel more about ourselves as we kick goals or fall over… small steps forward … It's a journey, not a sprint. And every time we fail to meet a goal or fulfil a wish ... we find another layer of "Who am I". Why do we want to find ourselves?

Because we have "the potential to become" … to be MORE than we currently are. But where was it, who held it, how could I find it? You will discover that it isn't found out there anywhere! It's found in you, in your thoughts, how you perceive yourself and your world.

We have a purpose in this life. Do you have a vision, wish or desire? Something you yearn for but seems out of reach? Your vision is part of your journey. To embark on this journey toward our vision we must be open to and ready to change. The journey has many challenges and demands along the way. If we don't embrace change, we stagnate. Change IS growth. It feeds our soul and leads us to our purpose, to that which we were born to do. Remember when you learned to crawl, then walk, then run? That was change! You grew in your capabilities. Again it was a process of change to attain those new skill sets. Some changes are easy, some hard and some we fail. My point is, change is everywhere. Embrace it. It's paramount for your evolution.

So, I ask YOU. Who Are You?

Are you constantly changing, evolving and growing? Are you ready to?

Be open to change and learning new ways of approaching life and people. You will fail. That's natural for learning, growth and to peel back those layers to reveal you and your potential. Important also is what we do after we fail that matters. Check-in, reflect, talk it through, get up and keep going!!

I want YOU to be the grandest version of YOU. Life changes. Learn to roll through the changes. You are AMAZING. Flow with the changes. Be the YOU you're proud of!

About Me

I know all about peeling back layers and finding myself … Growing up I felt different from my siblings. I looked different. The only tubby child with auburn hair, freckles and hazel eyes. I felt inadequate, isolated and wondered whether I was adopted. That made me melancholy. On reflection later in life, it should've made me happier to think my parents wanted me so much that they adopted me. Ah ha, the things we say to ourselves!! Our perceptions form our thoughts, our feelings and our actions!

I married young, divorced two years later. I believed there had to be more. I craved excitement so I changed my situation. Easy? Hell no, but I was motivated. A number of years later, another relationship and two boys later, I left him. The relationship was fraught with so many differences, coupled with being in an emotional and physically abusive relationship. Leaving took all the strength I could muster. He'd told me it would be the last thing I would do. I was petrified and worse still, I was too embarrassed to tell anyone. I remember thinking my parents would see me as a failure and I rejected the idea that I was in the wrong relationship. Eventually, I reached out to my parents, tail between my legs, gathered their support and moved back home away from those flames that threatened my emotional and physical wellbeing. I did not want my boys to grow up in an abusive and unhappy environment. It was this desire that gave me the strength, motivation and courage to leave.

I continued to raise my two boys for 13 years on my own with the support of my now passed Mum and Dad (RIP xx). I built a home, began to study and worked part-time. I pushed myself. I had something to prove! That *"I was enough"* … that I could make these changes, give a better life to my boys and survive! I still didn't find myself. I survived day to day.

I had many changes, roads to travel, bridges to cross. Some good, some not. I *'burned out'* at work and fell into a depression. I found out I was not superwoman. How sad! Counselling sessions later coupled with antidepressants, I finally felt better.

Through ill health, frustration and still that sense of adventure to learn and find more in my life, I sold my home in New Zealand. My two boys and I moved to the Gold Coast, Queensland Australia. No easy feat as a single mother. But life was exciting. It was a new adventure. A new country, a new life but alas it was so very hard, a real struggle. I couldn't find employment, financially we struggled, used all my profits from the sale of my home just to survive. I also tested employment in unsavoury arenas to survive. Who was I? I was lost, that was what I was! I was down and out but no one would ever have known. I wore my mask very well. It hid a myriad of sadness, discontentment and melancholy. Was this my life?

In this lost state, I met my now ex-husband. I thought he was my knight in shining armour. Oh my, ride in and save my sorry self. I had struggled long enough! I had lost my self-confidence, and, felt like a failure. I was sinking financially and stressed more often than not. He entered my life at a vulnerable time. Another pivotal moment on my life journey.

We moved to Central Queensland and I fell into some fabulous management roles in aged care, disability and child safety which saw me travel a great deal. I loved my experiences, the changes and my growth. I loved the people I met and the good that I was able to do for and with others. My husband worked in the coal mines, 7 days on, 7 days off. I travelled while he was in the mines. This time away from him, coupled with the skills and the people I associated with, changed me. I grew. I blossomed. My self-esteem and confidence grew. I learned more about myself. I was more than I thought I was. I did have the potential to become more!

I had wings, I can fly.

This marriage ended. It had to. I couldn't remain in an unhappy unfulfilling relationship any longer. My husband had no idea how I felt even though I cried myself to sleep more nights than I care to remember. We fought often, not celebrating our 50th birthdays due to these emotional outbursts. Pent up anger, frustration and resentment released itself at many points during our relationship. His constant denigration, controlling actions and behaviour left me miserable and again I wondered … Who Am I?

It was only the weeks that I travelled that I could express ME. I was passionate about my work, worked hard and loved travelling. I could not be ME when I was at home. I was told not to act like 'that' (but 'that' was me). I felt smothered and although I put on the face of happiness to others, I was not. I was miserable. I took a risk and gathered the courage to leave, finally, after years of unhappiness. I questioned myself … Another failure? 3 relationships … all failed. Was it me? I broke his heart. Riddled with guilt I resigned myself to leave with very little. My personal belongs, my car, $20k and a yellow sapphire ring. Another mistake in my life! I had also lost my contract in the child safety industry so I had no income. My message … No matter our circumstances, do not feel obliged to be in or around toxic people who drain our energy and leave us shattered, dishevelled and beaten. Be aware of those who try to hold us down, and hold us back!

I was so crushed that I thought I didn't deserve more and was unworthy of leaving with my fair matrimonial share. I'd put 16 hard years into that relationship but I walked away with little so I would not destroy his life. Even with my self-esteem and self-confidence again trampled, I had a deep down small, albeit righteous belief, in myself. That little voice that whispered "Ange, you can do it, yes you can!". However, I didn't realise how hard it was going to be to start again and survive in my mid-fifties. Yes, life was tough and with many lessons.

So .. off on another journey of discovery. Who am I? I had absolutely no idea but I knew I wanted a different life, a better life. I looked forward to finding out what that was going to be. And here I am, stronger and more confident than ever!

So many of us avoid risk, avoid stepping outside our comfort zone. Our inner voice says "don't do that, you will fail", "what if 'this' happens", "others will laugh at me", or "who do you think you are". Well, I say, what IF 'this' happens and it's an outstanding success? So often we talk ourselves out of what might just be leading us to our ultimate success, the next steps toward our vision, or the best thing we've done in our life. Some see failure as a negative and may not ever venture out of their comfort zone. They accept what they have as "their lot, this is it". But I'm here to tell you that THIS is NOT it. You ARE enough and you can reach for the stars, YOUR stars, YOUR vision, YOUR shining light …

Will it be easy?
Hell no, but it isn't easy staying in the same place treading water either!

I floundered in so many entrepreneurial ventures I've lost count, lost insurmountable amounts of money ... I've grown through adversity. So can you!

Who Am I? Am I enough?
Yes, I am! And so are You!
I'm constantly gaining more insight. It's been a long hard journey and my hardships are not unlike yours … that's Life! Challenges are ongoing but I'm stronger now and better equipped to pick myself up. I have gathered the tools to be able to do so, and I can show you how to do the same!

Reflecting, I've learned that our beliefs impact our lives from an early age. Our perception and perspectives of "WHO AM I" shape our thoughts, actions, attitudes and behaviour. These can stop you, start you, redirect you …

CHANGE is inevitable - Embrace it.
You've read it, you've heard it .. If you want something different for you, your life, your family, your career, your lifestyle, your relationship, then start doing something different.

To change successfully it's not about the desires of others, what's happening in your situation or your environment. It's not even about our behaviours or our actions. It's about what we think of, why we feel that way, and how we perceive and relate to the world we live in. Read that again. That is the essence of successful change! YOU hold the key!

You have to be "ready for change".

You are the creator of your successes and your failures. Once you are hungry to change something in your life, once you know you want more, you must change. That's when you know you're ready. You're motivated to change. You've recognised a desire (or a pain point) and you want it to change. You are then motivated and may well be ready to make that change. But how do you go about that? Great question! I have a solution that will give you the grounding and knowledge to be "change fit" .. To reach for your stars!

What is "*change fit*". It's understanding your capabilities and being ready to succeed, to understand the process, the demands and the resources to make it through change.

Every change, no matter what it is, brings demands. If you can't meet those demands you are more likely to fail. I wish you to succeed. My passion is to see you win!

Who Am I?

I've learned about being change ready and change fit. I'm now armed with the knowledge, skills, tools and resources to seize opportunities, understand how to overcome the rocks in the road, fall and pick myself up quickly, climb that next hill and smell sweet success, self-fulfilment and self-satisfaction. These have not always been massive changes. Some are small, such as changing a job, improving your relationship, an exercise or diet regime. Regardless of what change occurs. Embrace it, learn about it and achieve more. Become a better YOU today.

What stories do you tell yourselves?

Yes, "self-talk … I'm not pretty, no one cares, I can't, I'm dumb, I'm fat, I'll look stupid

' and so the chatter goes on.

Stop it !!

Our mind does not know the difference between what is real and what is imagined. Take a moment here. I want you to look yourself in the mirror and say "I am enough" and believe it! Say it with conviction every morning because you are! This is change, a change to how you perceive yourself.

Be kind.

I can help

Embracing change is how we find ourselves, feel fulfilled, find our purpose, and meet our vision.

It would be a privilege to connect with you on your journey. If you'd like the opportunity to embrace change and transform your life, believe in yourself and be more successful at fulfilling your goals, your desires and becoming a better YOU, contact me.

Pick up the challenge, poke at it, and tame it.
Let me help YOU find your wings!

Co-Author
Angie James

Angie James is a **Change Fitness Practitioner & Change Readiness Consultant.**

Angie states that change fitness is at the growing edge of our understanding of what makes people successful at change. She loves holding the keys to empower others to have more control over their lives and become more successful in the process. She has always gained satisfaction from helping others and now, through utilising a unique program, tools and resources, she focuses on 7 key change strengths whereby clients average 40% improvement in 12 weeks.

What could be more valuable than that?

Angie knows that "Success is what happens when we change and become the best version of ourselves. It happens when we become masters of our own lives."

Facebook: https://www.facebook.com/angie.james.581
Instagram: @angie_james61
LinkedIn: http://linkedin.com/in/angie-james
Website: http://angiezbiz.com/
Twitter: @AngieJames61

"

No matter what your situation in life is, you always have the choice to choose to either pick yourself up or just let yourself suffer in despair and keep free falling in life."

~MARGIE O'KANE

Pippies On The Beach

Making a difference in the lives of millions, one woman at a time.

by Margie O'Kane

"Forgiveness is your gift to yourself – from yourself."
~MARGIE O'KANE

"It was the best of times, it was the worst of times, it was the age of wisdom, it was the age of foolishness, it was the epoch of belief, it was the epoch of incredulity, it was the season of Light, it was the season of Darkness, it was the spring of hope, it was the winter of despair, we had everything before us, we had nothing before us, we were all going direct to Heaven, we were all going direct the other way—" Dickens's famous opening sentence introduces the universal approach of the book, the Tale of Two Cities, (book one), the French Revolution, and the drama depicted within.

This was how I described my life during the late 1970s. I cannot compare my life to the French Revolution, however, it was my revelation and my revolution.

"Hey Margie", a voice called out. It was the manager of the Hospital where I was the Director of Nursing. He motioned me into his office. "Yes"? I said happily. "We no longer require your services".
No preamble, nothing!

I never heard what was said after that. I immediately had numbness and tingling in my hands, I could hear my heart pounding in my ears. I became nauseous. I felt hot as if my skin was on fire. I felt like I was not present in the room. My throat closed. I could not swallow.
I walked out of the room. I was devastated.
I was a single mum. I needed to work.

Once I had my composure back, I walked out the front door feeling the eyes of everyone on my back and went straight up to the General Hospital and said to the Director of Nursing: "Pat I need a job"! "Great," she said, I need a Night Supervisor would you like it?
Let us step back!

I want you to imagine a young woman of thirty-three going through the hurt and heartache of a failed, violent marriage. Keep in mind that the period was the 1970s when women were treated differently. Although inroads for women's issues had been made by 1970, society still viewed men and women as two different characters. Men did not like the fact that women were coming out of their social norm, and were fighting for their rights which they believed they didn't belong in. According to men, women belong at home with the kids cooking something good for dinner.

Two months into the marriage my then husband was a victim of a hit and run car accident. He suffered a major right frontal lobe head injury.

The frontal lobes are considered our emotional control centre and home to our personality. The frontal lobes are involved in motor function, problem solving, spontaneity, memory, language, initiation, judgement, impulse control, and social and sexual behaviour.

It took many months to nurse him back to physical health.
In 1977 the amazing joy of my life was born. I can still visualise the moment love and protection surged through me. During the months that followed my self-esteem was unconsciously being eroded as I juggled with supporting us, managing an infant (I was so grateful she was a good baby) and the unpredictable behaviour of my husband. I felt I was trapped.

My child was my priority. I was not going to bring her up in that environment. However, I was paralysed. It was my father that came to my rescue making the decision for me. One day a removalist turned up, packed me up and we left. My biggest sadness was that I had to leave my dog behind. I still get teary when I think of this time.

In 1979 I decided to get full custody of my baby. I could not trust my then husband's mental state and if he took her away I would not have a leg to stand on. Going to court, I was made to feel like I was not relevant in the big scheme of things. The magistrate grilled me. Why should I have sole custody? Who would look after her? I explained that I had a job and that my family would help me with my child. Remember it was in the 1970s and as a woman, I was the one who had to prove I was fit to be a parent. My husband's mental state didn't enter into it. But to my joy, I won!-

On reflection, however, I was so grateful to go through this experience as the outcome of this experience was that I started to become interested in women's issues, which in a way has become my life's work. Before this, I went with the status quo. I was raised in the '50s with "Father knows best!" I was thirty-three with very low self-esteem and self-worth. I started questioning issues and began observing the world around me.

My then husband came into my life off and on for the next few months as I allowed myself to feel guilty regarding his head injury until I realised that his behaviour was also who he was before the head injury. When I got divorced I was criticised by many.

At the time I was 'sacked', I was the Director of Nursing at a Private Hospital in a reasonably sized town where I was well known. I had been in the position for a couple of years doing my best with very little support. There had been many managers come and go, and there had been many issues that I had to resolve. I found out later that I was the butt of malicious lies and innuendo. But the heartbreak of it was that it was my best friend who went against me, the person I trusted the most, who I loved as a sister, and who I relied on.

I was blind, I didn't see it coming, even when I was warned what was happening. I didn't believe. I trusted.

What do you do when your best friend betrays you?

Can you remember one time when you felt betrayed?

Recall that hot flush of recognition when you first realise that someone you knew very well would act one way and didn't? What to do? How not to become bitter or wary? Funny how one betrayal is often closely followed by another wrenching experience — or so it seems.

Getting the sack and getting divorced and getting custody of my baby all happened during this period.

The saddest thing about deceit is that it often doesn't come from our enemies or people we don't know but rather from those close to us. As can be expected, this hurts a lot.

The worst thing about being deceived is not what was said, but what the lie brings with it. When a feeling as important as trust is broken something inside us dies. Being betrayed is different than being hurt; You lose your direction, your compass, you don't understand, you feel distraught and confused. You feel extremely stupid and ridiculous. You must start at zero to rebuild yourself and go back over a difficult path. To me, it was almost a fatal wound and I wasn't sure how to rebuild myself.

My first reaction was to re-run the wrenching situation in my mind, over and over, digging a deeper rut in my memory.

The situation dominated my thoughts.

I became practised at denying the emotional pain I was experiencing. I learnt how to keep the pain at bay so I could continue to be a mum. I was also at this time an external student at a University. I had no idea how to care for my emotional self - however, this was about to change.

I began to recognize that I possessed the strength and resilience and value to heal this hurt over time. I decided to stay true to my deepest values and began to focus on creating more value in my life. I reached out to friends and other loved ones recognised human frailty in myself and evaluated my options for a better future. Once I faced the painful truth of the betrayal and my feelings about it, I was able to start the process of healing. I went through a gamut of emotions. It was challenging to stay true to myself.

This was a catalyst for my self-discovery journey

From this time, I learnt to walk tall with eyes straight ahead, laughed and smiled. I read many books on self-improvement, attended seminars, studied various modalities, psychology and leadership programs. I spent hundreds of dollars on mentors and I learnt to become like self-raising flour and rise above it all.
I learnt that betrayal doesn't kill you.

I then found a professional person who listened to my frustrations. This vetting helped me release my negative emotions about the situation. Over time I become less emotional and less negative about what had happened.

I have never received an apology form the person who betrayed me.

When I was first introduced to Dance In The Fire of Life, my intuition immediately brought up a time in my life that perhaps still needs further understanding of my individual life lessons to enhance my forgiveness process and enrich my life further. My intuition never lets me down, so I quickly realised I had to allow this healing and forgiveness to take place through this book and trust that if it heals me, it will heal many.

It is in the writing of this chapter that allowed me to become willing to forgive the person so that I can move on. For over forty years I have been a prisoner. I buried this incident and pain. However, it manifested unconsciously in other ways. Finally, I started to think of it as a lesson learned. Now I know the signs and symptoms of betrayal, and I can pinpoint them in the future. I will be more in control if it happens again.

> "Forgiveness is not always easy. At times, it feels more painful than the wound we suffered. To forgive the one that inflected it.
> And yet, there is no peace without forgiveness"
> ~MARK TWAIN

Once you realise that your failure to forgive hinders the flow of love into your life and the circulation of this essential energy throughout your body and mind, you are capable of forgiving others from a place deep within you. You allow yourself to acknowledge consciously that the giving and receiving of love is strictly up to you. It does not lie with anyone else, irrespective of past or current circumstances. Personal power is initiated and then develops further as you recognise and then internalise the reality, which is, that it is in your best interest to forgive and to accept forgiveness.

From there, you can more simply acknowledge that the benefit of forgiveness is specifically yours. There is really no one else, nor any other thing to consider. Forgiveness is your gift to yourself – from yourself.

It's time I gifted myself with forgiveness too:

Dear M.
It has taken me a long time to write this. My intention in writing this letter is to release any hurt so that I may move forward in peace and freedom.
For the past 40 years, I have been living a good life. It is this reason I want to thank you sincerely for giving me the chance to really grow as a person. Without this incident happen-

ing, I would have continued with an uneventful, routine life. I still may have been the same town, the same mindset, in the same little circle.

I was devastated when the incident happened. I still don't understand why. I may never know, and I am not sure I now want to. In many ways, I was so naïve and didn't see the warning signs. I never once believed what the staff were saying. I trusted you. I loved you as a dear friend.

The incident was a catalyst for me to get out of my comfort zone, study and obtain knowledge and become a champion for women's and girl's rights. I learnt to smile and walk tall, stand my ground. I become the person I was born to be.

I had the courage and resilience I never knew I had. I faced further adversity easily but most of all I learnt to know myself, believe in myself, trust myself and love myself.

It has been a while now since I've seen you. We're in different places, and our lives are different, everything is different. But today I thought about you. Even after all this time and this distance, somehow hurt and anger was still there, and I am not sure why. I am doing this for you and for me. There's a happiness, a lightness I'm missing due to the unconscious anger I had for you. I want that back in my life. I want to be able to smile, laugh and skip without feeling that a part of me is being held back. I guess I'm looking for the freedom that comes with forgiveness. So today, I'm letting go of the hurt I've held onto so tightly. I am sorry it took me so long to understand the weight of forgiveness, and I am so sorry I didn't learn to forgive you sooner. I forgive you and I'm sorry. I hope you understand this.

Fondly M.

There I have done it! Writing that letter wasn't too hard. I have kick-started the healing process and broken the chains that were holding me back!-

I have practised forgiveness at other times. Why then, has it taken me longer to resolve this? On reflection, I believe my unconscious was keeping me safe and there was a lesson I was not ready to accept. Until now.

The moral of my story is you can stay in the status quo and get the 'stuffing' kicked out of you or fight your way back to the light. You can climb out of hell, one inch at a time.

No matter what your situation in life is, you always have the choice to choose to either pick yourself up or just let yourself suffer in despair and keep free falling in life. You have a choice. You and only you can make the choice, and nobody can take it away from you or help you make the choice unless you choose to let them do it. Make the choice, choose what you want in life and create your destiny.

Keep your head high no matter what happens. You'll be alright. If the moment hurts, do not fall victim to its pain. Look ahead. Focus on what can be. Focus on dreams. You'll make it.

You don't aim to make dramatic changes in your life. I don't believe that anyone can change into a better person with the snap of your fingers. Make improvements inch by inch. Learn to walk before you run and always remember to make the inch happen

To you all, my sisters, the message I leave for you today is that you already have the strength, courage and knowledge to have all you need in life. Being you makes a difference to yourself, your families and the community you live in.
There is nothing new I am telling you. It is the wisdom of the ages. However, it is important to be reminded now and then as this helps you focus on what you want, not on what you don't want. It is so easy to get caught up in life that we forget to remind ourselves that our story matters.

I would like to end my chapter with a story I love sharing. I always tell the story of the "***Pippies on the Beach***".

A woman was walking along the beach, it was a morning after a violent storm had lashed the beach during the night. This woman had a sadness about her. She was thinking about what was wrong in her life and she thought "Water soothes me, so I'll have a walk along the beach." In the distance, she saw a young girl bending down and throwing something into the water. As she got closer she noticed the beach was strewn with Pippies that had been washed ashore following the storm. So, she said to the little girl "What are you doing"? "I am saving these Pippies she replied". The woman said, "You cannot help them all, there are thousands". The little girl bent down again and picked up another one and as she threw it back into the sea she said. "Well, I can help this one and this one" as she continued to pick up and throw them back into the sea. The woman continued walking along the beach in deep thought when she looked back for the girl however the girl was no longer there. She looked around and could not see her. She suddenly felt cold all over as the realisation came to her. I too am here to help the one that may resonate with my story. She then ran up over the sand dunes with a lighter step and when home, sat down and started to write her story. This day she started, 'I vow to love myself, to treat myself as someone I love truly and deeply – in my thoughts, my actions, the choices I make, the experiences I have, each moment I am conscious, I make the decision that I love myself'.

What 'vow' can you make to yourself today that will permanently impact YOUR life, your self-esteem and your feminine resilience in the most positive way?

"

I decided to stay true to my
deepest values and began to focus
on creating more value in my life."

~ MARGIE O'KANE

Co-Author
by Margie O'Kane

Margie O'Kane is a talented educator, speaker, visionary and mentor who has spent her life in service of others and has a fervent commitment to making a difference in people's lives.

In her career as a Registered Nurse, Midwife and Consultant for over 50 years, and as a Manager and Director of Nursing, she has trained hundreds of people in leadership, communication and clinical skills.

Margie has travelled widely to rural and remote areas throughout Australia supporting the local health authorities on clinical issues and leadership. She is a skilled auditor in many various Quality Standards.

Apart from her many Nursing and Midwifery qualifications, Margie has a BA Health Administration, a Master Trainer in Neuro-Linguistic Programming and a Grief Counsellor.

Her skills as a Master Trainer in Neuro-Linguistic Programming and a Grief Counsellor have helped her to mentor and consult to many, particularly to women in their 70's who she feels are made invisible by society, to encourage them to believe in their wisdom and skills and to share them with others in a meaningful way.

Margie's Vision is to create a global movement of 1 million baby boomers to become women of significance. Women who want to spend the rest of their lives being an inspiration to themselves, their families and their communities and share their stories, wisdom and skill and leave a legacy.

Website: margieokane.com
Email: margie@margieokane.com
Twitter: Twitter.com/@margieok
Instagram: Instagram/okanemargie
Facebook: Facebook.com   margie.okane - margieokanespeaker
Linkedin: www.linkedin.com/in/margie-o-kane-82bb2b48

"

To rise from the ashes of the Phoenix means to make a miraculous comeback. It is my belief that, like the Phoenix, we are reborn through our various challenges."

~LINDA D'ABATE

Phoenix Rising...
Emerging from the ashes of life's challenges like a rekindled flame
by Linda D. Abate

When Vicki first shared her idea for this book, the title 'Dance In The Fire Of Life' instantly captivated me and I instantly envisaged a phoenix rising from the ashes. In mythology, a phoenix is an immortal bird that, when it dies, bursts into flames and is reborn from its own ashes. "To rise from the ashes of the Phoenix" means to make a miraculous comeback.

It is my belief that, like the Phoenix, we are reborn through our various challenges. Each challenge contributing to more of who we are and every pivotal moment in our lives leaving us more powerful and transformed.

Making a difference in the world is something that I'm passionate about, especially making a difference in the lives of young people. A couple of questions kept coming up for me whenever I thought about writing this chapter: Who would want to read whatever I write? What could I include that could make a difference in someone else's life? There are many experiences and challenges that I have gone through which have given me strength, taught me so much and transformed me in some way. After all, our life experiences are what make us unique and special. (So, how do we really understand another person without having lived all of their life experiences?)   On reflection, I can see that through the difficult times in my life, I have had to search within to find what has been necessary to get me through.. Whilst I have been blessed with support from a wonderful family and friends, the choices have had to, ultimately, come from within me.

There are some 'golden nuggets' that I have found, along the way in my travels in my own life, which I like to call 'tools' in My Life's Treasure Chest.

These 'gold nuggets', have been life-saving to me in moments where I have had to face challenges or where I was feeling totally disempowered. I'm talking about

days where I wanted to crawl into a hole, get into the foetal position, rock myself to sleep and never wake up.

I have chosen to share myself openly, humbly and honestly with you with the intention that something you read here will resonate with you and should the need arise, you can open up your Golden Nugget Treasure Chest and recall whatever it is that you need to get through your challenging moment.

I will share with you some of life's challenges, some of life's treasures, a beautiful story about butterflies and the importance of belonging to a 'Tribe'. I hope you enjoy it.

Am I dreaming? Is that the phone ringing?... it's so early in the morning? What's going on?

"Hello, John… what? … Hang on! What do you mean you're coming straight over to take us to the hospital to say goodbye to dad?"

How can this be? My father is too young. He can't leave us now! I'm only 24 years old. Who is going to walk me down the aisle when John & I get married? My brothers and sister and I are too young to lose our father.

The hospital feels like an eerie place at this time so early in the morning…
"Beep… beep… beep…"

Can someone please stop that noise! After so many years of hearing that very sound coming from the equipment in ICU, I can't deal with it anymore!…
This wasn't the first time. My father's numerous hospital admissions began when I was in my early teens.

Fast forward 2 years and I'm sitting in church, just married to the man of my dreams. Tears well up in my eyes as I recall the numerous times my father spent in the hospital, thinking that this day would never come.

 My father delivers his speech and leaves everyone in awe…

He proceeds to thank one of the priests who performed our wedding service. That moment in itself was quite emotional for the entire family as this was the very priest who performed my father's Last Rights on the night that we were called into the hospital, years earlier…

During his speech, my father included these words: "there is nothing that you can't do- as long as you believe in yourself- you will succeed" these very words have remained and supported me during many challenging and difficult moments that proceeded.

You see, when my father was in the hospital fighting for his life, what got him through was his drive to be there for his family. It was stronger than anything. He still says: "Who can stop you but you? If at first you don't succeed, keep on trying. Believe in yourself"

The experience of my father's numerous illnesses and the way he overcame them has taught me resilience and belief in myself. The strength that my mother displayed, taught me that I could be an unstoppable force of nature. It's something that I have instilled in my own children from a young age. My father's 'words of wisdom' were valuable to my brother Anthony, as he underwent his battle with cancer. When Anthony shared with me that he had been diagnosed with cancer, he referenced the impact that our father's words & our mother's strength and determination could have on his journey to overcome this terrible disease, or, at the very least, prolong his life. The optimism and strength that our parents instilled in us, propelled Anthony forward and kept him motivated to fight his battle. Unfortunately, he finally succumbed to his illness after 3 years, but it wasn't without a fight. When Anthony was in his final weeks, and we realised the extent of his illness, he shared with me what an impactful difference having our father's resolute and determined mindset as an example for his life had made to his fight. He didn't believe that he would have lasted as long as he did without it.
"Beep… beep… beep…"

There's that familiar insistent sound of hospital machinery… The anxiety builds to a crescendo and I can feel my heart pounding in my ears. Look at that tiny, fragile little baby lying in the humidicrib! The size of his wrists can't be much larger than the width of my thumb and he weighs less than a packet of sugar. I can see his veins through his transparent skin. This isn't how pregnancies are meant to go! We have only been to 2 antenatal classes and who knew that our baby boy would be born 8 weeks early?! The fear is now crippling me as I ask myself: will he ever grow up, go to school and play with his friends in the schoolyard?…. Will we EVER get out of here?!!!

The way I feel today, I don't think I can bear another day.

From a distance, I notice there is a woman coming into the special care nursery

with her toddler. I can hear one of the midwives saying that it's one of the mum's of a baby who was also born prem.

Wow! So there IS hope that we might get out of this place! I have to go and talk to her. In that moment, I recognised her as an earth angel sent to me at a time of need!

When this woman shared with me the normality of life for her and her beautiful young child since leaving the hospital, including the rosy future she foresees for her family, this gave me a glimmer of hope. To this day, I wonder if she realises the impact that she had on me?

Yet another day in special care nursery and who is THIS woman coming in with her baby? I realise that she too needs to have her baby here for a few days and all I kept thinking is: 'No worries honey, you DO get out of here… '

We only spent a few days together at the hospital and little did that woman know that she would alter my view on how we all have the ability to impact each other. Incredibly, years later, a woman walks into my office at work and I instantly recognise her as the same woman from the hospital whose child was also in ICU and she shares the impact that I made on her… At a time when she was feeling low and saddened in having to bring her boy back into the hospital, what I shared with her had made an impact on her stay in the hospital. In her experience, my situation seemed far worse than what she was going through. My son was so tiny, I was dealing with my own issues and yet, I was there supporting her…. Wow! I had no idea! It made me wonder, how many other things do we inadvertently do or say that impact other people in such a profound way?

What could the ripple effect of our actions have on the world?

Many years ago, someone told me that one person couldn't make a difference and that there was no point in trying. I beg to differ because I believe that every person has greatness within them and, given the right tools, are capable of anything that life throws at them.

"Beep… beep… beep" Yep, car horn works. My heart is pounding in my ears. I feel the saliva building up in my mouth. The 'new car' smell fills my lungs. I can't believe this, I'm finally behind the wheel driving my first car- in my 30's! I am about to drive down the steep curvy road that I have feared for so long. It's ok. If I can make it down the hill and back again, it will all be ok. Here I go…!!!

Wooo… Hooo!!! I've done it! I have conquered that irrational fear of driving that has had me stopped for nearly 20 years! Thank you, mum and dad, for your 'words of wisdom'… if it IS to be it is up to ME…"

It made no sense! I got my licence when I was 19 and then something stopped me from driving. Through the many books I have read, courses I have participated in and discussions I have had with others, I discovered that fear is the main thing that stops us in life. All too often, we choose to avoid working towards our goals in order to avoid the FEAR!

'Fear', I have discovered, by definition is: "emotion or state induced by perceived danger or threat, whether the threat is real or imagined". One thing that really stood out for me is that it's 'perceived'. I used to think that what I was 'fearing' was real and that it was something that was actually happening TO me.
What I have discovered is that when I recognise the fear in a particular situation, it is the way that I deal with it, that makes the difference in my experience of that situation.

In the thesaurus, I found some antonyms of the word 'fear': assurance, calmness, confidence, ease, faith, happiness, joy. So, in the presence of any of these other states, can fear to be present? For example, where there are calmness, confidence and joy, can fear exist? In situations where I choose different ways of dealing with my fear, and different ways of 'being', I actually overcome my fears.
Changing my mindset is what makes a difference to me. Recognizing the fear and acting on it, stretches me and pushes me forth. For example, in my fear of driving, in taking action and getting behind the wheel, the fear loses its' power. For me, it's conquering one 'perceived' fear after another. By the way, the model of my car was a 'Conquest'!! Not intentional, but awesome all the same.

> "I am the master of my destiny. I define my own future.
> I am not a victim, I am a conqueror."
>
> ~TERERAI TRENT

How can I be 100% responsible for my life!?' After-all, there are going to be situations that are beyond my control. Looking into it, I've discovered that taking responsibility for me, my thinking, my reactions and my decisions, is in fact, very powerful for my life. (This gives me more power in life). It gives me choice.

In not being a servant to the 'effect' of my circumstances, then I am the orchestrator of my life and I can create life the way I want it to be. Waiting for someone else to be responsible for my life or passing the responsibility of my life on to another,

risks that I am putting my life in someone else's hands. There is no power in that.

> " Every experience in life is a learning experience and gives us a choice whether
> we're going to be victims or survivors"
> ~Dr Edith Eger -Holocaust Survivor

We have choice at any time. In any moment, we get to choose how our life is going to go and we can generate the emotional state that we wish to evoke. It's like the saying: if you tell yourself something enough times, you will begin to believe it! Why would you NOT want to use your internal dialogue to empower yourself, rather than disempower yourself?

Making different choices might feel uncomfortable. It's in embracing the uncertainty of a different action and making different choices that change and transformation occur. You will always have the same results when you are basing your life, your life choices and your decisions from the past, and you will never reach the potential that is awaiting you.

Learning and growth always occur in what we don't know otherwise, how can anything be different if we keep doing and experiencing everything the same way? This may seem obvious, but not always easy to take in. When things get tough, it's what you choose and your way of being that makes a difference.

My brother Anthony and I worked together in our family business and when he died, I had to look within and do what I had to do & be who I had to be in order to keep our business and family going. In that moment, I discovered strength, creativity, direction and leadership that had never seen the light of day! What an incredible discovery of SELF that moment was for me!

Everyone can feel great when things are going well. It's doing all that needs to be done when things are tough, that makes us extraordinary. It is said that 'extraordinary people' are ordinary people making extraordinary choices and taking extraordinary actions.

> "When the caterpillar thought it was the end of the world,
> it turned into a butterfly"
> ~Deepak Chopra

Life is not without its struggles.
This is a story about a little girl who finds a cocoon with a butterfly struggling to

break out of it. She calls her mother to come and have a look. They watch for a while and still the butterfly hasn't emerged from the cocoon. So she pleads with her mother to 'help' the butterfly. Her mother uses some small scissors and carefully cuts a slit in the cocoon. Out falls the butterfly, with its large body and small wings. They wait for its beautiful wings to dry and flap around, but the butterfly just lays there.

Although the girl and her mother did what they did with good intention, they didn't know that only by going through the necessary struggles can a butterfly emerge to be beautiful, with strong wings. The struggle to push its way through the tiny opening of the cocoon pushes the fluid out of its body and into its wings. Without the struggle, the butterfly can never fly.

Like the butterfly, our struggles are sometimes necessary for life. It's through our struggles that we gain strength to face our challenges.

"It is so nice to find your tribe, or actually,
what happens is, your tribe finds you…"
~Lucille Clifton

Look for your tribe of women to support you.

From a young age, I discovered that I had amazing, strong women around me who could support me. In facing a challenge, I realise that I'm not alone and that they are there for support. Ultimately, the choices I make are mine & come from within me, but it's reassuring to know that I have supportive, strong women who have my back if and when I need it. Find or create your tribe. It may be women you already know or women that have just come into your life. Either way, remember that the women you choose will be your tribe to support and empower you when you need it and vice versa.

"It is said that girls with dreams become women with vision. May we empower
each other to carry out such vision …"
~Meghan Markle

In closing, I am humbled to be co-authoring with Vicki Gotsis Ceraso and the other co-authors, connecting as women globally to support, nurture and love each other. In a world where its commonplace for people to bully, crush dreams and tear each other down, it is refreshing to be creating solutions.

My extensive reading and researching over the years has led me to the conclusion that we come into each other's lives for a reason, sometimes never realising why. We all have an impact on each other through what we say and do.

It's by no coincidence that you have picked up this book and there is no coincidence that I have shared my story with you...

Remember to ignite the fire within you. Like the Phoenix, everyone can rise from the ashes. It's in those pivotal moments when you are faced with challenges that you choose to run and hide or face the fire head-on, break through the flames and come out the other side, transformed.

" Don't die with the treasures you have to share with the world, still in you.
Live your life- don't just exist.
Create your own destiny or path in life, don't wait for it to come to you"

~LINDA D'ABATE.

Co-Author
Linda D'Abate

Linda D'Abate calls herself a catalyst for transformation. She loves helping and witnessing people she works with transform. Making a difference in the lives of others, in particular- young people is what get's her jumping out of bed every morning.

Linda has created a community project, **Furnishing Lives With Love**, beautifying the living spaces of foster kids with much-needed furniture, colour and some pizzazz.

Inspired by her community project, Linda has taken her thirty plus years of working in her own business in the furniture industry and together with her Life Coaching and NLP experience and is now assisting people in not only transforming their mindset but also transforming their home environment. She is also about to embark on a creative journey of sorts where she will share her expertise on her own Youtube Channel & Website as well as in her new venture into Mindful Art Workshops and products.

Linda is happily married, has 2 adult children and comes from a large extended Italian family. When she is not working in her business & looking after her family, Linda loves cooking and entertaining.

Facebook: facebook: https://www.facebook.com/linda.dabate
Facebook: https://www.facebook.com/Design-Style-Hub-465976273805442/
LinkedIn: https://www.linkedin.com/in/linda-d-abate-08b600ba/

"

Believing in myself was the most significant success strategy I could have bestowed on myself."

~Pina Cerminara

Stepping Out
From Behind The Shadows
by Pina Cerminara

Have you ever entertained the idea of being somebody else? You know, someone beautiful, smart and confident. There was a time where I certainly had. As a young girl, I would flip through the pages of magazines of perfect girls and want to have their body, their mind, their image, their clothes and mostly, their confidence. I would dream about it, yet sadly believing that it wasn't going to be. How could it be? For most of my life, I felt different. Not different in a good way, like special. No! Different like weird and unusual. I was ashamed and embarrassed by it and hid from fear of being found out.

Allow me to take you back in time with me to truly understand where I'm coming from:
I'm a happy 5-year-old with pigtails playing with a friend in the schoolyard. I'm feeling free-spirited and happy up until my friend and I are stopped by two older boys. I felt intimidated by them as they stood aggressively before us. I am frightened. I wonder - What do they want? I hear him angrily yell something at me while pointing an accusing finger. "Wog!" What did this mean I thought to myself and why is he referring that to me? While I understand now that this is a racist term used for Italian and other European migrants, I didn't understand it at the time. I was an innocent little girl who has been singled out, ridiculed for being me. Why is this so? I didn't understand it and was left feeling bad, shamed and embarrassed by it all.

This was a pivotal moment in my young, formative years that put me on the path of believing that I wasn't worthy and left me convinced I was different from everyone else. So, began my fear of being found out and a life of hiding.

"Never be bullied into silence. Never allow yourself to be made a victim. Accept no one's definition of your life but define yourself."
~ Harvey Fierstein

I am 12 years old and I remember it like it was yesterday. I am, for the most part, a normal teenage girl feeling self-conscious about my appearance and wanting to fit in with my friends and be just like them. When I looked in the mirror I would always be comparing myself to other young girls and secretly questioning whether I was good enough, pretty enough, smart enough and the like. I thought there was plenty of room for improvement, but generally, I accepted that I was OK.

It's a gloriously sunny afternoon in my backyard and I am enjoying my time quietly playing with a tennis ball. My younger brothers and sister were also playing outside having fun, until my brother and I accidentally collided. What a life changing moment that was to be for me!

My brother and I physically collided with his head going up and my head going down; sinking my two front teeth into the top of his head. Ouch! The pain shot through my mouth like a dagger. My brother is 5 years old and is screaming at the top of his lungs and my mother is desperately trying to calm him. During this chaos, I try to soothe my aching mouth and as I rub my tongue against my lips, I feel my teeth missing. Oh no! Where are my two front teeth gone? I race inside to look in the mirror. My teeth are broken! Not just a little broken; so badly broken that they were a mess. I screamed and cried for hours. I wanted to be swallowed up. I didn't want to leave my room. I am now even more ugly! I don't want to be seen. EVER! Where can I hide?

Of course, I had to have them repaired and somehow restored. But unlike today's fixes, mine was of horror and disgust. I hated how they were repaired; with two silver caps. Imagine that! I am a self-conscious teenage girl who is interested in boys, wanting to feel pretty, with silver caps on my teeth and a metal mouth smile. I stopped smiling and talking. I hid even further and deeper.

As much I tried to keep my mouth shut, the silver caps became evident to the kids at school. I was teased and taunted for months on end. I felt like a freak. These are the years where what your peers think is important. While I wanted to be like the other girls, I couldn't feel anything more than ugly and different.

I'm now thirteen and I am so excited! I'm a junior bridesmaid for my uncle and his new bride. It is a lovely wedding day and the bridal party are out in the gardens getting ready to have photos taken. I am filled with pride and happiness for this wonderful day. My much-loved uncle comes over and whispers something to me. "Don't smile with those teeth" he said. "I don't want you to spoil my photos". It broke my fragile heart. On a day to feel special, this was another day of an intensified feeling of being ugly and weird. I wanted to go home, run to my room and never come out. I didn't want anyone to look at me ever again!

I eventually got my teeth repaired, however, it never repaired the self-worth I had lost, nor did I gain any confidence back either.

I don't remember when it started exactly, but another confidence crusher began. As I am growing and developing into a young woman, blushing became the next addition to my woes. It wasn't the occasional embarrassed blushing like most people. Oh no, it was often and consistent. It took over many of my conversations with people. It affected me so much that I felt ashamed and struggled to look people in the eye. It was awkward and uncomfortable to have someone look at me when I was speaking. I would feel the heat that would come from my face turning red and I would burn with embarrassment.

Even as a young adult the blushing got worse. I would blush at anything and everything. I was laughed at, teased and taunted each time I blushed. I didn't know how to control it and it exposed my lack of confidence, low self-esteem and I became awkward. I didn't want anyone to know what was going on the inside. I created a 'mask' and developed the 'persona' of being someone that I knew I was not. I believed it was safer to avoid drawing attention to myself. Keep quiet. Don't speak too much. Don't stand out. Don't draw attention to yourself. Don't let anyone know how you really feel or who you really are. It was a constant conversation I had with myself that drove me further away from gaining confidence. I continued to hide and be quiet.

> "Once you become self-conscious, there is no end to it: once you start to doubt, there is no room for anything else"
> ~Mignon McLaughlin

I had spent all my school years at the back of the classroom. I did everything I could to get away with not having to do school presentations. I dreaded school assignments. It was traumatic to get in front of the class and be criticized and ridiculed for being 'red like a tomato'. I didn't ask or answer any questions in the classroom so that I would be saved the embarrassment and further ridicule. I hated the word 'red' so much that I never wore clothes of that colour. I didn't want the reminder. I learnt how to play small in order to stay safe and I excelled at it.

This way of being continued on into my working years. I was the quiet one at meetings hoping that I didn't have to say anything. I just wanted to blend in with the board room, table and chairs. I didn't want to be noticed at all. While I was good at my work, I chose not to advance too far up the career ladder. I didn't want a job where I had to speak at meetings or do presentations. So, I kept myself small and stayed in jobs that weren't that challenging nor fulfilling. All the while there was a cry inside and a longing for more. It was like holding down a bird in flight by a chain. I longed to feel the freedom to fly, to soar, to achieve and to have self-confidence. What would it take I wondered?

As well as believing I was different, I also believed that I was shy. I thought that was why I blush so easily, couldn't hold eye contact, wouldn't speak up, and why I wouldn't stand up and be noticed. I thought it was part of my personality and genetics. It was a label I accepted, yet I wanted so desperately to reject it.

I wanted to get out of the internal prison that I created for myself. I knew that I could have more from my life. I wanted a bigger, brighter and happier life. I wanted to be confident with people, to show up and be seen and heard. But how?

Fast forward over 20 years to today and I am so proud of having been instrumental in changing my life in a significant way, despite everything I have experienced, which could have kept me imprisoned with my wings clipped and my dreams crippled!. Most people don't believe me when I tell them that I was a shy girl, hiding at the back of rooms, lacking confidence in myself.

> "It took me a long time not to judge myself through someone else's eyes"
> ~ SALLY FIELDS

It was when I decided to go into business for myself that everything had to change. I was new in business and was determined, committed and oh so excited about it. Being in business was something I had dreamed of and I had the opportunity to make it a reality. Or could I?

As I began the entrepreneurial journey, I questioned and doubted myself on hundreds of occasions. I was advised that I needed to get myself out there, network with other business owners, meet new people and get good at marketing and social media. What? Put myself out there? Be up front and centre? Who ME? No way!

I was both disappointed and terrified. All of my fears and insecurities came to the surface. Am I good enough? Am I smart enough? Will I be laughed at? Will I succeed? What will people think of me? I questioned whether I could just be in business and hang out with my computer, speak to a few people, and it would all just happen. Couldn't it work like that? Well, there was a firm NO and I was encouraged to push through my fears, embarrassment, shyness and all the other excuses and rationale that got in the way of my confidence.

After a number of years of being in business, I had to learn about confidence and having a voice. I learnt why I need it, what to do to get it, how to increase it and how great it feels to have it. It inspired me so much that I wanted to help others do the same. I'm grateful for the opportunity to show that it IS possible to turn your life around! My life experiences and lessons have helped bring hope to others. Years of personal development taught me some simple and powerful ways to build up my self-esteem and confidence. It takes a strong desire, a real WILL and WANT to make changes to your life. Otherwise, it's just a wishing game. Here are four elements:

1. Change YOUR Mindset

I created a powerful intention to change my thinking. I had to change the thinking behind the behaviour which is where real transformation happens.
What you say after "I am…." holds the key to who you believe yourself to be. "I am shy" – whether it is true or not, ruled the way I believed myself to be for far too long. I wasn't born shy. I was moulded into shy; not only by me but also from others, even my loved ones. "I am different" – had to be removed immediately. Once I began showing my true self to others I realized that underneath our 'masks' and 'personas' we all have fears, insecurities and barriers. We are all the same drink, just different flavours. The biggest change in mindset was believing that I could get over myself and be confident and authentic.

Believing in myself was the most significant success strategy I could have bestowed on myself. It's been one of my greatest gifts. I now believe that who I am IS different - in a special way. I also believe that my true self is powerful, lovable and enough. I cannot imagine my life being anything else.

"Nurture your mind with great thoughts,
for you will never go any higher than you think"
~ Benjamin Disraeli

2. Baby Steps

I was surprised to find out that confidence is a skill and something that you learn. It's not something you are born with; it's something you develop over time. Just as I have learnt so many things in life, I can learn 'confidence'. Other people learnt it; so why couldn't I? I put faith and trust in my ability to learn.

What worked best for me was taking baby steps. By creating small or mini goals to get through each step, I was able to push through my fears. When I went to events, I would start practicing with people I didn't know with a firm handshake, introducing myself with a great big smile. When I got really good at that, I took the next baby step of talking to a small group of people. I was persistent in taking action and that became my superpower; PERSISTENCE.

Eventually, I got to do small presentations then, bigger ones. It took time and consistency of practice to get to that point. My mother would always tell me that "every beginning is hard". So true! Each baby step began as "hard" and then it got easier.

3. Put Yourself in the Right Environment

I had been doing 'comfy' for a long time eventuating in feeling stagnant in my working career. Working in my own business is where I grew the most. I uncovered my true self. My authentic-self surfaced and started to shine brightly.

Being an entrepreneur required me to be part of business networking groups. The idea of having to present myself and my business would literally make me vomit. I dreaded the lead up to any event but I knew that this was exactly where I needed to be - to push ME and help ME grow. I simply kept attending.

My advice to anyone going through crippling fear is put yourself in the environment that involves taking action and pushes you out of your comfort zone. There is no growth and change where it's 'comfy'. 'Magic happens outside of your comfort zone'. Well, for this silver toothed, shy, red-faced girl, it has certainly seemed like magic.

4. Acknowledge Your Journey

I had always avoided having to 'say a few words' at family celebrations. I would shame and berate myself of not being a good mother or daughter. It would be that constant reminder of who I didn't want to be. Here was another belief that

I have had to remove from my thinking. Not only did I not speak up for myself, I didn't speak up for my family.

I recently had the privilege to deliver a speech to the biggest group of people so far. It wasn't the biggest crowd by some people's experience; however, it wasn't the size that mattered in this case. It was my son's birthday and I was to deliver my first family speech to over 100 guests. It was a big moment for me. While I wanted my speech to be special for my son, I wanted it to be a moment that I would be proud of ME.

I stood in front of all these people holding firmly onto the microphone. I took a moment to settle and check in with myself. I searched for the tummy-churn, the sweats, the shaky knees and trembling hands, they weren't there! The shy, embarrassed girl had grown into a confident, self-assured, driven woman who is proud of her journey and of the woman she has become.

I was congratulated on my speech, the delivery of the speech and my confidence. I even enjoyed the experience itself. Who would've thought? It was in that moment that I stopped and reflected on how far I had come. This was another significant moment for me. I acknowledge my success in overcoming a strong, stubborn and determined mindset which has held me back from true self-expression and potential. I could not imagine allowing this belief-system to continue having a hold over me and not giving myself the opportunity to stand proud and be heard.

> "You can have anything you want if you are willing to give up the belief that you can't have it."
> ~ROBERT ANTHONY

Today, I am playful, adventurous, happier and at peace with myself and my life. I have an unshakeable self-belief and trust in myself while I experience deeper and more satisfying relationships that add joy to my life.

It's funny where life can lead you. While I spent most of my life hiding in the back of school rooms and board meetings, I now spend most of my working day being seen in front of groups of people. I get to teach them life and work skills and use my own stories and experiences to show them that all is possible when your 'WHY' is big enough and you really want something. I never expected that I would land a job where I present and facilitate learning and mentoring. It is in this space that I speak confidently, openly, have fun and laugh. In fact, I laugh a lot! I love that I am free to be me, warts and all. I don't hide and shy away from

who I am nor the challenges that I faced. I am **FREE!**

I am reminded that coming from the back of the room to the front of the room took **DESIRE, INTENTION, PERSISTENCE** and **COMMITMENT** in order to make changes, live a life of confidence and having the freedom to feel good about **ME!**

Be fearless in stepping up and into to your own personal power. You are different in a beautiful, unique way. Don't allow others to have you believe otherwise. It is YOU and only YOU that has the power to create the changes that will give you choices and opportunities in life. I have been blessed to share my journey and know that it has inspired others to make changes and live a more authentic life. You can do it too. Believe in yourself. I believe in YOU.

"You become what you believe. And to believe that you are created by the power that's greater than yourself means anything is possible"

~OPRAH WINFREY

Co-Author
Pina Cerminara

As an entrepreneur, professional coach, mentor, a co-author and a workshop and program facilitator, Pina specialises in upgrading people's thinking and accelerating their skills, talents and behaviours which help them to live a purposeful, fulfilling and happy life.

Having founded her business in 2013, Pina's interest in people and human behaviour has been insatiable resulting in her becoming qualified, knowledgeable and a highly sought after experienced personal and professional coach.

"My passion is to help every client achieve and succeed as I know beyond a shadow of a doubt that when I empower another, I will be rewarded in watching them soar".

Pina is a believer in lifelong learning and is always expanding both her personal and professional skills. When Pina is not working, she loves to travel, cook and walk along the beach. The things Pina loves most in life are her family and friends.

PINA CERMINARA
Personal & Professional Development Coach and Facilitator

Instagram: https://www.instagram.com/pinacerminara/
Facebook: https://www.facebook.com/pinacerminara2/
Linkedin: www.linkedin.com/in/pina-cerminara-a9409460/

"

Often in the moment of an experience
we don't understand where it
is taking us or what change in course
we will make."

~TARA BULUM

Everything Happens
to Reveal Our Purpose
by Tara Bulum

What happens when a child's world is torn apart and turned upside down, a few times over?

Who can they turn to when there is no-one at all to support them and they don't understand why this is happening?

When I was a very young child I thought my life was wonderful. I had a great family and was living in a nice house.

As a 6-year-old little girl, I realise I'm told, too frequently, that I have to be "a good girl" and because it is my parents are telling me what to do and how to behave, I don't think anything of it.

As I am starting to get older I feel like I am often being watched, and getting disappointing looks from my parents when I do something "unacceptable", unladylike or noisy. I often hear my father saying, "Children should be seen and not heard".

At 8 years old I am feeling like I don't need my parents telling me what to do and how to do it, or how to behave, after all, I am walking myself to school now. I'm a big girl! So I push (in my own way) to have more freedom, to be noisier and to know when I can get away with it! I play being myself as if it is the role of another person when I am in the company of my parents or other adults. *Isn't that what all children do as they try to work out what their role is in their family dynamics?* It's a little like when I am playing, teaching the class of my toys in the bedroom my sister and I share.

My Mum and Dad shout a little louder at each other and a little more frequently than normal. I have no understanding why or what all this thick feeling is in the air. To begin with, I don't even realise it is only at home that I feel this.

My Dad has decided to start a business from home, doing the same thing he does at work, but for more than one company. I am nearly 10, I don't like the idea of having to share a room with my sister again. Yet we have to as Dad is putting his office in their bedroom and they are moving into our old bedroom. For Mum, this means she doesn't have anywhere to do her hairdressing anymore and has to do it in the kitchen or outside.

I love sitting on the bench or on one of the chairs watching Mum cut hair, tease it or style it, making people look good and feel great. When they leave I can see the change in the way they carry their body, like their head is higher and shoulders more relaxed. They seem more content and happier, at least about how they look, maybe it was the conversation too though. I love feeling that with them like there is something to like about themselves again and be a little proud of.

REFLECTION 1:
What we love doing and revert to when we can, is often our life calling or an essential part of it.

When someone's contributions to their family or community are not appreciated and valued it can deeply affect their self-esteem, if they let it, they are not centred and don't know themselves well.

I am now in grade 6 and I am super excited I get to go to my first school camp. I am also very nervous about it. I don't have many close friends and the girls who normally pick on me are going too, though they are not sharing my room. I am wondering what new things I will get to do.

It's now the night I get home from the camp, I climb into bed feeling very tired, yet exhilarated from all the things I showed myself I could do, even though I was scared. I'm deeply slumbering, in a dream and happy about the camp. Suddenly, I wake to voices that are trying to whisper, yet are angry at each other. I'm alarmed and off guard, my body tenses up, my brain feels like it is shrinking with tension and intense energy. I sneak out to the hall to hear what is being said, I am disappointed that I can't really hear well. I can't really understand the words, but I can feel the energy of it - intense and heavy. It fills my entire body with dread and fear.

I want to go back to bed but sit there feeling like I am glued to the floor for what feels like a very long time. All the while, my mind is whirling and whirling around faster and faster, trying to think about what I can do to stop this and fix the fear of becoming a reality. I don't want to realise or accept there is nothing I can do. I want to talk with my parents, but have no idea what to say, or that they will even hear me, as they are not even listening to each other. I eventually walk up to their bedroom door and just stand in the doorway for a while; at first, they don't even notice me. I finally pluck up the courage to call out, it took a few times of doing so before they finally turn around. They are trying to act as if it's a normal conversation. Moments pass quickly and when I think back, I don't remember what was said or how long it took for me to calm down, though it seemed quite a long time. Sometime later I go back to bed, still hearing some discussions going on and a while later I fall asleep.

A few days later I get up in the middle of the night and go into their room, I am shocked that Mum isn't there. I was unaware she had been sleeping on the couch since the big argument. Several days later she finally admits it, she said it is only while she and Dad are sorting a few things out.

A Month or so goes by and they hardly speak to each other, when they do it's very tense, loud and unpleasant. They are hardly ever home at the same time and some weekends one goes away, for what seems like strange reasons, maybe even made up ones.

One particular Saturday we'd been to a friend's place during the day and had fun. We get home and are quite tired, but it feels like Mum is rushing us into bed. A few minutes later the doorbell rings and there is some strange man standing there. He comes in and introduces himself, "Hi, I'm Lynton. Who are you?" I don't want to answer, I don't know this man and I don't think I like or trust him. He gives my sister and I a few gifts – Smurf colouring books and characters. My body is filled with dread, anger and grief, as it seems my fear has become a reality – my parents are not together any more. This is not only scary, but it is also devastating. I feel like my world is caving in and that my parents don't love each other anymore, so how could they love me? As this has happened just after I went on camp; I am wondering what did I do to cause it? Maybe I wasn't ladylike enough or quiet enough, perhaps I should have tried harder and did what they wanted and kept myself in control.

A couple of months later Mum, my sister and I move to a few blocks away, it took a few weeks to settle in. The only good thing was that it was closer to school. I never felt really comfortable there, it didn't really feel like home, it was cold and empty, even though Mum had all the furniture we need.

Months have passed, it is now October and I am starting to get used to where we live with Mum, but I feel really sad. It's near Christmas and I've heard frequent heated discussions between Mum and Dad about who is having us for Christmas

and who is having us for New Year. Every time I hear them talk like this it makes my body tense up and I shrivel up inside. Finally, it has been decided, Christmas is with Mum and New Year is with Dad.

It's now just after New Year of the next year, we have lived in the unit with Mum for a year or so now. There are often different people visiting. Last night she told us that someone special was coming over tomorrow night for dinner and we better be on our best behaviour. I was unsure and wary of who this was and why we had to be SOO good.

REFLECTION 2:
What we are exposed to regularly becomes our normal and expected. When we have expectations and we trust in them without doubt, they always get delivered, good or bad.

When the visitor arrived, my sister and I didn't feel comfortable.
About a week later he is visiting again. When we are sitting down eating at the table and he says "Your Mum and I are getting married and you're moving to Bendigo.". I felt so shocked that I didn't' know what to say! I was distressed and horrified that Mum had decided to marry this person we didn't know much and we'd told her we didn't like! As well as having to leave the good friends it has taken all of my primary school life to make!

It's a few months later and we have moved to Bendigo. Every day I dread waking up, wondering if today would be another day of abuse. I am going to get severely bashed by my new stepfather on most days.

We are sitting down to dinner, another part of the day that absolutely terrified me and made me tense up all over, knowing my sister will probably inadvertently say something that would again mean I would get a lashing later. Tonight we get the usual dinner, which I often didn't like, vegetables and a small amount of meat. For years before him, Mum didn't give me any or many vegetables I didn't like, as she knew I hated veggies. Tonight though my stepfather was in a really bad mood and I was the victim of it. I refused to eat the dinner in front of me, food I didn't like (more flamin' veggies, I have had enough of them and him). Rather than have it served for breakfast the next day, as usually happened, he decided he would force me to eat it that night. He had a way of making sure Mum agree with everything he said and did. Anyway, this night he cracked the shits "big time" and yells at me for ages to eat my dinner. He keeps telling me to hold my nose so I can't taste the peas, then suddenly he jumps up and grabs my jaw, forcing it into a locked open position, while telling my Mum to grab my nose so I can't taste the blasted peas, and she does so, without hesitation! I don't know if you can work out what this means, but let me spell it out for you. My nose is held shut and I have my mouth locked open, so I can't move it at all. Now someone is shoving a fork full of peas in my mouth. I can't breathe through my nose and I can't gasp for breath and I am too small and weak to push anyone out the way. I feel like I am inhaling peas through my throat, I am turning blue and I feel like I am going to die. Eventually, something happened, I don't know what or by whom, I wasn't aware of what was going on around me, but someone let go and I could breathe again. GASP! I didn't want to die! Unfortunately, this is a night I'll never forget.

REFLECTION 3:
People will do whatever it takes to protect themselves from their greatest fear, even at the cost of their own family. All that we do satisfies a need or drive, even if it is only momentary. Unless we are self-aware and have a strong intention and purpose that feeds our core self and nurtures us, we don't think about challenging it or try and stop it, we don't even see how we can.

While I have my own life at 26, I feel like something massive is holding me back (or lots of big things really and I am frustrated that I don't know what they are or how to deal with them), similar to being on a leash and having a shield between who I am and who I want to be, my child self and the successful independent adult. I am at work, about to pack up and leave for the day. In a job, I don't love, but can do, in a place that is unrewarding and where I feel like I am being slowly strangled. I get a phone call from Mum saying "I just wanted to let you know that Kevin my stepfather died a few days ago.". When I ask Mum how she is, she puts on her 'tough me' act, with a response of "Why would it matter to me? I'm not surprised or upset." I proceed to ask about the funeral in an attempt to have her go under that barrier and recognise her feelings. When doing so I received a strong message to go to the funeral. The conversation, in my mind, is in seconds, may have been minutes in reality –

> Me: "But why would I want to go to his funeral, he was worse than awful to me?"
> Inner Voice: ***"You just need to go."***
> Me: "How will it help me? I don't see why I'd go."
> Inner Voice: ***"You just need to go."***
> Me: "But I don't understand?" I am getting frustrated at this point, but I know I need to listen.
> Inner Voice: ***"We know you trust us, don't you? So go!"***
> Me: "Yes, you know I trust you. Don't you?"
> Inner Voice: ***"Well show us how much by going."***

Next, I asked Mum when and where the funeral is.

She doesn't understand, wondering why I would want to go to his funeral. I share with her that I don't know why, but just know I need to go. I invite her to join me, and at first, she makes an excuse not to come. When she realised I was going anyway, she decides to come with me.

At the funeral, all the family friends who all stopped talking to us when Mum and my step father split up, including his first wife and their children and current wife were there. The children from his first wife knew me because they had been to stay at our place a few times, but they never acknowledged me at the funeral, it was as if they didn't see me. Only one person says hello to me. For most of the funeral, I don't really feel like I am there; I am taken to another space in my mind where I am given a totally new perspective as to why he was in my life and what it meant for me. I was told many times he was a catalyst for me, to break my shell and form a new one. It became extremely clear at that moment, I am here as a significant catalyst. I see that is what he did for me, though it is not obvious at this moment, in detail what he was catalysing. Agghhhh, I suddenly knew and was comforted by the understanding this is why I had to come to the funeral, to understand that my purpose in this life is to be a catalyst for the change in others, not in the same way he has done with me, but much more gently.

REFLECTION 4:
I find myself now moving into becoming more of a catalyst for change and self-awareness. This realisation came to me once I committed to being a Business Coach and Mentor. I felt I was exactly where I was meant to be. I felt that my background, my history, everything I had been through in my life had enabled me to help others in a unique way because when I help business people with their businesses, I am now able to help them on a personal level first which builds a solid foundation for their business as well.

Often in the moment of an experience, we don't understand where it is taking us or what change in course we will make. In fact, it is only through knowing ourselves and asking ourselves the sometimes difficult questions that we gain a deeper understanding of why, what it means for us, who we are and what we are here to do.

When I have been asked, "What if you could go back and change it, would you?" My clear answer is I don't have any emotions, other than gratitude, for what has happened and those who were involved. As strange as that may sound, it is absolutely true. All of these experiences have shaped me into the woman I am today and I am very happy with who I am.

The other reason I would not want to change anything is because it was during these physically and emotionally horrible experiences that I learned how to disconnect from the physical environment and take myself to a different place, maybe even a different time. It also gave me the strength to stand up for myself and my convictions later in life. To be completely honest, I love who I am now! To change this part of my life would change who I am and why would I want to do that?

My love and empathy for my mother is immense. As a wife and as a mother she went through so much too and she honestly did the best she could do with the understanding she had at the time. In fact, I am extremely grateful for all that she sacrificed for us, her children. Because of her, I am a better person.

We all have our own unique journey, it is not right or wrong, it just is. It is not our job to judge what and how others live their lives, but for us to live our own lives and hopefully lead the way by example. As humans, this is the main way we learn; therefore it is the main way we will change the world. For some people in the world part of the life purpose is to play an active role in that; in the way, degree and volume that others cannot or will not. Your experience and perspective in life is yours alone; the rate, method and approach at which you grow during your journey in life comes from how open, honest and transparent you are with your self-awareness, self-communication and self-appreciation.

May your heart and mind be opened by the experiences, understandings and reflections shared with you in this chapter and the others in this book.
May you take on new adventures and insights from them.

With great appreciation, thank you for reading.
Tara Bulum

"

In fact, it is only through knowing ourselves and asking ourselves the sometimes difficult questions that we gain a deeper understanding of why, what it means for us, who we are and what we are here to do."

~TARA BULUM

Co-Author
Tara Bulum

Tara Bulum, of Plan It Biz Success, has worked with business owners for over 15 years helping them achieve a strong sustainable business through utilising systematic approaches to reach milestones, improve efficiency and profitability.

After spending 15 years in various roles in the finance industry, a volunteer counsellor and then qualifying as a life coach Tara has had the privilege to learn a great deal about people. Her most rewarding and inspiring aspect of being a Business Coach is seeing how clear decisions and changes can improve a business owners inspiration, motivation and results; connecting with their own value and the difference they can make for others. Seeing people grow can be a lot of fun! Committed to her own personal and spiritual growth for over 30 years, Tara has truly enjoyed being present when people open up to their potential and stand in that space with grace and integrity.

There is not much that Tara loves more, apart from her husband and two young children than spending time with others who know their purpose in life and are committed to achieving it, even if they are not sure how. This is important to her because we all aspire to be more and can be inspired by those around us.

Website: www.planitbizsuccess.com
LinkedIn: www.linkedin.com/in/tarabulum
Facebook: www.fb.com/PlanItBizSuccess
www.fb.com/groups/ImproveMyBusiness

Dance In The Fire of Life!

"

I no longer put off things to do until I get married. I have blocked loneliness' call and placed myself on the do not call list. I am no longer existing but living out every tick of the clock. I have hung up those singed dancing shoes and replaced them with the barefoot freedom of positive self-esteem and premium self-worth."

~B. JACQUELINE JETER

(from 'Don't Be Afraid To Dance Alone: Partnerless Is Not Powerless')

Don't Be Afraid To Dance Alone:
Partnerless Is Not Powerless

by B. Jacqueline Jeter

Dance in the fire of life. Wow! When one thinks about dancing, one thinks about fun and joyous things. You think about rhythmic, free-flowing undulations. What comes to mind is the 'Cha Cha', Latin Dancing and even the Waltz. When I think about fire, I think about something that is hot. It can be a good thing and it could be bad, depending on the circumstances. So, when we put 'DANCING' and 'FIRE' together in a sentence, we could easily be challenged for a moment trying to work out if this is a good or bad thing. What is interesting, however, is that I, just like you, have had pivotal moments during my life where I have come face to face with the flames that life has thrown onto my path. It is at this point that we have a choice to either dance with and eventually through these flames or allow them to destroy us. The fire that I had to dance in during the past 30 years (because I'm 52 as I write this), has been the fire of being alone.

Often we hear people say, 'I'm alone. I'm not lonely'. However, there have been times that I have really fought loneliness and as a result, endured depression. I always imagined myself to have a lot of options from which to choose because I'm very eclectic. I'm very outgoing and have a very effervescent, and bubbly per-sonality, and I like to be around people. I like to be with my family. I had a very loving mother and father growing up and that cocooning of just having the time we had, I wanted that sameness in my marriage. I wanted that with my husband, to be able to do things for him and serve him and also he does things for me. For years I watched shows like the Cosby Show where the husband and wife got along. To me, it was real. It wasn't that pie in the sky thing. They went through real issues and I always longed for that.

As a Christian, you're told to pray for God to send you the right person, to send someone who's going to be the perfect match for you. We have these ideas when we're very young about how our wedding is going to be. We never think about how a marriage is going to be, just the wedding piece. Yes, you have it all planned out! You're going to wear a beautiful dress, the service is going to be in a beautiful church with flowers everywhere, your best friends are going to be your brides-maids and your sisters will be your maid and matron of honour. Even your hair will be perfect. It will be up with some cascading curls, or maybe you'll have it down with flowing pretty curls and you will wear a tiara that has the veil attached to it and you'll walk down this beautiful aisle with your father by your side to the man of your dreams. He will stand there beaming with joy about the choice that he's made and you'll both take off into the sunset and enjoy your beautiful honey-moon in paradise. When you come back, Your relationship will be perfect. Even your arguments will be sorted quickly and perfectly and you'll walk hand in hand into the sunset of yet another beautiful day. What a wonderful plan, but what if the other player never comes along or takes his time coming along? What then?

That dream and that strategic plan of mine, all in my head, of the day I get married or when I meet my husband has shifted many times throughout the years. About 18 years ago, I really thought that I had met him. I was 30. He came to me, I didn't seek him out. We really clicked. He was a very loving, very giving and supportive person. As we started to grow and talk more, he was the first to mention that he wanted to marry me and that he didn't think it was going to be long before it happened. He initiated all those discussions and decisions. So as we continued to get to know each other, it was confirmed how perfect we were for each other by both of our friends and some of our family.

Everything was moving along beautifully so you can imagine my surprise the day he turned to me and said that he wanted to take a 'break'! My first response was a break from what? Life? This isn't some cry for help, is it? 'You're not considering harming yourself are you?' I mean, after all, he COULDN'T possibly be talking about US!. He was like, 'no, from us'. It was as if someone took a steel toe boot and kicked me straight under my sternum. All I could do was cry and run from the room to my car and drove home. During this 'break time', there were sever-al times when we came back together and fell apart and came together and fell apart. And I have been left wondering what the reason was. I know now, 20 some years later, because he and I are now friends, that he was scared. He wasn't ready. Fear makes people behave in unrecognisable ways. Even though he put all the pressure on to get married, his fear to commit caused him to run all the way into another woman's arms only a week after! within several months of meeting this woman, they were engaged. The pattern then repeated itself. That engagement fell through, but they were still together and were re-engaged three times in the expanse of the 10 years they were together.

As you can imagine, It took me a while to get through that because it made me question my self-worth. The song 'what is wrong with me?' hit platinum on the charts in my mind. Why, after all this time has no one come to the table and said, 'Jackie, you are a magnificent woman. I choose you. I don't want anybody else I just want to have this jewel of who you are to myself. Now I'm not saying this in a narcissistic way, but I'm a damn good woman. I'm loyal, brilliant, beautiful, successful and enterprising. I was 'raised right' (meaning that I had a loving, stable family, that they poured the love of Christ in me and they showed me how to treat and love them and others.) My mother was my greatest teacher. I learned by watching her how to care for and love my potential husband and be an excellent wife. She taught me to make my home a sanctuary of peace for myself, our children and my husband, to ensure my home was clean and that I knew how to prepare a home-cooked meal.

I'm a woman who loves the Lord, a woman of honour and grace and a real Christian, a Proverbs 31 woman, so why do I not have my husband here? Why do I not have those two kids that I often dreamed about? My mother never told me that. She told me to do my best in school, which after all wasn't that the point of going to college? So now I'm matriculated through college and I'm at that 30 mark and soon I'm past the 30 mark and I'm approaching 40 and there have been people who have been interested in me but not that one that I've longed to meet. What is it about me? Am I my too fat? not fat enough? Is my hair too long? not long enough? Am I too dark and too pecan? What is it? Am I too brilliant? Am I not being open enough? Should I be looking outside my race? My whole plan was to marry a successful African American man as I believed that we would be more compatible. Should I be online dating? What should I be doing so he can find me? Am I being too passive and saying and thinking that a man is just going to come along on a white horse and say, 'you are my queen'. Am I trusting God too much in this respect? Of all the teachings poured into me about allowing God to write your love story, perhaps I am being too focused on that. So as things transpired, what I decided to do was just throw myself into my career.

One of the worst times in my life was when I went through a very traumatic experience alone. I was date raped. I went through that date rape with the thought that I'm okay for you to take that portion of me, but you can't capture my heart and give me yours??? All these things that happened to me made me harder. Not in the way I interacted with people, but harder on myself. I became very protective of myself in how I engaged with people. I only showed them so much of my heart, but there was a constant struggle because I knew that was not me. That was not who I was. I'm the kind of person who is that touchy-feely person. I'm the kind of person who, on movie night, I want to be snuggled on the sofa with you or touching you. That's the kind of woman I am and that's the kind of relationship I want, one where the husband is loving and supportive. Does he have to make a lot of money? No, I don't care about that piece because for me, money will come and money will go. In fact, that was proven to me as after 23 years with a company that I thought I would retire from, they decided one day they were moving their operations somewhere else and in doing so, almost 3000 people were out of work in one fail swoop. So now I'm looking at that loneliness and rejection again. Because remember, I had thrown myself into my career and that had become my 'boo', my 'bae', the lover that kept me warm at night. My dreams and aspirations with my career, the fat paycheck and major bonuses had become the warmth.

And here I was, dancing partner-less. I read in a magazine about a woman who actually planned her wedding and went through with it without a husband. She gave herself a celebration. She didn't call it a wedding. She was approaching 50 and she did not see herself getting married any time soon. Her father was getting older and she wanted her father to walk her down the aisle and to have that first 'father-daughter dance with her him. So she planned and spent thousands of dollars to have this elaborate celebration that people actually came to as if it was a true wedding. All the while, the first dance, the cutting of her celebration cake, and the toast was to her only, but she was happy and she had checked off her list that she had had a wedding celebration.

As ludicrous as her actions were, there have been times I've thought about that. I have so wanted to experience that celebration of getting married and no longer feeling like I have missed out on something very special. Well, my parents have been deceased for a while, so I will never have that first dance with my father. I will never have him walk me down the aisle. I've had to come to terms with that and it is okay.

But back to this dancing and this fire. Life throws at us many curve balls. The book of Job in the Bible talks about this. He says after he goes through all his turmoil; ' Man, born of a woman is a few days and those are full of trouble.' A lot of times in the Christianity world and churchdom, we're told that once you come to Jesus and once you give your life to him fully, then all things will fall into place and everything will be beautiful. You'll be skipping to the city and running through the sunflowers and the birds will be chirping at the right time in the morning and everything will be perfect.

People fail to tell you that your faith will be severely tested. I know mine has been. Through it all, I can rest in knowing that one of the main things giving your life to

God provides you is the confidence, courage and persistence to go through trials in life.

This fire of loneliness has permeated my life. I went through a very angry time in my early twenties when my mother passed away from Multiple Myeloma cancer. She passed away even after I and others prayed. At that time, I did not understand the healing process of God and what faith and everything meant really.

I'd been to church, but I really hadn't had the true experience with the Lord to have him give me an understanding of the scriptures. I thought His word says that if I pray to God, because He is a healer, and His word says that the person you are praying to be healed, is already being healed, I took that literally. I prayed so hard and so much for mother to be healed and yet she was not. 'So God heal her' I would often hear myself plead. My mother was a beautiful woman of faith. She prayed every day, sometimes three or four times a day. She never complained about her pain. She danced in that fire. Now here she lay, suffering internally from painful cancer and knowing that she'll never see her baby girl grow up into the amazing woman she is today. I can't imagine what was going through her mind, knowing that she's leaving her husband and her family behind but I do know probably at one point she was she was thinking; 'I see you, Lord, calling me home'. I was 20, my mother left me. It is a hard thing to say even today because I needed her so much more at that time and the sad thing was it was a couple of months before my 21st birthday. When we were gathering her things, my father gave me her favourite Bible, the one she used all the time, the one that she read to me out of. One day as I picked up her Bible, a prescription fell out. It was a prescription that was written on my birthday a year before, the day her cancer came out of remission. I treasure that scrip and that bible. It is as if a piece of her is still living.

The fires kept on coming as time went by. My father passed away several years later. After that, I felt like I didn't belong anywhere. You see, my siblings were all married and had their own lives. I didn't fit. I was the odd one out. I was the one who was still standing without a chair when the music stopped. The fire of loneliness kept on burning.

Then one day, I had an epiphany that would be the fire extinguisher to this loneliness. I fell in love—with God and with ME! I came to the realization that I didn't have to live as if I needed the validation of a husband to be the awesome wonder that I was created to be. I began to see ME how He created me to be—fearfully and wonderfully by the Creator of all things. So here I am in 2019 at the young

age of 52 living my best life. I no longer put off things to do until I get married. I have blocked loneliness' call and placed myself on the do not call list. I am no longer existing but living out every tick of the clock. I have hung up those singed dancing shoes and replaced them with the barefoot freedom of positive self-esteem and premium self-worth. Loneliness is a state of mind; not a state of existence. Have you ever felt lonely surrounded by a room full of people? It is about how you see yourself. I had to reset and look at the awesome things about ME and not what I wanted others to see. The fact is, some people may never see all of your awesome essence and this is ok. The tragedy comes when YOU don't see it. A rose doesn't compete with the beauty of another rose, blooms in its own fragrance.

I had to come to the realization that my life is not dependent on someone else living it, instead, it is dependent on ME living it. I challenge you to stop existing and be intentional about allowing your uniqueness to impact all around you. Each morning I awake, I look myself in the eye in the mirror and proclaim something about myself that I feel and know to be amazing and powerful. Pause here and write down things unique about you that you will intentionally celebrate.
I had to learn to appreciate ALL of me-- the good, the bad and the ugly. I had to learn that my scars told a beautiful power-story of success, resilience and strength. Guess what? Yours do too. I challenge you to look at each scar (physical, emotional, mental) and write down how each made you stronger and what you learned about yourself. It's is time for you to tell your own story!

If you have been dealing with the fire of loneliness and rejection, lift up your head, square your shoulders, look yourself in the mirror and say ' Hey jewel. You are amazing, beautiful and powerful just the way you are. You are too priceless for validation from anyone. Go live your life to the fullest!'

'After all, validation is for parking'
~ ANONYMOUS

Co-Author
B. Jacqueline Jeter

As the CEO and Founder of the personal development company, The Ripple Effect Coaching and Leadership Development Group, Jacqueline's passion is to empower women of all walks of life to realize their full potential and excel in their life's passion and purpose. She is also the Founder and Visionary of the non-profit, ReignDrops as the Encouragement Ambassador and offers encouragement through practical life experiences to help others discover the triumph and strength in the world around them, despite the situation they are facing.

Having already appeared in three other anthologies, Jacqueline will be publishing her debut work, Altar Blockers, later this year.

Jacqueline is a licensed minister, teacher and faithful servant in the kingdom of God at Wake Chapel Church under the leadership of Bishop J Jasper Wilkins II. In her 'downtime' Jacqueline likes reading, travelling, spending time with family and friends, philanthropic activities, and listening to music. She is an avid sports fan, especially with anything associated with her beloved NC State Wolfpack. She currently resides in the Raleigh, NC area.

Website: www.hisreigndrops.com and https://www.amazon.com/-/e/B07D-PQPJW6
Twitter: @ReignDropsBJJ
Instagram and Twitter: @bjsquare
Facebook: https://www.facebook.com/jackie.jeter

"

When it comes to life, it's either look at nothing or look at everything! Look back on those pivotal moments that contributed to your life and how they are still creating your future. I encourage you to look within. Are you 'just living' or are you ALIVE right now, striving to experience life fully and question everything?"

~Julie Opperman

You Were Born To Shine
Courage. Self Esteem. Personal Development. Success. Influence. Motivation.

by Julie Opperman

Each one of these words is very powerful 'influencers' in the lives of many these days. It seems that wherever we look, these words are glaring back at us in the form of advertising, promotion, motivational quotes, blogs, articles and so much more.

Not only do these words serve to influence us, they also cajole us into believing that this is WHO we should be, or who we should WANT to be, or what we should be DOING. I believe that these words have an incredible power attached to their meaning. They can motivate and inspire but depending on where people are in their lives, they can also intimidate and make people feel less than. To some extent, this is what happened to me when I found myself drawn to contribute to this book. The self-talk that was going on in my head went something like this: "What makes my story, my life, different from anyone else? Why would anyone want to hear my story, do I even have a story that is worth sharing? Don't be so ego-driven to think your story is worth reading." Then I recalled something I read; 'You were born a hero, and somewhere along the road you just forgot or were told, who you are'. We all have pivotal moments in our life that have a major influence on the trajectory of our life and I have realised that not only do I have a story that is valuable, but a story that is unique and one I am happy to share. Like you, I was born to shine but in my case, life got in the way.

I encourage you to develop courage. Courage has been the foundation which has held me up in the most challenging of times. Courage is taking a leap, exposing your vulnerability and creating the possibility of dancing with and through the fires of life, ultimately stepping into your own unique brilliance. It is in the midst of difficult times in life that IF we are courageous enough to trust that these very challenges gift us the opportunity of self-development and discovery of our greatness that we begin to change the way we see life. We actually begin to live and enjoy the journey!

I find I am now grateful for the moments in my life that changed me and enabled growth. Without those moments I would not have strived to learn or develop courage which has in turn given me joy and freedom.

Even when the story isn't perfect, even if it's more real than you want it or believe it to be, your story is what you have and what you will always have. You cannot change the past but you can change what your story will be moving forward.

I was born 100% authentic, loved unconditionally, surrounded by family and more love. We lived down the road from my Gran and around the corner from my aunties and uncles. I was enveloped in love, family learnings and history, played on the streets, ran to school with friends, had family Sunday lunches, sleepovers and fun. I was a child, free of worry and free to do whatever I dreamed.

What an adventure! Six weeks across the ocean, what an experience! Those weeks were a long time for myself and my siblings. We were 10-pound Poms, heading to Sydney to make a new life in Australia, the land of opportunity and beautiful weather, which matched the equally beautiful lifestyle. I didn't realise this was the start of a new life and the end of something that I wouldn't recognise until recently is the disconnection of family ties from that fateful day in August 1971. It wasn't until years later when I realised that time signified the loss of something that is intangible and immeasurable but it sits within. Imagine being 7 years old, not really knowing that this moment in time would be the first … and not the last that makes me who I am today.

Note to my younger self:

Be brave. You will be different, you will have to make new friends, you will need to be resilient and see this adventure as the beginning of who you will be in the future. Know that those family ties will always be there, you will stay connected, by love. The networks you craved will make you the person you are today, your parent's sacrifices and efforts to make a new life are also part of what made you who you are today It takes a special kind of courage to reveal yourself, know that you will fit in, you will know when you fit in. You will see yourself in others, you may need to search, however, you will find your soul connections, your tribe and one day you will just know, your internal heroine will emerge and you will be home!

The next pivotal moment in my life: I am 16 years old and my fun, carefree teenage world is turned upside down. One day I had a boyfriend, the next I was involved in his family's dramas. This is a huge fire I danced in this part of my life and I look back on this sliding door moment and wonder why I didn't take the other door that eventful day? I got caught up in something quite intense at the time and I was swept up in the drama. Without going into too much detail, as that story isn't mine to tell, but what is mine is the impact this had on my life. Until writing this chapter I didn't realise the enormity of the impact this experience had on me. My husband's brother was swept up in a significant murder investigation in the late 1970s in South Australia and was consequently imprisoned for a long time, claiming his innocence, but nonetheless, he was convicted and the impact this had on the family is hard to describe. The difficulty I have had putting pen to paper has made this journey even more real. We think we have dealt with our past, our emotional states and our dramas but have we? As I write this it becomes real again and I have now realised the impact and I cry a little for the innocence I left behind but I also cheer this girl on for the strength that made her who I am today.

I'm changed by a new role, a new identity and it's hard to explain how I was pulled into thinking I was in love. Did I even really know what love was? I married without really knowing who I was. The years of distress within his family made me forget my dreams and I really didn't know myself. The 'secret identity' started quite quickly, 'be happy, look happy' I put on this facade of happiness and normality and I started to believe it was true but somewhere deep inside I knew the truth. I ignored my true self and took on a fake copy of me. Everyone loved me but I couldn't feel it. As I reflect back on this time, it felt like I wasn't really there. I was living - but I wasn't ALIVE. I didn't even see the impact it had on me at the deeper level, I didn't really know myself.

Looking back over that time, I wonder how I made the choices I did, how I took on the responsibility that I did and recognise that I was not ready emotionally, after all, I was just a teenager. The decisions were made for me and suddenly I lost my voice to speak up. I didn't mean it to happen, it just happened. I was partly brainwashed into thinking my thoughts and feelings didn't matter and my voice got lost behind the influence of others and wanting to please. Underneath I was still that girl who knew she wanted to go after her dreams but she let someone else make her decisions for her and that is when the fear of speaking up took over. I realised I had been surviving instead of living. The fear of living my life the way it was intended, alongside the fear of living in abundance, an abundance of love and letting my light shine was so remote to me at that time, that I could not see it even if it was sitting in front of me!

On the outside, I had a good life. We had the all Australian dream. We bought a house we wanted we had it all, the picture-perfect life, or so I projected to everyone looking in. But on the inside, it was a different story. It was like a painted

wall that was slowly cracking and peeling in front of your eyes but you don't really notice the cracks until it started to fall off. I wore the mask so well I couldn't even see. I used the mask as a security blanket, to hide behind.

So what was wrong? I kept the mask on, especially for me, and for my parents my family. I could not let them know, my thoughts told me they wouldn't approve, so I spent the following nine years suppressing what my heart was telling me, suppressing my emotions, ignoring them. No, I was lost, I was fearful, I WAS wearing a mask.

There was something inside of me that knew something was not sitting right. I was not feeling okay, I wasn't happy and at the time, I didn't know what was wrong but this feeling was just getting stronger and it was revealing itself as shame and blame. I was feeling ashamed for the life I had accepted and I blamed myself for it all.

I had to leave this life and this marriage but there was so much at stake. I didn't want to hurt my daughter, my family, my husband. He wasn't a bad person. We just got together too young and were not able to cope with his family's extraordinary circumstances. I was afraid of being judged. What will my family and our friends think? How do you just let go of a thirteen-year relationship, and then how do you face people you know? These are all questions which were going around in my head. I was going to get blamed and I did not know if I could handle it. I can deal with my own blame, but not when it came from others. I made the decision anyway. It was the first time in a really long time I had made a decision for myself, the most difficult decision was telling my family. I had made up all these stories in my mind of what I thought they wanted for me of what other people wanted from me but what I discovered was that all they wanted was for me to be happy. What I found when my life fell apart, when that painting of my life was in flames, when I stepped out a little from behind the mask, I found something I never expected to find.

I found ME, I found the part of me that is the real me.

Advice to that young woman:
Don't be hard on yourself. You were at a vulnerable age, you thought you were in love. Accept what happened and learn from it. Perhaps you had to lose something of yourself so that you could become the person you are today. You became stronger, you fought for your child and you grew as a person. 'Courageous' is a word I see in you. It's time you saw it too! Your life matters, there is only one YOU!

I woke up that day like any other day. I was 29 years old, been married for 9 years and had been with him half my life. My daughter was three years old. That particular day, I just realised I wasn't happy and I was going to speak up. I hadn't planned it. My life wasn't going how I wanted it to. My soul again was disconnected and I couldn't see a way out without breaking up a family. I just knew it was the right thing to do and that it will it be worth it in the long run! That day I made the decision to leave, it was one, if not the biggest decisions of my life. I was a woman who was about to break up her family because I could not breathe in that life anymore. All I wanted at that time was for my daughter to be ok so without even realising, I took on a new persona. A new identity. That of the strong woman. 'Nothing will get through me, be strong for your daughter, don't cry, don't fail, you must succeed otherwise the turmoil you went through will be for nothing, close up your heart and just get on with it.' I didn't take time to grieve what I had lost, what I, through my own choice had given away. I didn't take time to sit with what I had done because I was in my new identity now. How quickly we can move from identity to identity but how hard is it to find YOU again!

My life started to expand as I started to get closer to the real me, although deep down it still wasn't the whole me. I still had to be the strong mum, the person who had it all together, the one that didn't fail, the one that wanted to please everyone. In 1987 I met my partner who then became my husband. He loved and adored me, but did he really know the real me? what if I showed up as the real me and he didn't like what he saw? I still need to be strong, keep the mask in place just in case. When you shut down your heart, it's hard for those trying to get in. They keep knocking and slowly they break down some of the barriers. Grief is a word that comes to me from a place deep down inside I have grieved for missing out, for what I put myself through, for wasting so much time going through life in a robotic trance, not using my senses to see, smell, hear and feel the love, the beauty, l, the praise I grieve for not allowing myself to feel or show my vulnerability.

I don't hide behind my mask anymore and I am my true whole self, turning 50, becoming a grandmother, finding myself, constantly learning has given me the ability to grow into that woman I was destined to become and having people in my life that love ME not just the person on the outside, but for the real me, I am so grateful!

Today
I've let go of my secret identity, in fact, it's been slowly peeling away for many years I just didn't realise it - it feels amazing, scary, courageous and invigorating all at

once!. I'm still a work in progress especially when it comes to allowing myself to feel love, actually feel it, to enjoy that feeling of being so secure and safe in my own skin, you just want more, and be selfish enough to say I deserve more. I now have my own business, I give back where I can, I go out and SHINE. I now embrace gratitude and I am so grateful to, my parents who themselves were courageous leaving behind the security to follow a dream. I feel gratitude when I look at my beautiful, caring and loving husband, my beautiful girls who make up my world and I am so proud of who they have become. I am so grateful for my granddaughter who is my joy, and all the people who I choose to have in my life now, my life helper's they know who they are, the books I read and the Landmark Educational Seminars that empowered me to somewhere beyond where I thought I could be. Discover the magic behind gratitude in your own world. It will change your life!

If you too are a woman with a mask on and have a secret identity that keeps you hidden, I recognise you. , Drop the mask, allow your true self to shine. Surround yourself with people who love you and want the best for you. Surround yourself with people that encourage you to shine. Take on personal development whether it be inspirational books or courses, get yourself a mentor or mentors do whatever you are able to do, do whatever it takes. Once you start shining it takes a lot to dim that light, be out to live an extraordinary life.

> "Our deepest fear is not that we are inadequate.
> Our deepest fear is that we are powerful beyond measure.
> It is our Light, not our Darkness, that most frightens us."
> ~MARIANNE WILLIAMSON

Lessons in life won't always be comfortable, but instead of focusing on the uncomfortable, if we focus on what the lesson is here to teach, it will lead us to the next step in this journey we call LIFE.

I now understand we are all the same, we are made up of trillions of cells, we are all adapting and living in this world. We all have fears, insecurities & masks. I still have many unwritten chapters in my life and now I have the courage to be nothing more or no-one else but ME. I hope you too can see that within yourself.

This is my chapter, my life, it's now your turn to look at your own life and work out where you're heading and what changes you want to make if any?

When it comes to life, it's either look at nothing or look at everything!

Look back on those pivotal moments that contributed to your life & how they are still creating your future. I encourage you to look within. Are you 'just living' or are you ALIVE right now, striving to experience life fully and question everything?

Pivotal moments create your life, it's time to embrace them, love them & let them go.

Who says we can't have it all and be all that we can be? We have to believe that we are able to be anything we want to be, stand for whatever we believe in and above all else, believe in our brilliance!

Be your own hero, shine bright and do whatever it takes to make that happen, it will be worth it!

Co-Author
Julie Opperman

Julie Opperman is a passionate Melbourne-based Entrepreneur who loves helping people with their health and their wealth goals through her Global business and business partners with a BioTech company to distribute a cellular health technology. Julie also is also self-employed in Business Management and is currently working in the Commercial Real Estate industry where she is known for her relentless work ethic and dedication to helping people.

Julie is driven by an unwavering entrepreneurial spirit, where she entered the industry in the health and wellness a few years ago and recognised an opportunity which included her love of connecting, networking and also being a health advocate.

Julie is on a mission to help others attain optimum health, self-empowerment, and personal success that has a permanent impact on their lives.

In her spare time, Julie enjoys bike riding with her husband, reading uplifting books, and exploring new places. Above all, she cherishes spending quality time with her loved ones. She is happily married, the proud mother of two successful daughters, and a very proud grandmother to a beautiful girl.

LinkedIn: https://www.linkedin.com/in/julie-opperman/
Instagram: https://www.instagram.com/julesopperman/
Facebook: https://www.facebook.com/julie.opperman

"

What I'm realizing is that with my fitness background, I've learned ABOUT my body, but I've never KNOWN my own body…or myself."

~Holly Wade

Dance of a Warrior
by Holly Wade

Fighting tears, with shakiness in her voice, mom says, "Your dad could die," a lot for a 12 year-old girl and young boys to take in. She had called my brothers and me into the living room for this serious discussion that I imagine, a parent hopes to never have. As the only girl, the eldest child, and a responsible little first grader helping in my parent's grocery store, I've always felt a duty to take care of everyone in my family. I gently spoke up. "We already know that, mom."

To ease the burden of others, I've practiced wearing a smile on the outside when my insides are ripped apart because I don't want people worrying about me. This was one of those moments, trying to show my assuredness when only a few minutes before, my brothers and I had discussed death as a possibility.

A few weeks before Dad was diagnosed with Crohn's Disease, an autoimmune disorder that affects the intestines. Doctors don't seem to know much about Crohn's, but recommend surgery to remove the diseased part of the intestine, along with a lifetime on Prednisone. It seemed hopeful. However, in a few short days after surgery, his body had become septic, causing our concerns.

Dad survived and Crohn's took center stage, dictating daily life for our entire family: bland meals, ever-changing plans that create disappointment and unpredictable holidays. I HATE Crohn's for so many reasons.

I couldn't wait to get out of this house and get on with my own life.

College arrives and as I continue to take care of my athletic body, I can't get rid of my belly bloat. It's a constant reminder that I can't get six-pack abs, meaning I can't get that 'perfect' body so I hide my mid-drift under bulky shirts. I feel sluggish and achy. I brush it off, thinking it's from teaching as many as five intense group fitness classes a day.

By the end of my college career, I'm beyond exhausted. When I'm home during breaks, all I can do is lay on the couch. I'm stressed with a lot on my plate, but in the back of my mind, I can't help but wonder why I'm feeling this way. My friends don't seem to struggle like this!

Mom notices my lack of energy and weight fluctuations, bluntly stating: "I think you have Crohn's".

Images flash in my mind of vacations lost, terrible mood swings, and dad lying on the couch with a cold washcloth over his eyes from the side effects of prednisone. I shout, "NO! I DON'T!!!"

This disease isn't going to rob ME of MY dreams of travel, big adventures, and running a company.

The moment I notice blood in my stool, my heart races, I get a lump in my throat, and whisper, "God, no!"

I've seen the toll that surgery and medications have taken on dad physically and mentally. He's been nothing more than a guinea pig for pharmaceuticals. All I can see is that he's a skeleton with the side effects of those drugs doing more harm to his body than the Crohn's itself. This latest drug requires a monthly infusion that is starting to kill the nerve endings in his face, hands, and feet. It's heart wrenching and infuriating to watch.

The way it stands right now, if I'm diagnosed while still on my parent's insurance, I will be labeled with a "pre-existing condition", limiting my ability to get my own health insurance. So I sleep and pray a lot.

"God, help me find a healer. Not just a doctor. But someone who can get me well, not like dad."

After grad school, I land my first job with insurance benefits. Barely able to put one foot in front of the other, I've stopped teaching fitness classes altogether to reserve energy and try to consume extra calories. It seems that no matter what I eat, I'm doubled-over a couple of hours later. The only thing that seems to relax my gut is a long nap, not always possible. Though I'm worried about what lies ahead, I down-play the severity of my symptoms.

It seems that I catch a cold or the flu whenever they go around. I'm in the doctor's office quite a bit, mentioning that I have zero energy. Even though I've listed that dad has Crohn's on the Family Medical History Form, it's not pursued. They order a blood draw, noticing that my white blood cell count is up some, but it looks like whatever my body was fighting is on its way out. I feel like I get a pat on the head and sent on my way like a good little girl, not taken seriously and no closer to an answer.

The problem is that no one, not even the four Specialists I've visited, will look inside. My trust in Western Medicine is shot!

Thankfully, my Chiropractor is concerned. When she asks how my appointment with the doctor went, she's livid that no one has done an endoscopy. She says, "I've got a woman I want you to see. Her card is on the counter out front."

When I get home, I immediately dial the number on the card. We set the appointment date and time. She says, "Oh, by the way, I don't work out of my office that day. I work from my home. The address is..." I pause and say, "What?!" She repeats her address. She's right across the street!

Relief! We begin YEARS of working together helping my body detox, absorb nutrients, unpack stuffed emotions, and rewire the patterns between my brain and body.

My first assignment is to adjust my diet: no flour, no sugar. My chest tightens in panic as I make a mental rundown of my basic diet: cereal, toast, sandwiches, pasta, and low-fat ice cream. WHAT am I going to eat?!!!

I'm determined to become the poster child for natural healing.

I fully immerse myself into every book and article I can get my hands on to learn how food heals my body. I hadn't given myself a chance to like cooking before. After all, I've intended on being a career woman, traveling for work. Surprisingly, I discover that time in the kitchen nurtures my soul. Besides, fresh food tastes soooo much better! Thanks to Food Network, I'm figuring it out beyond reading a recipe.

Crohn's is a funny animal. One day you feel on top of the world, and the next you're back to square one. I hit another cycle, motionless on mom and dad's couch for a week. We're at our wits end as the medical community sure hasn't helped.

Hope arrives with a connection to a Gastroenterologist who doesn't mess around. Another answered prayer! He runs the full battery of tests over the span of a couple of weeks, confirming that I have Crohn's Disease.

At first, I feel a sigh of relief in having an answer.

Then disheartening memories from growing up play in my mind, remembering how Crohn's impacted our whole family. The Perfectionist in my head says, "See? You really ARE flawed! Who's gonna want you now?! What kind of partner wants a life sentence with THIS?!"

I vow for different.

Slowly, I regain my energy.

I start Pilates and Yoga to strengthen my body. Oh, how good it feels to move my body, even when walking. It's as if I'm coming back to life! I dip my toe back into teaching, which I have missed immensely. I'm starting to build a relationship with my body and realize that even though I've felt what's going on in my body, I haven't always been able to interpret it.

As I learn more about energy work through my healer, I'm integrating it on my own. I recognize which foods, thoughts, or people give me energy and which drain it. I commit to changing that deadly concoction of perfectionism, people pleasing, and overachieving that causes my gut to shut down. Setting boundaries helps, though it's not easy for someone who is achievement oriented.

What I'm realizing is that with my fitness background, I've learned ABOUT my body, but I've never KNOWN my own body…or myself.

My career takes me on a new adventure from Nebraska to Virginia where I know no one!

Plunging into my work, I enjoy the challenge of growing the group fitness and wellness program on a college campus.

Thankfully I'm able to continue treating the Crohn's holistically., I find a Holistic Center, an Osteopath, and my healer in Nebraska and I continue working over the phone.

After living in the area for 4 years, I discover salsa dancing. Talk about feeling fully alive! I light up as it gives me an outlet and social life I haven't experienced while living here.

At the same time, I'm feeling stagnant at my job. I would love to help individuals similarly to the way how I've been helped, but I have no idea how to leave the security of my job as a single woman.

Things spiral quickly from the highest of highs to the lowest of lows.

It's 2014 and my body is struggling. With no reserves, my body shrinks quickly. EVERY aspect of my life has stress: physical, emotional, financial, social, environmental, and career. A healthy person would struggle under those circumstances, let alone someone with a chronic condition.

The weight of my worries are paralyzing. I'm afraid to go to my Specialist because I don't want to admit that I've stopped taking my meds; they became pricey and I wanted to trust that my body could heal on its own. The way I currently look makes me afraid to go to the ER, thinking I'll be misdiagnosed. At work, we're in the midst of an expansion, so I don't feel like I can take necessary time off. My family is in Nebraska while I'm here alone. Not to mention that during my last hospitalization, my doctor warned me that the next time I would need surgery. It all terrifies me to death!

As my body struggles to keep food down, my fears intensify. I eat breakfast and lunch, and by mid-afternoon, my gut is churning with double-over cramping. Vomiting is the only way I find relief. The first time I purge to alleviate the pain, I crumple into a ball on my cold, bathroom floor sobbing.

I'm confronted by well-meaning co-workers asking whether I am aware that I look like a skeleton. What they don't realize is that I'm not blind to my receding body. My well-practiced smile appears. Inside, I'm scared shitless!

I'm ashamed, feeling like the biggest fraud as I've built a reputation on campus for healthy body image and eating disorder education.

I fly to Nebraska for Thanksgiving, wondering if I'll pass out in the airport as I run from one terminal to the next. My once fit body that easily carried me now struggles for each step! It's hard to breathe and my heart feels like it will burst through my chest.

When my family sees my skeletal body and sunken facial features, they flip out.

I'm devastated, yet offended, when I discover they've had a secret family meeting regarding my own life. One uncle offers to fly me to Mayo Clinic for treatment. Of course, that's not what I want! The responsible little first grader inside wants to show them she's strong enough to do it herself while the adult woman realizes she can no longer manage on her own. Melting into my mom's shoulder, I tremble, deciding to give up my career to seek help.

A friend discovers an eating disorder treatment center in Denver. As emaciated as my body is, I recognize that I need experts to refeed my body along with doctors to address the Crohn's. Bingo! They treat eating disorders medically as well as psychologically. I send an email on Friday night, expecting no answer until Monday. Not only do I have a reply the next morning, I'm approved by insurance and have an admittance date within a week.

My parents drive to Virginia, arriving on my 40th birthday, to help me move back home. As I open the door, mom gasps, thinking "My God, we're too late!"

I pack for treatment.

Admittance is straightforward and we're all anxious to have help. My parents head home thinking, "We have hope!"

After my initial physical, I'm introduced to my treatment team when there's a knock on the door.

"We have to get her to the hospital stat!"

My doctor calls my parents and says, "You got her here just in time. She didn't have another day."

My 5'6" body barely weighs 90 pounds, yet my belly looks like a pregnant woman ready to give birth. X-rays reveal that my stomach has ballooned to 15 cm., mostly air, a life-threatening scenario if it bursts.

I receive the best of care, partnering in my own health, which is how every patient should be treated. I see three teams of specialists every day: gastroenterologists, surgeons, and internists. I also have a psychologist. For the first time, I trust the medical community with this team of doctors, confident that everyone has my best interest in mind.

After days of running the full battery of tests, often feeling like one step forward and two back, Dr. G. walks into my room and closes the door. She sits on my bed next to me, placing her hand on mine, and says, "If you were my sister, I would want what's best for you. What's best for you is surgery."
The floodgates of emotion I've been holding in stream down my cheeks as I try to smile through the disappointment. I feel that somehow I've failed, not being able to heal myself. I did all the "right" things. How could my body betray me like this?

I have gone from being the woman who loves being active and living fully to being strapped to a hospital bed, hooked to about every machine imaginable, fighting for her life.

How am I going to make it through surgery?!!!

When my surgeon comes into my room to go over plans, he asks if I have any concerns. I nervously chuckle, "A few." He pulls my chart from his pocket, reassuring me that all of my numbers are improving. I'll stay on the PICC (Peripherally Inserted Central Catheter) line, a thick-walled IV inserted into my bicep, dripping my 'bag of food' directly into my bloodstream. This ensures that nutrients go straight into my body to continue building it up.

A bit cocky, he shrugs his shoulders saying, "I've seen worse."

One of the problems is that the affected part of my small intestines is tucked behind other organs, meaning doctors haven't gotten clear images of what they're dealing with. They need to entirely pull my intestines out to examine every inch. They'll only remove something if absolutely necessary because cutting out anything creates more scar tissue, often making things worse down the road. However, they've also mentioned having to remove as much as 16 feet.

What does this mean for my future or quality of life? An ostomy bag? Disability?

I open my journal.

F-ing Crohn's!!! I HATE YOU!!! You've imprisoned me long enough!!! You've gotten in the way of so much of my LIFE. I've wasted time, energy, and money on YOU.

I've placed so much hope in being cured and truly believed that I could get rid of this f-ing illness. I'm angry at myself for letting this go too long. I was just so afraid to do it alone.

I pray, journal, and meditate, keeping my spirits up as I mentally prepare for surgery. For the first time in my life, I fully understand SURRENDER. I have absolutely NO control. All I can do is trust the outcome and figure out how to live with whatever that ends up being.

My doctors all assure me that 90% of my success comes from my attitude, pointing out how I've shown up through the ups and downs of this entire process. I have a

wall full of cards and daily messages of encouragement on Facebook reminding me that I'm well loved and supported.

The day of surgery arrives and I'm relieved to be the first of the day. I'm wheeled to the surgical unit and prepped. I watch the anesthesiologist put on my mask. As he counts down from "10" I know nothing after hearing "8".

"Holly. Breathe slower. Breathe into your belly." I hear a voice, but can't speak as I feel the pressure of my diaphragm pressing on the fresh wound inside of me. My instinct is to react, with a quick, shallow inhale that doesn't sting so badly. I wince, fighting tears. As I open my eyes, a nurse is on my right talking; Mom on my left patting my hand.

Surgery went smoothly, lasting about 90 minutes.

Eight strictures (areas of damaged tissue) were discovered; four were so constricted that air couldn't pass through. No wonder I couldn't hold food down! Surgeons opened those areas, kind of like plastic surgery to my intestines, so that there's no longer a traffic jam. No intestines were removed though. The good news is that what is healthy is "pristine", and the bad news is that what is sick has been that way for many years.

How freeing to finally release the guilt I'd held onto for not doing or being enough, and fully forgive myself! What I HAD been doing DID work, sustaining my body enough to get to the hospital. I now realize that there is no shame in needing medical intervention.

Dr. G. says that what I held in my body was "a responsibility of having to be OK all the time." Boy, was she right! Looking back, I realize how much of my life was spent trying not to be a burden by making sure things seemed alright to the outside world, even when they weren't. I put pressure on myself thinking that I had to do it all, including healing myself. It became too much.

When I look down at the battle wound on my belly, I'm reminded how I fought for my life and fought for ME, for years, not just those four months in the hospital. Knowing that I have that kind of courage and resilience within myself, I recognize that there is very little that I can't do. Trust, hope, help and surrender are always available. I've embraced being a warrior for my health and my life and so can you.

Co-Author
Holly Wade

Holly Wade is a Holistic Health and Life Coach. She helps mid-lifers who notice they can no longer get away with old habits to reclaim their health and create a vibrant future. Holly has always enjoyed movement and uses dance and yoga along with other modalities to help others connect to themselves. Now she is the owner of Holly Wade Wellness which helps people view themselves as whole so they can restore their health and reclaim their life.

She got into this line of business in 1996, after her hospitalization and in realizing that helping people take their health back is her calling. My favorite part of having an online coaching business is mobility, because it allows me to work with people from anywhere in the world.

I'm a, dancer, writer, and Holistic Health and Life Coach from Nebraska. The things I love most in life are salsa dancing, nature, and hanging out with my special people.

I've been a Fitness and Wellness professional for 25 years, and love helping people feel comfortable in their own skin.

The kinds of people I'd like to meet are ones who are passionate and courageous. That's important to me because it inspires me to be even more bold in how I live my life.

Holly is a regular contributor to We Are Beautiful Magazine and Kai Magazine. She is also a Master Trainer for the World GROOVE Movement. She is available for live speaking engagements or programs as well as 1:1 Coaching and thrives on the real life experience.
You can find her at www.hollywadewellness.com
Facebook Personal Page: https://www.facebook.com/holly.wade.35
Facebook Business Page: https://www.facebook.com/HollyWadeWellness/
Instagram: https://www.instagram.com/hollywwellness/
Twitter: https://twitter.com/HWWellness
LinkedIn: https://www.linkedin.com/in/holly-wade-wellness/

"

*I learned over time, not all questions
have answers.
They are what they are,
simply questions to evoke thinking and
therefore, many times they are rhetorical.
I learned to let go, to accept and not place
any expectations on what was,
what is and what will be.
This provides me with astounding peace,
a skill I am ever grateful to keep
in my toolbox of life."*

~PENELOPE HALL

The Naked Hustle
A Raw and Personal Story Of My fight for Freedom, Peace & Connection.

by Penelope Hall

Little did I know at such a tender age, that my life would be paved with the rawness of fiery lessons, a plethora of trials and judgements and a whirlwind of emotions capped with crucial experiences. I was left standing naked in front of my one mirror of life, staring at the vast and curious, or, you could say, fast and furious, depth of a life that truly was NOT meant to be owned by me. Yet, as I peacefully absorb my reflection after a myriad of lessons learned, I am much clearer as to how these experiences helped me evolve into the woman I am today.

#1. Security, Alignment & Congruency

As a child I was much loved and at a young age, I became independent in a positive way. Our life was filled with experiences from family travel to international school exchanges. People, culture and language always fascinated me and held my interest.

During my own life, pre-children, I was always up for a party, conversation, fun and socialising. The more people I met, the more experiences and the more I felt fulfilled. Yet something was missing. I continued this lifestyle until I could no more. I became someone else, I wasn't living my values, but I didn't know it at the time.

Today, I am a mum of two amazing daughters, Taite and Regan and they are my best friends. Our journey of breaking free from control has been a monumental team exercise. These two young people have grown perhaps more than others their own age. If any of us are searching for a definition of resilience, you would be amiss to look past my two incredibly strong little people whom I love immensely and share my life with.

Together with my beautiful children, slowly but surely as we have ventured on our path, we lost our security, our alignment and our congruency. Our life was tipped upside down when I changed the locks on my home to ward abuse off. Eventually

forced to sell my house and now, overwhelmed with physical injury and mental exhaustion, the next obliteration was to accept being in the line up for charity food. I now believed I was a failure. Any residual peace extinguished. My soul destroyed. Family court and coercion are a bitter platter of human degradation and humiliation.

I was in a place that wasn't on my "life plan". This thing we call Life is a continual growth-check and often on the very street we reside.

#2. The Hustler's Choice: Foundation Laying For The Dreamers

Why do we settle for something less than what we should be living? Often, we get so wrapped up in living a certain way, accepting certain things that we would not consider to be 'normal' that they eventually become part of our life to the point that we forget how abnormal they are. We do have a choice to recreate the magic we may have felt inside if we indeed had it before.

The truth is that we don't know what we don't know, so how do we recognise our lessons and become aware whether our dreams are drifting away from us or towards us? If we equate learning from our life experiences as not only the quintessential survival which carries us swiftly, safely and soundly to our future but also our monitor for feedback on how we are tracking, then we have discovered that our lessons from our life experiences and it is these life experiences that are the guiding lights illuminating the way forward to our future.

So, the sooner we learn that life experiences are this quintessential "feedback", the sooner we are on our path to greatness, or so I found during my own experiences.

The solid foundation that supported the very core of who I am in life had cracked a very long time ago. Whilst my beginning was all connected, my middle and end were vastly different from the life I had imagined for myself. When life challenges you at the deepest level of your being, whether it throws domestic violence and deep financial instability at you like it did me, or whether it pauses your life due to ill health or other struggles, you feel so removed from where you were heading in life and where you are meant to be. I had become resolute that the unfulfilled life I was feeling from the inside, was to be my life, always.

Transitioning from young person to adult, I often queried whether dreams really do come true? Can our fiction turn into reality? For me, it wasn't until I attended a 3-day immersion personal development conference that I realised I did have the choice to create the perfect life for myself and subsequently my two children. I decided that my dreams were worth becoming the reality I had always wanted. I began to own the word 'tenacious' and to unleash my inner fire. My new resolute was now concrete. Abuse was out the door and I no longer allowed it to define me.

Every time I recall my firm life-changing resolution, my WHY appears over and over. If you are anything like me however, once you have discovered the answer to one question, it is instantaneously replaced by another. So how do we find the answers to them?

I learned over time, not all questions have answers. They are what they are, simple questions to evoke thinking and therefore, many times they are rhetorical. I learned to let go, to accept and not place any expectations on what was, what is and what will be. This provides me with astounding peace, a skill I am ever grateful to keep in my toolbox of life.

The aforementioned conference saved my life. It triggered something powerful inside, something so incredibly forceful that, at the time, I just had to go with it. Have you ever experienced rock bottom where the only way is up?

#3. Unanswered Hustle: My Why becomes Clear

When I think of the word hustle, I think of dancing and movement. A shake of the body, a rattle of sass, a damn fine piece of person who is damn fine in her entirety, ready to shake, rattle and hustle along, ignited by the fire of determination and resilience, hustle style.

The Hustle in Motion. (by Penelope Hall)

She loves to dance, for the life she was given, and dance she did.
Why did the music stop? For the dance she did, is no more.
In the riches of faith, the dust of love, she rode well.
In the squalor of dark, losing the way, she rode no more.
It was the sign of peace she grew to mourn.
Her longing for home, her whispers and cries.
Life's misunderstanding dare to beat.
Bring The Hustle to her, for she adorns it well.
The Hustle of Freedom, no room to dwell.
Her own Hustle, it's hers to keep.

#4. Rebellious Hustle or Cornered Complacency

I much prefer the dance moves of a spicy hustle, the rhythmic tunes and sways of moving my way, and dancing to the beat of my own melody. I was never complacent, although it may have appeared so. Pretending to be someone I was not, became so much a part of who I was, but it never felt right.

I had never stopped believing I could have it all and that tomorrow's dreams will come true. For I am her, I am that girl. My beliefs did change during this time of "dreaming" because I was told over and over how worthless I was.

Often the question is asked, "why didn't you leave sooner?" For me, it's a complex answer to a very serious question. Mental exhaustion and belief you are a failure and truly worthless embeds into your mindsets' psyche. Once you place children in the mix of abuse and entangled emotions, life is hard, torrent and about as raw and as naked as it gets. Living a life classified as abuse seems to define us in a judgemental human society. Unfairly, but it does.

So, why didn't I leave sooner? Why did I keep attracting the same controlling relationships into my life? My first lesson once I was aware, was to get the hell out of there and to change who I attract into my life. By now the trail was littered with upturned friendships and those controlling ex-lovers.

Often I would ask myself if I was inviting rebellion into my life and if so, was it due to the possibility that I was settling and becoming complacent? It was the realization that perhaps I was becoming complacent which is not a behaviour I wanted to accept that resulted in me taking a stand and changing the locks on my home.

I was terrified but determined.

#5. Judgement, Transition, Freedom & Truth: Time to create peaceful Hustlers' music.

It was time. I wanted more and I was going to get it.

I had to fight hard for my freedom.

I slowly but surely transitioned from rock bottom to living with purpose. Before any noticeable transformation, however, I had to investigate who I was. I urged myself to find the right hustling shoes to dance in the life I desperately sought.

That very decision to change the locks on my home sent me straight to what I would imagine hell on earth to be. I was ridiculed, defamed, spat on, laughed at, ostracised, abused mentally, physically, verbally and emotionally. I was judged, slammed, labelled and targeted. I was shattered.

Interestingly, I have experienced more than one abusive relationship. The lessons for such attractions have been catastrophically detrimental and a harsh reality. I kept going back for more. I believed they "were my people" until I realised they never were.

During one relationship whilst living overseas, I was told to by someone whom I thought loved me to "get the fu*k out of here, this country doesn't need you", which was then followed by a glass thrown full throttle at my face and head. At other times our home contents were thrown, turned upside down or broken. This was abuse. I just did not recognise it. My child was hit on the head and her bike helmet cracked, this was abuse and again, but at the time I did not recognise it as a sign of narcissism and control. A further incident of stabbing my daughter's favourite doll with a carving knife in front of her then intentionally throwing a hard toy at her head which penetrated the wall behind her was obviously abuse again, still, I did not recognise it.

A further person standing over me, demanding I find an extra lover for a seriously explicit sexual encounter. Yes, ALL abuse. I had no black eyes, yet I have been abused.

As time went on, and my eyes were now fully open, I sought to find my true life values and to live by them. FREEDOM & CONNECTION are the shining lights. Freedom provides me with the "MORE" I had been searching for and CONNECTION provides me with friendships, love and good times.

Forgive my sidestepping for a moment, but as I look back over that time in my life, it is a haze. I guess it's because I am not proud of the fact that I allowed myself to be treated the way I was, allowed my children to be treated the way they were and all because I did not realise any of this was domestic abuse. I was also so scared. I did know that this behaviour was wrong. The truth is that at the time, it was easier to remain in the mess, much because my own dream of "a family unit" had not disappeared from my mind. I grew up with divorced parents and did not want this for myself. Finally, I broke. I had to get out and make a totally new life for myself and my girls. Like a puzzle, I gathered the pieces of my life, looked at myself in the mirror, naked and raw and asked some really tough questions through teary eyes. I began to create small changes by understanding and initiating choices. I began to wake up!

So, perhaps you are experiencing life as an abused woman right now. You may have set a brave goal for your own freedom path or have taken one more violent encounter too many. Life IS worth fighting for. Your VALUES are worth LIVING and your heart is worth the softness of pure and unconditional love. Liking YOU is a good first step, loving YOU naturally follows...in time.

#6. Before heading home let us do "BRAVE".

Writing this chapter brought further change. I thought I had dealt with everything and I had nothing left over from that time I needed to work on. This surprised me. Changing those locks in 2013 plus two car accidents in the same year forced me to pull on every human survival resource to self-preserve. Yes, discovered I have SUPERPOWERS and so do you however, it takes time to move through emotional disconnect, guilt and sadness. If I can share one thing with you, it is to be patient and kind to yourself and never, ever assume that your issues will not reappear from time to time. Life presents us with moments, feelings and memories which can trigger old wounds and re-open them and this book had done just that for me. This is not necessarily a bad thing. I believe the only reason a wound will reopen under some sort of emotional duress is because it had not fully healed in the first place.

In the midst of writing this chapter, I allowed myself to further change my life. I stood up and said
" You can do this, it's OK". Spending what seems like thousands of hours immersed in personal growth books and events, where I was encouraged to challenge myself by breaking boards with my bare hands, arrow snapping with my neck and fire walking, have all paid off. While writing this chapter and reliving so many challenging times, I submerged myself in those feelings of achievement and I finally crushed my fears and limiting beliefs about who I am, to almost be rebirthed. I now know where I'm heading because I have forgiven myself, accepted the lessons and let go of the past hurts. Those wounds will finally heal uninterrupted.

If you could take a sneak peek at your life 5 years from now, what would you see? Are you at peace, happy, fulfilled, living with passion & knowing your purpose? Would you be able to forgive all that has transpired in your life and accept the lessons?

Once you forgive the past and accept the lessons, it's time to implement new habits, make lasting changes and choose to free yourself. I now OWN my life. If you too chose to OWN your life, conquer stress, anxiety and lack of self-worth, keep moving forward. I found and firmly placed passion and purpose back into my daily routines via some of the most useful and result-based life skills ever to draw upon. My beautiful children are thriving and happy (it's been a long road), PLUS, I birthed my personal development business called Penelope Jay which includes our online e-Academy called Mindset Mindfit, regular live events and a podcast channel. Adversity certainly changes lives. It did mine.

Being BRAVE for me means dealing with some of the questions that were pending in my internal inbox. Acceptance is part of the healing process. I taught myself to accept that some of the questions will never be answered, and this is OK.

This chapter has been a pivotal BRAVE moment because it shook me up, helped me to forgive and understand me on a deeper level and I really like what I have found. If your life, is anything like mine and you have been living in a defensive, angry manner, it's time to let all that go. Let go of the blame. Take full responsibility for your own actions and make better choices for yourself and your family. We are better parents when we first give to ourselves and learn to sometimes say 'no'. Try it, not only does it feel good, it will change your life!'

B **Be you**
R keep it **Real**
A share lots of **Adventure**
V live by your life **Values**
E re-engage life's **Energy**

The second chance I had hoped for and worked so hard towards arrived. I am on MY own stage of love, understanding, support, rapport and inclusion. No judgements, no critics. My 'Teenage' event was certainly a life-changing 360-degree pivot for them and for me. Beginning conversations with young beautiful teenagers and their parents/carers and hearing their responses to some confronting questions was exhilarating! My daughters were my co-hosts and yes, they are pretty amazing. I've been brought back to life and it feels out of this world! To the people who have stood by my side, the ones who did not judge or turn their backs, I say thank you. Notably to my mum, my children and a handful of friends. I love you, x.

#7. Finally, my own Hustle comes to Life. The Hustle of all Hustles.

As long as I can recall, I searched for more in life. Since climbing over life's obstacles, I stand firmly and proudly on my podium of life, I am Number One. I am my More. Have you ever felt yourself, time after time tripping and falling into a dimness of your own light? At the same time though, never quite believing this is all life is? Well, don't give up. Keep believing!

I have now secured more than enough answers for my "why" to be defined. I like

who I am. I say 'no' to control and I am not a victim of life in any way, not intellectually, emotionally or physically. I no longer require validation, I now utterly provide this to myself. I am my own stamp of approval!

I have found my Home-base, my inner peace, the comfort, purpose and validation we are ALL looking for, and the journey of my discovery has uncovered the following lessons/treasures:

*Let go of hurts quickly.
*Do not set expectations or conditions.
*Be gentle on yourself and stop being your own worst critic.
*Learn forgiveness as this is an act of service for you.
*Love passionately.
*Change means growth.
*Read, as knowledge encourages self-growth.
*Share yourself with the right people.
*DO NOT JUDGE yourself or others.

Mostly, I think one of the biggest treasures is the ACCEPTANCE of who we are and where we have been. I firmly believe nobody is forever broken. For me, time and self-development education paved the way to my freedom. I am now capable with little or no emotional collapse to navigate swiftly through just about any situation.

I would like to leave you with one final thought:
We are the dancer, the hustler, the lover all rolled into one. You too own your own SuperPowers and you are unequivocally your life's 'More'.

Co-Author
Penelope Hall

Penelope Hall is a naturally creative, caring, self-driven and a tenacious woman who loves to travel, thrives on her main purpose as a mother and has lived in over 5 continents throughout the world.

Penelope started her own journey in personal development the moment she changed the locks to her home in 2013, to once and for all lock domestic violence out of her life, and subsequently her children's.

She has been in business for 16 years, mainly in the travel industry, has worked in the corporate world for many years both in Australia and overseas while gaining qualifications in Psychology & Counselling, NLP, Masterminding, Speaking and Life Coaching.

"Human behaviour, cultural uniqueness and language coupled with an innate ability to look outside the square and to avoid making a judgement has been my passion if not my obsession.

Being impacted by domestic family abuse wasn't enough for me to remain in the shadows. I accepted my past, fell in love with my present and know the future is going to be one hell of a ride. I am one strong woman, mum, friend, daughter, lover and business leader."

Youtube: https://www.youtube.com/channel/UCGd2xWtgJocf-gwObWAYig
LinkedIn: https://au.linkedin.com/in/penelopejaylifecoach
Instagram: https://www.instagram.com/penelopejaylifecoach/
Facebook: https://www.facebook.com/penelopejaylifecoach/

Dance In The Fire of Life!

298

"

My life has given me ample opportunity to believe, without a shadow of a doubt that we are all eternal and we have been in this physical plane many times before, via reincarnation. For me, there is no longer a question, as there was in the past, about the reality of reincarnation. Instead, there is a firm belief that I know too much about life, instinctively, to have not experienced it many times before."

~Adrienne Gaha-Morris

From Darkness Into Light

by Adrienne Gaha-Morris

The title of this book, Dance In The Fire Of Life resonates strongly with me because that is exactly what I had done during the period of my illness. I learned to dance in this fire that life had thrown me into and I came out the other side! It is possible to come out the other side after staring death in the face. I am proof of this!

As a young girl, I went through a frightening illness. Frightening for me, my parents, my family, my friends and the medical people looking after me. I will share this part of my life with you shortly but what I would like to point out is that this illness and my ongoing challenges within it, awakened in me the realisation that WE as human beings have a lot more control on what happens to us, in the first instance, and also control the impacts of what happens to us moving forward. We are capable of moving out of the darkness of our challenges and into the light.

I believe that when it comes down to it, all people are good, and I believe this from the centre of my being. Humanity, however, has been misguided over the millennia, which has left many profound scars upon the human psyche. We walk around this planet not believing in ourselves, in our innate capability to change anything in our life that does not suit us. We for the most part, never allow ourselves to discover our own power and to stand proudly and powerfully within it in order to heal our lives. Now is the time to heal and this is why I have outlined, towards the end of my chapter, practical ways to leave behind all the turmoil, heal our physical body and in turn, heal emotionally.

As a result of staring death in the face, my biggest motivation, in much of what I do, is to share my experience in the hope that people who are feeling like there is no hope, who feel overpowered by their struggles, become inspired by my journey and begin to have a spark of hope that then expands and explodes into an all-knowing confidence that anything is possible!
Allow me to explain

During the Christmas holidays of 1995, when I was 12 years of age, I became sick. I was diagnosed, in early 1996, with an inoperable condition in my brain, and my future was put in jeopardy. I spent my teenage years in and out of hospitals, where I had a number of touches and go experiences, and the medical consensus was that I wouldn't pull through.

I was barely a teenager when I had a shunt put into my skull, running down to my abdomen (most absorbent part of the human body). I experienced three noted bleeds in my brain, but it was suspected I had more minor ones. I had a stroke, resulting in complete paralysis of my right side, for about 4 hours, and the gradual change from right to left-hand dominance. I had notable memory problems and a couple of experiences of organic brain syndrome.

When I was 19 I became critically ill. At that point, the doctors decided to use a massive dose of experimental Radiotherapy, on my brain, that eventually fixed my neurological condition.

Throughout my illness, I always knew it wouldn't be the end of me, as so many people thought. Yes, even at the tender age of twelve, I was determined to get through this. This tenacity and bloody-mindedness saw me trudging through the darkness of my teenage years and into a life no one thought I would have. To add to the surprise of what I was capable of, I also had three children, which was a shock to most people when I fell pregnant, and they were then born through another process of discovery.

My illness and the threat of death looming upon me gifted me the belief that wherever we go in life, we should be growing and moving, not stagnating; this is one lesson my illness taught me and to this day, I live by. What I have discovered since, is that in order to grow, move forward and ensure we don't stagnate, we need to discover within us, courage. As a teenage girl, I discovered that I had the courage of a lioness!

Throughout my pregnancies and births, I saw what I was capable of within myself, and I made significant discoveries about how I felt I should be treated as a woman, around my births. When I was having my first child I was obediently listening to my obstetrician and letting him dictate how things progressed around my pregnancy. The experience, of birthing my second child, in a private hospital, was a complete eye-opener for me. I had sought out, when pregnant, the most alternative obstetrician in my area, so I would have the best chance of having a successful VBAC. Due to hospital policy and the fact that it took a long time (51 hours) to birth her, I ended up strapped to a bed with a monitor and then a suction cap extraction of my babe. By the time I'd had my third child, through all the research and inner knowing I'd tapped into, I felt confident to birth my baby without medical assistance and at home. Long births were on the cards for me (my third was 36 hours) because I had misaligned hips relating to my stroke and not walking correctly on my right leg for so long. Being given the time I need, however, results in a baby coming out! During my last birth, she dropped down in my pelvis very quickly and then was out of my body two pushes later.

That very same tenacity that saw me get through my illness in my teenage years was still there and I drew upon it when I knew I needed to speak up and express my needs when it came to birthing my children. This gave me such an understanding that, as a woman, I must stand up and demand what is to be with myself. I want and to live my life the way I want without being dictated to by anyone, but also with the grace to know when I am wrong.

Having experienced ill health and the risk of life not continuing for such a long time, gave me the opportunity to think about life, and our existence, in a totally different way to the way I would have. I understood the deeper meaning of our existence, which I believe I would not have, had I not experienced health issues.

My life has given me ample opportunity to believe, without a shadow of a doubt that we are all eternal and we have been in this physical plane many times before, via reincarnation. For me, there is no longer a question, as there was in the past, about the reality of reincarnation. Instead, there is a firm belief that I know too much about life, instinctively, to have not experienced it many times before. I have also had a few past life experiences with lightworkers, that make so much sense about who I am. Recently I was told that I have had past life experiences in the Bedouin tribe, in North Africa. This makes so much sense to me because I never felt I belonged in Australia. Also, when I went over to Senegal (NW Africa) in 2016, I felt like I was returning home, yet I couldn't explain it at the time before I had this experience. Everything felt so familiar including their way of life. It was all so natural to me and yet I had never been there, in this lifetime before.

There is so much more available to us when we are living life from a spiritual perspective. We are all one, eternal and from one source, so fighting and killing others seems very perplexing to me.

When you have been through as much in the way of life challenges, as I have, and particularly for as long as I have, you start to come to certain ways of understanding the world around you that may be different to the way other's experience life and understand life. For this reason, I would like to share some of my life insights with you.

I see the need for the human species to let go of ego, and more specifically to let go of the fear that is attached to the ego. Fear plays a major part in clouding our judgement and influencing unfounded behaviour in people, start arguments, break up families and can be responsible for starting wars, all over the world. As I have said before if you can entertain for a minute, the thought that we are all eternal, then you too will recognise we have nothing to fear and ego has no place; it just breeds fear. At present, there is so much hatred in the world, which stems from fear and ego. Imagine if there was no hatred, fear and violence in the world? Imagine what the world would be like If we all loved and cared for everyone? If we all helped each other out when we were feeling lost? What a different world this would be!

It is simply a normal part of life that we will all, at one time or another in our lives, find ourselves in difficult situations. It is important to deal with all negativity and challenges in life, completely, so that you clear them and they don't continue to impact on our lives. It may be simple to you, but one thing I find invaluable, in dealing with difficult situations, is the ability to take a step back, even if it is just for a moment and reflect on what is going on within that situation, before making a public response. The times in my life, when I have done this, it has always worked out better in the long run. Another thing I do, when I know I'm heading towards a difficult situation or a conflict of some sort, is that I ask upstairs/god/higher-self etc. to ensure it all works out for the highest good of all concerned; and that never lets me down. It can be that simple!

My experiences, with having had a stroke and mental disturbances and all the challenges that came with them, have convinced me that they were 'given' to me or perhaps 'chosen' by me, so that I can understand, from a very deep standpoint what it is like to go through such experiences. Even today, I feel a deep knowing that as horrid and as frightening as these episodes were and all the other challenges that were borne from them, on some level, I had to experience what I experienced. This illness, together with the multiple challenges that came with it, changed the trajectory of my life. I became a much more empathetic person, who could really feel what other people were going through with their own challenges, physical or emotional. Ego is something I recognise instantly within myself and within others and I am able to control it and ensure it does not cause any harm. Challenges both physical and emotional, therefore, can help us on many different levels and in an authentic way.

Because of my illness, I am now beginning to help others going through something similar. This is interesting because as a result of many years of trying to help myself, I have created a program, based on my own experiences in healing from a stroke, particularly healing in the long term and nothing makes me happier than knowing

I will be helping people all due to the fact that I found the key to healing myself and am now able to share that with others.

When I first had the stroke, as a young teen, I was much more interested in partying than performing repetitive exercises to regain ability down my stroke side. I have renewed hope, since starting my program; a hope that I had lost previously. The ecstatic joy, that overcame my body, as I implemented an exercise that meant I was walking from my leg and not my hip, was profound. For people who have not experienced such debilitation, they cannot even imagine the sheer joy that is felt in even these perceived small wins.

When you experience a stroke, your body forgets how to function and afterwards, you need to relearn how to do many of the things we take for granted. I have had some amazing shifts with this program and slowly, but surely, I have seen the side of my body, which has been affected by the stroke, WAKE UP. Nothing will give me more pleasure and satisfaction than to help a fellow stroke inflicted person experience healing through my extensive experience and program.

As I began to heal myself, I was awakened to the discovery that through physical healing comes emotional healing and it changes your entire outlook on life. Confidence levels rise and hope enters your life once again! There simply is no better feeling than living fully and purposefully once again. I am more than happy to share with you more information on this program. My contact details can be found at the end of this chapter.

I never realised before my illness started, the profound effect my family and other loved ones, had on me. At least in part, their wishes for recovery, that I intuitively felt around me, are one thing that brought me through the darkness into the light. Another way this love was shown to me was through my mother. She possesses, within her, the ability to love unconditionally and fully. When I was in the hospital, in my teenage years, she was always by my side. Whether that be on a recliner chair or foldaway bed, she was always with me at night. Throughout the day, when she popped out for a breather, it was always ensured that someone was by my side. This, I believe, was one of the things that saw me through; unconditional love. My mother was like a mirror of love that I too have made sure I carried into my mothering and projected on to my own children so they to grow up to be well-adjusted adults who know they are loved and that they are capable of doing and being whoever they want to be.

Another suggestion I would like to make that may be of benefit to you or a loved one is meditation. The meditation I use, after searching long and hard for one that resonated with me, primarily focuses on tones. This has had a profound effect on me

recently. Have you ever heard a sound, that was coming from inside of you, maybe after a loud music event or concert? I used to think this was a bad thing, but how I was wrong! If you focus on the tones, that comes from inside you, it's like opening a doorway to the divine (source, god, higher-self etc.). I used to only be able to hear them when it was very quiet (like at night time) but once you get the hang of it, you can hear these tones whenever you please. I find them very calming, centring and grounding.

I have been exercising daily meditation for about a year. The differences I've seen in my life has been profound, to say the least... Meditation centres me, grounds me and has given me access to a peace that I wasn't aware of before I started. After a session of meditating, I feel a rejuvenation of my being, like a nap but better. I feel I have been conversing with the Divine and doing what's necessary to enliven myself.

I'd like to finish this chapter by posing a few questions for you to think over:
- Where do you see your existence going, in this life?
- Did you set goals for your life and if so are you on your way to achieving what you would like in your life? If not, can you think about some goals you would like to set now?
- Can you see yourself, if you don't already, setting aside up to half an hour a day for self-development (meditation, reflection, practical analysis of your life)?
- Can you relate to people and see things from their point of view?

So, after pondering on these questions, your answers will then help you to discover and understand so much more about yourself. I would suggest putting these questions out, during your meditations, and allow your higher consciousness to dive deep into the wonders of your life. In doing so, I know you will make some meaningful discoveries to enhance the enjoyment and understanding of your own existence. By dancing in the fire of life, I have become resilient and have encountered all of life's obstacles with strength and a deep sense of understanding and empathy of the struggles of others.

Everyone has a story to tell. I am not the only one. I do urge people, particularly women, to put their fears and shame to one side and share their stories with other women because this is the best way to help and give hope to another woman.

If my story stirs the fighter spirit in just one woman and encourages her to believe she is able to impact upon even the grimmest of situations in her life in a positive way, then I have completed my purpose here.

Let's join hands and together, leave the darkness behind and dance into the LIGHT!

Co-Author
Adrienne Gaha-Morris

Adrienne Gaha-Morris and is a mother of 3 (12,9 and 6) who has had a rather colourful life and now lunges forward to shift people's views and influence them to see the world in different ways. Adrienne has a passion for enlivening and connecting the spirits of all she works with.

Adrienne is qualified in massage, spiritual healing and in selenite swords and is proud to state teat she is also the Ambassador for a worldwide organization, Heaven Town. Adrienne is always keen to answer peoples' queries and make a point of looking at their problem from all angles as she makes a point of always collaborating on her client's dreams!

"I have an urge, from deep within me, to see a tangible shift on this physical plane of existence. On a micro level, I look for things that bring about a shift in people's worlds. Whether that be a smile on the street, or introducing a new view to someone I'm speaking with. From little things, big things grow."

Facebook: facebook.com/agahamorris
LinkedIn: linkedin.com/agahamorris

"

Networking is never about you, it's always about the person you would like to connect with". People always love to talk about themselves, make sure you take a genuine interest in listening to people, don't fake it, people will read you like an open book."

~Kristina V Herreen

Become The Diva You Were Born To Be
Communicate and Connect Genuinely
With Integrity and Respect
by Kristina V Herreen

When I was a little girl I was always in trouble. I spent my first year of life in hospital as I was born with heart disease and when finally home, I was a handful for everyone around me.

I can still remember being that outgoing and a no fear kind of kid, chatting and interacting with just about anyone, stranger or not. I remember Mum running after me, as I happily rode to the shops just in my underwear on the back of a pushbike, enjoying a free ride to the shops. I was just a very happy and jolly little girl who found everyone friendly, enjoyed being the centre of attention and making people laugh. I had a lovely childhood with great siblings, horses, animals and friends around me all the time. The word shy was just not in my vocabulary….I had no idea what that word even meant!

School was great but I was not very academic so I left home at 14, lived on a farm, went to an agriculture school, eventually studied at university and became a counsellor and marketer, got into health and fitness and lots more.

I learned that I was the type that wanted to be around people and help people. To be at a desk was just not my thing. I really was just constantly looking for that right fit for me and it felt like it was alluding me. I understood that I would not be happy until I did find that "spot" in life that was meant for me.

During that same period I gained a lot of weight and lost a lot of self-esteem and that outgoing and fun girl was just no more. She seemed to disappear into thin air! So what happened?

Now that natural feeling that I would find that "me spot" in life started to become a distant dream and I started to listen to what others wanted for me, instead of lis-

tening to what I wanted for myself and my happiness. That once clear, strong need to work with and help others were now starting to become a grey area and I was losing grip of my previous clear future. I started to have self-doubt and with that, my self-belief was on the rocks as well.

It would take years before I was able to have the courage to rediscover and move back into that "me spot" after all, years of self-destruction and pain had made that a distant memory.

Life is life and your life is all about your circumstances. Yes, we can change a lot but we still have our own personality and own conditioning and that will shape us further into who we are and who we become. I did have a great childhood but my parents and my family had their conditioning and they brought all of that into our family, the good and the not so good, as it always is with everything. I became very body conscious and very aware of my looks and weight which affected my way of acting and suppressing around people. That meant that I was going from this happy unlimited young girl, with big dreams and no limitations, to a very insecure woman with lots of judgement on herself and a growing pile of limitations.

I can remember being 8 years old. I was with a friend and we decided we wanted to become movie stars…as we all do…lol…We were very excited about our decision and we told my Mum and the first thing she said, very nicely, was "That's nice girls, but that will not happen, only rich people become movie stars". Instantly, we just lost that excitement on the spot and that was it, we never again talked about becoming movie stars or dreamt big again!

I was raised to believe there is a certain order to life: get a government job, get married, have kids, get a dog and then live happily ever after…but I just had that inner calling telling me that I was here for something big, something that will help others, something that will make me special…so against all the odds, I have never stopped looking for that right vehicle to become that special person that I knew I could become.

Travelling alone around the world for over thirteen years with just a backpack, confirmed my personal philosophy that if I travel by myself I also have to look after myself and interact with people, I cannot rely on anyone else – "for it to be, it's up to me". Those years travelling around the world taught me to be grateful and to be ME, just me and to be genuine and true. People are not stupid, you try to be fake or put on a fake story, people will read you like an open book and you'll be toast…lol…

Why am I telling you all this? What has all this got to do with my part of this great book?. Everyone has a story and everyone's story is unique. Throughout my travels, I discovered that no matter where in the world I was, there was one very strong common theme amongst women. We like to look after others more than ourselves and that's probably the motherly instinct in us all, but the truth is that we need to look after ourselves before we can help or even assist others, that is true in life and in business.

When I came to Australia I become a wife and a mother in a city I had never been to before. A city that was and still is in many ways, very conservative. I did find it very hard to connect with people socially. Suddenly, I had an accent that was odd to many people so starting a business was like hitting my head against the wall most of the time.

That wasn't because of others judging me, but because I judged myself more than anyone else, something women seem to do more than men, unfortunately. It wasn't until I started to tackle my fears and got out there showing myself to others for who I really was and what I stood for, that things started to change. Life really changed for the better when I was at a business seminar one day and had the opportunity to speak to the speaker. He said to me; "You have an accent and you are a from a non-Australian origin, turn that into your advantage, what you have people would love to have".

That really made me think and from that day those words have always been on my mind and serve as a reminder when my confidence plummets or even when I feel like I owe this world…. these are strong words and they are one of the reasons I like to share my story and journey in this fantastic book with you. I now believe, understand and accept that I do have value, even though at times I may appear different to many, my differences are what attract others to me.

I meet so many women from all over the world, from different cultures and backgrounds, different religious beliefs and so on but we all have something in common. We all started somewhere….. we all are unique even if that uniqueness comes from where we were born, where we grew up, what we believe, not believe or just our skin colour or age. We are who we are and we should be proud of that and it will take you a lot closer to where you want to go.

So, you are unique, but how is that going to help you connect to others in a way that you really want? Be yourself and be genuine, the saying I love is "I'm not perfect but at least I am true"' . Be true to yourself and you will be true to others.

You may have heard this before, but heed my advice anyway; people will understand you and any business offering you may have if they like and trust you. That is so true and let me rewind a bit, "we all have a story"…."we are all unique…" Yes, and that is the same for the person you like to connect with as well, they have a story to tell…they are unique as well……right? To become an excellent Networker the golden rule is always this:

> "Networking is never about you, it's always about the person you would like to connect with". People always love to talk about themselves, make sure you take a genuine interest in listening to people, don't fake it, people will read you like an open book.
> ~ Kristina V Herreen

Getting back to us women, we are so much stronger than we think. Have a good look at yourself and start noticing the things that you are good at, and all that you have achieved. Give yourself a pat on the back and acknowledge your life as a great journey of achievements.

I acknowledge my parents for their love and support in raising and influencing me.e. My father taught me how to be a nice person and how to connect with others in a very friendly way. My mother encouraged me to take risks and do what I wanted to do.

I used my Dad's advice many times in situations where I had to connect with people and even when they put up a wall full of contradictions and judgments, I just knew that my father's advice was correct; I had to be very patient, listen and learn from that person and find out his/her story. Doing that, and again coming from a perspective of genuineness, it would always work out and I would eventually have that genuine connection with that person.

One of my greatest learnings came from the following experience; I asked to have a coffee with a famous politician once and during our time together, I asked him to tell me his story. At first, he was very defensive and asked me what business I was in and made sure I knew that he wasn't interested in my 'business'. I ensured him that I was not wanting to connect with him about business or what he can do for me. I told him that I simply wanted to hear his story, nothing else and that this was all about him. This man was someone who managed to get on the front page of the city magazine and even though he was not born Australian, he was respected and successful. I wanted to meet this man, learn from him and create a good connection. He agreed to a coffee and he gave me 20 minutes of his time. I prepared three questions that I wanted to ask him. When I got to his office he was still very defensive but after a few minutes the situation improved and he started to tell me his story. It was a great story and as I listened, asked him the three questions that would teach me something about his journey. We had a very relaxed conversation where he did most of the talking, just as I had hoped.

The twenty minutes passed quickly and as I was leaving, out of nowhere he asked: "Can I have your card, Kris?" Remember this meeting was not about me so I never offered any of my business cards or anything having to do with me to him. If I did, my integrity and being genuine would just have gone out the window…right?

My answer was "No, I prefer not to give you my card because I came here to find out about you". He was somewhat amused at my answer and after a friendly discussion, I had to give in and hand my business card to him. He placed my card in a huge business card holder and told me he would let me know of any events that may suit me. I definitely thought that I would be lost in his "card world" forever and he would have forgotten me by the morning.

I got back to my office and I thought that my connection with this man would be just momentary. How wrong was I!!!! A few days later l I started to get invitations to quality events from him. Every time I went to an event where he was present he came up to me, hugged me like I was a long lost friend, took me by the hand, walked around the entire room with me introducing me to all kinds of people, edified me to the moon and back! This is what can happen when you know how to connect and respect people, it really isn't that difficult.

I really began to understand the importance of listening to people. Everyone (including yourself) loves to talk about themselves and be listened to. I really understood the power of listening to and respecting people's stories, whoever they are and wherever they are. Find your person of interest, one by one. Sit down, buy them a coffee/tea, have no expectations, be genuine and you will have your network growing, like mushrooms, in no time.

Becoming a 'Networking Diva' and connecting people was not that natural for me to start with but after learning so much from the Chinese community, (me being a genuine "student"), taking on board constructive criticism as well as mingling with people from all backgrounds, networking and connecting face to face and online, is

just so natural for me. Who would have ever thought I would become the Networking Diva!!!

Networking advice:

Connecting face-to-face today is so underestimated as most people like to believe that the wonderful world of the web is the only way to go. I like to say that the web is fantastic but we all get to a stage where we need to make a connection face-to-face, and if we only make connections online, we and our businesses will be pretty much toast.

Connecting online is also this thing that most people think is just emails we send out to our database but we have to connect with people personally online as well, and that is **Attraction Marketing**, a skill whereby you have people come to you instead of you running after people. It's all about going back to basics and making it a good balance between the face-to-face connections and the online connections. Everything can be taught, don't worry. I used to be so scared to talk to new people. At University I would sit in my room for hours before I built up the courage to mingle with the rest of the students on that floor. My face became red like a tomato as soon as I talked or even looked at people, especially the opposite sex. You need to go outside of your comfort zone to move forward, and that's what I did. Little did I know at the time, but lots would I learn.

To be a part of this amazing book, *Dance in The Fire Of Life*, is an awesome way to connect with likeminded and extraordinary women, to encourage and inspire women who read our stories to pick up their game, use their talents and strengths and recognise that we all have stories that have shaped us into the person we are today. Let's unite and find the right way to reach our dreams and goals together! I still have a big vision in life, I know I will go to greatness -not in an egotistical way- but in a way where I believe we all have the ability to reach our true potential and I am on my journey to do just that! Part of my potential is to help and support women around the world to reach their potential and if we can help ourselves to help others, I believe we are all on the right track to achieving all that we want and need. Women can definitely make this world a better place and we can do it by finding the right connections, reaching the people we need to help us make that change. Whatever your dream of change is, YOU can do it. Never stop believing that!

The power of Networking is and will always be the same. "*Your Network is your Net Worth*", and we just need to build and build on that and its power will increase. Connect with others, particularly other women, help and accept help from others as well. That is the power of collaboration which is born out of the power of Networking.

What is your story? What do you have to tell others that will inspire or help other women?

This Book is a fantastic way to express our stories, visions and passions. This is a vehicle to inspiration so I thank you, Vicki Gotsis Ceraso, for offering me the opportunity to play my part in this book. I will be forever grateful.

Happy Networking
Kristina V Herreen
The Networking Diva

Co-Author
Kristina V Herreen

Growing up in a Swedish country town and with horses as her absolute passion, communicating with people was not something Kristina's was really very interested in. Therefore, the decision to start travelling was not one made lightly, however, it ended up being life-changing and the shy little girl started to shine.

With a professional background in counselling, personal training and weight consultancy, Kristina now loves to connect with people from all corners of the world, discover different cultures and different backgrounds.

The shy little girl who was lacking self-esteem is now known as the Networking Diva in Australia, and has become a sought after Networking expert who passionately teaches other businesswomen to do the same.

Facebook: The Networking Diva (FB page)
LinkedIn: Kristina V Herreen (LinkedIn)

"

My dream is that each person will, in turn, inspire the next person they touch to be aware of how we are each creating ripple effects to enable people to become more conscious of how their behaviour affects each person in that moment. It is this spark that lights up my soul!"

~Louise Keramaris

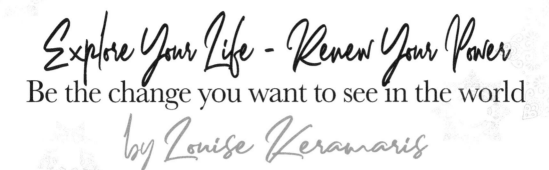

Explore Your Life - Renew Your Power
Be the change you want to see in the world
by Louise Keramaris

I felt very humbled to be selected to co-author and share a message – a universal message of hope to reach women all over the globe with the intention of stirring their hearts and souls.

It was quite an emotional moment – I was overwhelmed with joy and a wave of gratitude overcame me as I knew in my heart that this was something I felt compelled to do. I was so engaged with Vicki Gotsis Ceraso because I could relate to her Greek story and soul humour. I saw the kindred soul-sista calling out to me and I responded. I felt the need to respond to the rebellious, courageous one that pursued her passion and freedom at a "Whatever it takes" heart fuelled soul calling. Part of my calling and passion in life is to bring to light the truest truth - whatever that is and in every situation. To draw out the diamond in the making within each person I touch is what inspires me to jump out of bed each morning.

My dream is that each person will, in turn, inspire the next person they touch to be aware of how we are each creating ripple effects to enable people to become more conscious of how their behaviour affects each person at that moment. It is this spark that lights up my soul!

That moment between your thought and your action - the defining moment that creates your behaviour - when focused upon, is where we can really impact lives for the better and create a world to be proud of! Can you even begin to imagine a world where every human being is mindful of their behaviour, their intentions and in turn creates a lasting and profound shift in the hearts and minds of all they come across? Injustice, inequality, environmental degradation, human exploitation and even poverty will cease to exist. Imagine changing the course of the future of humanity and our planet!

In order to achieve this incredible undertaking, we must awaken and if necessary, heal that child within each of us. In my opinion, this is the best way to create a joyful

exchange, to focus on hope and take action to restore a balance on the planet. Each of us needs to be an earth custodian but also a custodian of our own individual existence on this planet and how we respond to the pivotal moments we experience. These pivotal moments can define your life. From an early age, I had a strong internal compass geared to my nature. I spent a lot of time on my own in nature and intuitively developed my truth and strength to stand my own ground. I have had at least 3 pivotal decisions that have taken me to the defining crossroads in my life. The first included choosing not to enter into marriage. I felt a power imbalance existed in the traditional marriage ceremony and energy that did not resonate with my soul. The second included ending two major relationships. I made a commitment that if I get to a stage where I lose all sense of myself and love for myself at the expense of loving another person (and this is not reciprocated) then this is the litmus test for ceasing a relationship. I got to a stage where I would have done just about anything for the other person at the cost of my soul. The key turning point was realising that the level and depth that I was seeking could not be reciprocated.

At my core, I continue to rebel against anything that does not feel *"true"* or of my *"nature"*.

The third pivotal turning point was choosing not to take the western medicine approach to address a diagnosis of breast cancer. I had undertaken earlier research about how the body can heal itself if you know the right thing to do and so was able to choose to take an alternative path. I also chose not to have surgery when I incurred a neck fracture. I decided that the best option was to take the least level of intervention to support my body to heal. Both of these decisions have been the best I have ever made.

I realise now that I continue to commit to the promises I made to myself during my teenage years. A key promise I made was that if I don't find a partner that is truly my equal with shared values (some might call this my twin flame) then I don't want to have children. I recall clearly saying this to myself "that I would rather be on my own than settle for just anyone". I keep coming back to such promises I made to myself which in turn drive my soul's direction.

There was an equal fourth tough decision but that this will remain a private one that I will take to my grave. I like to add a bit of suspense here!

I think I lied! There is probably a fifth equally tough decision which will definitely go with me to the other side! Meet me on that side and I promise I will share these with you!

Making the decisions that I made were not easy. These came from a place of valuing love, joy and freedom. I required an unshakable trust in myself that was only strengthened by my faith in God – the Creator. My faith has had a profound impact on my spiritual journey and I am forever grateful. The Traditional Owners of this Land here in Australia, have kept me safe and protected as I bless and honour them regularly throughout my life.

I would be amiss if I didn't also highlight my gratitude for my courage to walk my own path and at the same time, honouring my grandmother Theologia Keramaris, whom I am named after, (and my ancestors) my extraordinary loving parents (the Yin and Yang personified!) that sacrificed all for their children, my two brothers – Leon and Telis whom I love and adore – my family and extended family – in particular my nieces and nephews that keep me close to "my inner joyous child" including my dearest closest friends.

My community worldwide have shown me strength, resilience, passion, determination, courage and all the qualities I have embodied slowly on my journey. I acknowledge I am still a work in progress. This heroine's next chapter is unravelling right before her very eyes!!

I am that massive work in progress. I still have lots more room to grow; I have lots more mistakes to make - to learn from and even not to learn from; to meet more teachers and mentors I can learn from; to give back and to serve in some way to the world with what I've learned and experienced. Ultimately to spend more time being ME in the world.

What I can share with you is what life has taught me so far:

1. It is important that the actions you take are drawn from the depths of your values. My values are of love, compassion, humility, kindness, courage, care for the environment and humanity, self-respect and respecting all life forms. Paying reverence to the Traditional Owners of this sacred land and remembering the Elders (and my Ancestors), past, those present and emerging as the leaders – the children of today reminds me to be humble.

2. I invite you to aim at removing all the blockages and things that no longer serve you. Un-brainwash yourself of the programs indoctrinated through your early experiences in your family, school, peer groups, the media, television and all the subliminal ways our self-esteem and identity is chipped away so that we believe the lie that "I am not enough".

3. Recognise the many blind spots in your mirror and seek to dissolve them one by one. Reach for people and experiences that will bring these blind spots to view.

Actively choose to deal with them or if you choose not to then do this from a place of being really conscious and present. Embrace the NOW and recognise this is what is priceless, miraculous and truly a gift.

4. Live day by day with a BIG vision and put that out to the universe. My vision is to transform and inspire one individual at a time to create a ripple effect across humanity. Aim to make the connections personal and meaningful and bring joy and kindness in each moment. Lift each person a little towards their chosen path and reap the benefit of discovering self-satisfaction in knowing you have made a difference in someone else's life.

5. Change happens when we use our voice and are not afraid to be heard. I believe, as women expressing our voices, hearts and souls we mirror the essence of being vulnerable. This gives rise to encourage every woman to express whatever is within her soul. I have faith that as we empower, cajole, coach, pinch and strive to lift the feminine principle within each woman and man that in turn, we will see the balance returned to the most sacred mother of all - our mother earth!!! She is calling to us to create this balance by embracing, honouring and revering the sacred feminine that has been, for the most part, quite burnt and buried. It is from the ashes that a renewed fire will be born - a volcanic eruption much like what we see with the Haleakala volcano in Maui, Hawaii. The dance of this fire will emanate within each of us – at last! I love the fact that it is a dance as it restores a joyous ritual between women, between men and women and between men and men! Amen!

6. Emerge yourself fully in life for that is the best way to meet the role models that you require at the right moment in time. People often ask this question about whether I have had role models. I have been privileged to meet some outstanding human beings on this planet and I am grateful to every single person.

7. You are your journey so far! I was born in 1964 of Greek heritage (mixed with Italian and Persian - as far as I can tell from my DNA analysis!) and then my two brothers were born five and ten years later. A bunch of experiences and events happened to me, for me and at me for the first 54 years of my life. I was moulded by these experiences either positively, negatively or neutrally but nevertheless, they touched me in some way. As part of these experiences, I met a range of people including my extended family, friends, leaders, acquaintances, authors, film-makers, trainers, teachers, coaches, mentors and partners that in turn shaped me somewhat – probably a lot more than I care to imagine. I also journeyed to many different countries and met people from diverse ages, cultures, abilities, talents and backgrounds which in turn drew out my true nature.

8. Even though my background, my family and my upbringing may be different to yours, we are not really all that different as we have all come to this planet to have a human experience. In doing so we each inevitably are exposed to the daily stuff of life. Each and every day, I feel like a Humpty Dumpty of sorts. Some days I get up and some days I fall down – or more like roll around! Other days I am gathering pieces up by myself or with my friends and family or helping others gather up their pieces. Then on other days I'm putting myself back together and repackaging as I pray and keep going whilst I, in turn, help others to do the same.

And the story continues and unfolds. Sound familiar?

9. The moral to this story is to get focused on the important stuff in life; key relationships, spreading love, compassion, kindness and humour. Take action on the issues that you are passionate about and focus on your evolving purpose which is inherently about "service to humanity". For me, that gets repackaged every day! I pray and keep going, trusting that everything is unfolding perfectly for a reason.

10. Create a vision of the superpower you would dearly like to possess and aim at emulating that superpower at every opportunity. My superpower is to spread an infinite supply of LOVE and COMPASSION. When I truly look at another human being I do my best to see ME in THEM and come from a place of LOVE – ONE LOVE. I also look at all life forms in the same way. I aim to look with the eyes of love and see behind the masks and barriers people put up to cover up their pain and hurt. I aim to see deep into the beautiful soul that is within each person.

11. In order to see the beauty within others though, you need to see it in yourself first. Do this by being absolutely satisfied with yourself and your life RIGHT NOW. The present is the most satisfying as it is all we have. That is the only way to live, to be truly grateful and satisfied in the present. Everything that has happened in the past lead me to the NOW and this is very satisfying! I am still here today and I feel very grateful to be here. I am now a little wiser but in many ways, still very naïve. I am also more joyful as I harness my child nature more and discover a deeper, more sensitive soul. You too can discover your inner child and play in this wonderland!

12. Believe in Miracles. They do exist but we only experience them when we have an open heart and mind. If you have a strong faith, bring that forth in your life and allow it to guide you. There is nothing more sacred than being guided on a spiritual level.

13. Do not spend time with people that have closed minds and hearts. Having said that, I don't want to be closed minded or closed-hearted towards such people as I

truly believe that given time (and experiences they have?) their hearts and minds can truly open up! Please do not do anything that doesn't expand your energy and vitality. That's a pretty broad statement so if you want to find out you will need to ASK me!

The most central aspect in my life is to inspire and ignite the potential in each human being I come across, to be curious about their life and invite them to get out of their comfort zone by taking the first step. In a subtle way, I may nudge them to then take another step and then another... Before too long each person will have taken massive action towards their aspirations – to realise the vision of EXPLORE YOUR LIFE AND RENEW YOUR POWER...

You too can do can hold this intention of igniting the soul in each person by being more conscious of your everyday interactions everywhere with each person you meet. I am now more conscious and intentional in instilling these values in all my interactions – in my work as a coach, policy practitioner, mentor, daughter, cousin, friend, aunty or whatever role I hold in my family, community or workplace. I truly believe that as each of us embraces the 'miraculous' within us that we are truly unstoppable in what we can achieve. Set a big vision of the world you want to see for yourself and for future generations! I sense we are at a crossroads right now and have a massive opportunity to make these positive changes if each of us just stretches out of our COMFORT ZONES and takes a little step, a little action towards something new. It's time to open up our minds, hearts and souls towards what is truly possible!

My message is about changing one thing in the world to ignite a greater consciousness in each human being to then be the change we want to see in the world. This change is at its core, self-respect, respecting each other and respecting and honouring mother earth with the full set of values we each embody.

We are all energy beings and like the chemistry of miraculous grace that makes up our essence, we can impact on each other's energy and ultimately our neurology, our hearts and minds to activate our soul's expression in its fullest possible evolution. The point of infinite inspiration is truly embodying our infinite nature. I invite you to be in the spur of the moment and to embrace the adoration of ourselves and the planet that owns us and nurtures us. We must all do whatever it takes to honour our earth as she sustains our every breath!

I continue to strive to be a humble soul and do my best to release the ego and embrace each day as the gift that it is. I will continue to live fully until my last breath! I pray that each of you reading this takes something away to nurture your soul to activate your grace. Never take any moment, person, or experience for granted and trust that it is with you for a reason; to support your growth and the lessons you are here to learn.

Say YES to life and watch what happens! Infinite blessings and prayers to each of you reading this!

Co-Author
Louise Keramaris

Louise Keramaris **Founder and Coaching Director**
Infinite Inspiration *is a passionate result focused experienced Coach, Facilitator and Trainer, specialising in career development and transition, inner-work-mindset-personal growth and development coaching and delivering tailored training, facilitation and mentoring services in response to the needs of organisations, workforces and individuals.*

Louise has over 20 years experience in senior leadership roles across education (Koorie outcomes), early childhood, Aboriginal Affairs, Aged Care (community based) primary health, disability, sport and recreation, crisis support counselling and community services sectors in Commonwealth, State and local government and over 8 years experience in delivering coaching services.

She brings to her coaching, facilitation and training depth of understanding of the complexity of work environments, the qualities of positive strategic leadership, the needs of multiple and diverse stakeholders and effectively managing competing priorities. Louise understands the importance of fostering a culture of integrity, transparency, accountability and quality improvement.

Louise's level of compassion and emotional intelligence enhances her ability to work with people of diverse backgrounds and careers to draw out their values, support the right thinking and empower each person to lead more satisfying careers and lives.

Name: LOUISE KERAMARIS
Website: www.infiniteinspiration.com.au
Twitter: @Louise Keramaris
Instagram: InfiniteInspirationlk
Facebook: Infinite Inspiration
Facebook: Louise Keramaris

"

As I look back over my life so far, I have come to the realisation that if we change our perspective on life and view our challenging moments as gifts and blessings instead of burdens, then and only then can we really benefit from the gems of learning that lie hidden within these difficult times."

~ FRANCESCA THORNE

Flag & Barrel
Afraid to ask for Help!
by Francesca Thorne

To explain my journey over the last few years has been overwhelming, tough and most of all, I was afraid to ask for help.

My life hasn't been a fairy tale and it's still not, it's a journey. Even the thought of sharing my life journey with strangers, makes me feel so vulnerable. After all, who would want to read my story, if it still unfinished? That perfect last chapter where everything turns in good as in every fairy tale? Why would I consider that anyone is interested in reading about my life? What would I achieve, or what are they looking for? So many questions and fear from being open and honest. It might take me a long time before I feel ready to give it a try, but this time might never come. So here goes!!

I grew up in a small country town on a farm that had everything. We ate from the land always had food on the table, plenty to share what we had with others in need. We were always told that life is precious, we are blessed to be here to make the most of your life like a chapter in a book. They don't always have happy endings, but you must always remember you can't change the past, but you can learn from it, share it, embrace it and most of all love your life.

Growing up, something I have reflected upon was TRUST. As a young child, I was riding my horse Wimpy, winning the flag & barrel race. For those who don't know what this about, you have a 44-gallon barrel at each end of the circuit. In one barrel you have 10 flags on a pole and the idea is getting all ten flags from one end to the other, without dropping any in the fastest time. Wimpy and I knew each others role to achieve this. We won titles together for many years, as overtime she knew her reward at the end of the race. For her, it was a roll in the sand, a washdown and molasses drink. For me it was not about winning, it was building my skills and trust. This helped me understand, that when you want to succeed in anything, you need to embrace, trust yourself and your partner in my case "*Wimpy*", as she knew exactly what her role was as did I.

Coming from a European family of eleven siblings, me being the youngest daughter, taught me what not to do, say and most of all, to listen and learn as that is what life

is about. My father told my brothers not to get involved in transport, do a trade. As it's hard work and you need to be focused on everything you do and be prepared for hard work. They all choose a different path, but I did choose 30 years of Corporate Management in Transport & Logistics, Building and Constructions. I wouldn't have had it any other way, as I have worked with some amazing people in that life. Today I am in the Signage Industry, Director of a successful business with my husband, whom I am so grateful for. The diversity of my knowledge and life experience has made my working life a big WOW. Take the upbringing instilled in you and make the most of it!

I am the master of my mind, I always have been and always will be, as I am proud of my success. Looking back over the last 50 years, my life has made me choose directions and people I am grateful for, I am truly blessed. My husband and I have five adult children and four grandchildren and more to come... For those that have grandchildren, you will understand me.

Speaking of life experiences, however, one lesson I have learned, is that just because life looks like it is going in the right direction, does not mean that it can't unravel in an instant. The year 2016 was horrific for me.

In 2016 my life was turned upside down.....I trusted people with my daily living events, while I was lost in the crowd or cloud, I am not sure. I thought I surrounded myself with good people, but unfortunately, they were only interested in their own wellbeing. In April 2016 this turned out to be a winner at first, but on the front side behind closed doors, it was a struggle. A close family member fought each day for her life but was strong until the time came where life was cut short tragically to all. Help was there but they refused to stand up and say, "*I am struggling*". Suicide has taken so many lives over recent years and there is so much external pressure from daily demands on each and every one of us, that this disease seems to be overtaking human life.

When you are asked to stand beside someone you love and watch their heart crying with sadness, it makes you more determined to help others in need. While this was going on, the family seemed to struggle each and every day. We were all told "*time heals*", but no time was given and you think it's the end. When you have no answers, you have two choices, do nothing or decided to make a difference and take the '*bull by the horns*'. I have learnt over the years to have faith and belief. If you need strength or help in any way, just ask and it will come. So, here goes...

I often would sit and look up to the mountains around me which give me a sense of

332

the existence of something bigger than just myself out there, and ask, '***please show me the way***'. You learn to stand up, have faith and most of all, be proud of what you have achieved, with the support of your loved ones beside you. I was once told to unite in packs like the Lion on the mountain overlooking his heard "*The Protector*", which gave me strength and I hope this does for you too.

While we are there for everyone, our life seems so busy and we often forget about ourselves. This one morning I woke up and my world around me had collapsed. My soulmate was hurt; unable to speak, see or understand what had just happened. We had no idea what was going on around us, we were lost and scared. I sat by his bed in the hospital for days waiting for him to say it will be ok.

This particular day I walked around the hospital floor looking for answers and came across the chapel doors. I walked in not sure what to do, I sat down and looked up and asked for guidance, strength, answers and direction. As I sat there, a lady came in and was doing the same thing. We didn't speak to each other, as we were both immersed in our own feelings of helplessness and at the same time, focussing in building within us the hope we were both so desperately seeking. After an hour in the chapel, I stood up and so did she. We looked at each other and she smiled at me. She said, "*It will be ok, a long journey my dear, but keep asking and you will receive.*". I said thank you and we both left the chapel.

Later that day I had seen her again and she asked 'how are things going dear'? I said, '*the doctors came and explained what had happened, to give it time and things will be ok*'. I told her that my husband suffered an ischemic stroke and it will be a long road to recovery, but we must keep up his rehabilitation. She had tears in her eyes, held my hand and gave me a hug. She said, '*You are not alone*', smiled and left. This made me realise, as I am sure many of us feel the same, asking for help is not a failure, it's a strength!

I look back today and realise that my husband and I were reunited in this life together, after years of been apart from our childhood days, was for a reason. To be together through both the joyous part of life and the challenging parts, I trusted that things would be ok, as we were both given a second chance in life. The lady from the chapel on that particular day gave me the empathy and the hope that I so desperately needed and I will be forever grateful for that chance encounter.

Since that time, something within me shifted. I decided that it was important to retain our family memories and stories as these are our true legacy. Someone once told me something many years ago and it has stuck with me over the years. He said,

"Francesca, everything you need in this life is to preserve and share your family's life stories". We all need to understand, that "Our life stories are similar to a beautiful book. Once we collect them within our minds, they are destined to be our treasure to share so our loved ones we will cherish and have the opportunity to learn from them". I now journal almost every day and collect my own stories and experiences in the knowledge that they will be shared with my children and with theirs.

I have learnt with so many families living far apart across the globe, we are here in this life to rescue or be rescued, pass on traditions and priceless life stories to our families for generations to come. So you understand that no matter what we are faced with in life, there is always an answer or a direction to go. We owe it not only to yourself but to our children and grandchildren to preserve our unique family history. Until today, where we have an abundance of resources available to share and support us. We need to learn to talk openly, ask for advice and listen. It should not be a struggle and we should not give in to feelings of shame. The advice that was shared with me was '**You have to embrace your life purpose, don't take it for granted, learn from it**'. You can not change what happened yesterday, but today you can choose to be a better person.

As I look back over my life so far, I have come to the realisation that if we change our perspective on life and view our challenging moments as gifts instead of burdens, then and only then can we really benefit from the gems of learning that lie hidden with these difficult times.

The attitude I now take is this: "*Alright life, you might have knocked me down...but damn it, you don't get to win. I'm getting back up, and I'm going to kick your ass.*" We can all be heroes in our own lives so, if any of you are going through a rough patch in life, hopefully, this will help get you through it. Here's what you need to do: Firstly, you must understand that Sh** does happen and that's ok.

Whether your partner cheated on you, you're divorced, you lost your job, you ate six whole boxes of cookies and had to be rushed to the hospital, you got a DUI, whatever…these things happen, they happen to the best of us. It might have been your fault, it might not have been your fault. It might have been something that has been building up for years or something that just happened yesterday. No matter how it happened, when it happened, or why it happened, it happened. You know the expression, "*there's no use crying over spilled milk*"?

I have learnt over my life *what's done is done*. At this point in your "*sh** happens*" plan, you're probably thinking that you're the only person in the world that is dealing with this. You're not alone. We all have baggage we're dealing with – it's how we deal with that baggage that makes us who we are. I have learnt that you must vent or "*Get it out of your system*" in whatever way suits you

Call up your best friend and have a bitch. Go to a coffee shop with some mates and talk through it. Cry, scream, yell, drop as many "*what the f***'s*" as you need. Like my sister always said "*Let it go, let it go or let it flow*". Do whatever it is that makes you feel good even if you have to beat the crap out of a pillow. Do whatever you need to do to vent, as long as it doesn't put you or others t around you in danger. Whenever I get upset or frustrated, I find that exercise is the best medicine. In fact, I wish I could find a way to get angry more often because I can lift more weights, hit harder whenever that happens. If only they could bottle this stuff up…. One of my favourites is cleaning with loud music. Once you do let off some steam you will quickly realize, It's Not That Bad.

Ask yourself - Do you still have a pulse? Good! Things could be WAY worse if you did not. Even if you lose "*everything,*" you're still alive and you can still turn things around. Please remember this: It is NEVER too late, things are never as bad as they seem. Everybody has crappy days, but few of us have a real perspective on what a crappy day "*actually* " feels like.

Over the last 18 months, I have been involved with disability groups and learnt, whenever I think I'm having a bad day, I listen to these people share their stories and it is here that I get slapped in the face with a huge dose of reality.

Remember whatever happened yesterday is now officially history, Learn from it. It's done. **I'm a firm believer in that everything happens for a reason**. I spent thirty years in the corporate world pretending I was happy, before realizing how important it was for me to have friends that I care about around me at all times. I gave up that life in 2014 to care for my husband, work with him, support him and most of all our support network has got me through the last four years of my life, that had to happen to get me exactly where I'm supposed to be right now.

Whatever has happened to you in your past, be it yesterday, a month ago, or a decade ago, it's time to move on. Whether it's a lost job, broken relationship, tremendous weight gain, or anything else that is threatening to pull you down, know that it happened for a reason – it's a step that had to happen so that you can eventually get to where you need to be. It's all in your mind – make that a positive thing or as my husband would say; '*Don't Dwell on It*'.

> **"**
>
> **Remember whatever happened yesterday**
> **is now officially history,**
> **Learn from it.**
> **It's done.**
> **I'm a firm believer**
> **that everything happens**
> **for a reason."**
>
> ~FRANCESCA THORNE

Co-Author
Francesca Thorne

Francesca Thorne Founder & CEO of Australian Women's Network, Director of Magnum Signs

Fran's 30 years' experience in Corporate Executive Management & brings experience, particularly with Team Leadership, Mentoring & Training Focus, excellent Communication skills and Compliant Dispute Resolution with both internal and external customers.

Francesca had a trailblazing role as the first female Distribution Manager at a major national company based in Melbourne and this set the tone for a Proactive Mediator & Mentoring role with many Team Leaders & recognized work ethic to go the "extra mile". This enabled a combined excellent strategic planning ability, with strong collaboration with employees, to ensure client projects were delivered on time, particularly in sensitive Industrial Relations environments. Instigated a comprehensive Customer Service Relationship Management philosophy, throughout many sections of the business that revolutionized productivity in these day to day operations.

Fran left the corporate world in April 2014 to take up the role as a full-time carer for her disabled husband. During this time with the support of many practitioners, Fran has taken on the role of Managing NDIS as Support Coordinator, understanding and working in the community with people that have a disability. Volunteering with others in community program such as Woodend Lifestyle Carers Group, Carers Victoria and Acquired Brain Injury Program Management.

Fran has also recently taken on the role of managing Magnum Signs and is a board member of ASGA.

LinkedIn: https://linkedin.com/in/francesca-thorne-director-89557b20/
Instagram: https://www.instagram.com/awnfrancescathorne/
Facebook: https://www.facebook.com/frances.thorne66

Thank You

I do not know how to accurately express my heartfelt gratitude to YOU for choosing to read our book. My personal journey of collaborating with 27 Women from seven different countries and just as many time zones, has been one of profound learning and a new understanding of what is possible.

These incredible women have joined hands and hearts together in this awe-inspiring connection of the Feminine Spirit to take YOU and each of our readers on an upward journey of empowerment which we predict will result in a shift in YOUR thinking and potential for YOUR life.

Together, the intention of Dance In The Fire Of Life has been to give our readers a unique insight into the richness of the tapestry that is ingeniously woven together by an often challenging and confronting journey through this experience we call life.

I would like to personally thank each of my co-authors for putting their trust in me to steer and direct this beautiful vessel and collaboratively lead their individual life dances safely through the unpredictable flames of life - ensuring they leave sparks of light wherever they go and illuminating the path for the future generation of women to come.

Here's to our unlimited potential and willingness to be the light in the lives of everyone we meet which will, in turn, light us up to BE the women we are here to BE.

Thank you,

Vicki Gotsis Ceraso
Life-Vision Strategy Consultant, Author & Speaker

Creator & Founder
SheRises global
TogetherWeRise Global

A personal message from...
Vicki Gotsis Ceraso

So, you have read our beautiful book and I now ask you to consider if there is a call within your heart and soul to explore who you have come into this life to BE and to expand your unique light out into the world.

Reach out to me and I will help you write your own contributing chapter to one of my up and coming Anthologies, or, your very own Book, Workbook, Course, Keynote Talks, TED talk, and more.

Rest assured that under my watch you will not be producing something superficial in content and message as so many are doing these days. I am not interested in producing 30,000-word business cards. I'm interested in infusing each of my authors words with heart, soul, integrity and purpose.

I will help you unveil your brilliance and together, we will let the world understand clearly what it is that you have come into this world to offer through who you have come into this world to BE.

Join me in this rousing, inspirational and emotional united march of the Feminine Rising!!!

Together we can take measured and purposeful steps to catapult our individual lives as WOMEN RISING and ultimately transform the happiness and success destiny for the next generation of WOMEN RISING HIGHER!

vicki@sherisesglobal.com

VGC Publishing
VickiGotsisCeraso